Accession
36053107

D0549210

07

An introduction

and management ethics

University of
Chester

WARRINGTON CAMPUS
LIBRARY
01925 534284

This book is to be returned on or before the last date stamped
below. Overdue charges will be incurred by the late return of
books.

An introduction to business and management ethics

Michael R. Harrison

1838878

LIBRARY	
ACC. No.	DEPT.
36053107	
CLASS No.	
UNIVERSITY OF CHESTER	

palgrave
macmillan

© Michael R. Harrison 2005

All rights reserved. No reproduction, copy or transmission of this
publication may be made without written permission.

No paragraph of this publication may be reproduced, copied or transmitted
save with written permission or in accordance with the provisions of the
Copyright, Designs and Patents Act 1988, or under the terms of any licence
permitting limited copying issued by the Copyright Licensing Agency,
90 Tottenham Court Road, London W1T 4LP.

Any person who does any unauthorised act in relation to this publication
may be liable to criminal prosecution and civil claims for damages.

The author has asserted his right to be identified
as the author of this work in accordance with the Copyright,
Designs and Patents Act 1988.

First published 2005 by
PALGRAVE MACMILLAN
Houndmills, Basingstoke, Hampshire RG21 6XS and
175 Fifth Avenue, New York, N.Y. 10010
Companies and representatives throughout the world

PALGRAVE MACMILLAN is the global academic imprint of the Palgrave
Macmillan division of St. Martin's Press, LLC and of Palgrave Macmillan Ltd.
Macmillan® is a registered trademark in the United States, United Kingdom
and other countries. Palgrave is a registered trademark in the European
Union and other countries.

ISBN-13: 978–1–4039–0016–6
ISBN-10: 1–4039–0016–7

This book is printed on paper suitable for recycling and made from fully
managed and sustained forest sources.

A catalogue record for this book is available from the British Library.

A catalog record for this book is available from the Library of Congress.

10   9   8   7   6   5   4   3   2   1
14   13   12   11   10   09   08   07   06   05

Printed and bound in China

Contents

Contents

Acknowledgements

Any experienced teacher will be aware of a debt not only to researchers, theoreticians and writers in a given area but also to the ability of students and colleagues to challenge and inform. This is particularly true of the large number of thoughtful managers I have had the pleasure of working with in class discussions, projects and live contexts, where ethical theories have come up against hard reality and the complexity of evolving dilemmas. My past colleagues at Staffordshire University Business School deserve particular thanks for their contributions, intentional or otherwise. I would also like to acknowledge the comments made by the numerous reviewers of earlier drafts and the patience and persistence of Ursula Gavin, the editor at Palgrave. My wife and two sons similarly deserve thanks for their patience in putting up with an absent-minded member of the household with a tendency to hoard odd clippings from newspapers about strange happenings in the business world.

Preface

The purpose of this book is to provide an introduction to the language and concepts of business ethics and to show some of the benefits and challenges of applying these ideas in a practical, organisational context. This brief statement raises a number of issues, such as what is meant by 'business ethics', which will be addressed in the early chapters. However, we will assume from the start that the reader has an intuitive understanding of the need for an exploration of morality in business. We will also assume that such an exploration must provide a balance between criticism of business practice and constructive suggestions on how ethical behaviour may be encouraged.

A successful and fully functioning organisation is one of the most useful artefacts that society has produced. For centuries, the ability of people to work together in an organised way in pursuit of a common purpose has been the key driving force in converting ideas into large-scale changes. A primary way to obtain wealth and influence has been through running businesses and engaging in economic activity of some kind. This type of activity has also provided large-scale employment, complementing work funded by the state in providing public services. At schools and colleges one of the largest specialist subjects is the study of business, while management training is a major industry supporting companies and other organisations. This book is designed to support a consideration of the ethics of this activity, either in a group learning environment or through individual study. Such consideration might take the form of a taught module devoted to business ethics or be a part of other general or specialist modules in business.

An interesting question is to ask how well an organisation is performing. This question is confusing in that it might refer to two different meanings of the word 'well'. We may be asking a practical question: roughly speaking, is the activity effective in meeting the goals of an organisation? Alternatively we may be asking a purely moral or ethical question. This may refer to whether the activities were morally right or whether the goals aimed for are ethically acceptable. For many years, the discipline of philosophical ethics has explored the general area of personal moral evaluation in a careful and logical manner. When considering business ethics we must be aware of possible tensions between practical and moral behaviour, particularly when evaluating the actions of groups of people working in a formally structured way. The interpretation of traditional ethical theory into business contexts is challenging both to the business practitioner and the ethicist.

Thus, the sheer scale of business and organisational activity and the obvious ethical dilemmas posed by working in this field have prompted the increased attention given to business ethics in programmes of study. This may relate to the ethics of individuals working in an organisational context, to an ethical evaluation of the organisation itself or even to the business system as a whole. It should be noted that the latter are also the concerns of political, social and economic theory. We will mainly be concerned in this book with people working in an organisation and interacting with other people, such as customers, in the organisation's environment.

Moral conversation may seek to describe, explain, analyse or prescribe. However, philosophical ethics is a normative discipline, that is it aims to provide prescriptions for correct behaviour (always depending on some assumptions and background theories, as we shall see). This does not mean that this book intends to tell the reader how to behave ethically in organisations! It introduces the concepts, tools and techniques of ethics that an informed and responsible citizen may wish to use. Personal freedom and autonomy of action (within accepted social constraints) is an important idea in ethics.

A further point is that it is valuable to avoid, as far as possible, seeing ethics in isolation from other business and management disciplines. To see ethical analysis and strategic analysis, say, as separate approaches to a case study or real situation is far less useful than trying to use them together. While ethics may well challenge the assumptions underlying strategic analysis, and the politics of implementing strategic change may be difficult to reconcile with ethical constraints, there is a creative tension in using the two together. This is particularly evident in the more overtly competitive aspects of business activity, such as marketing. The inter-twining of ethical and other organisational theories, at an introductory level, is one of the key features of this book.

A final point is that we are here using the words 'ethical' and 'moral' as roughly equivalent in meaning. Like everything else in the subject, this is not universally accepted but it is the simplest way to proceed in a basic introduction which focusses on practical analysis. For a similar reason we will tend to use the phrase 'business ethics' to refer to the subject of this book, though as we see in Chapter 1 this is also debateable.

Organisation of the book

Structure of the book

The book is divided into four parts as described below. Each part contains an introduction which is mainly concerned with describing the purpose and content of the chapters it contains. The final chapter in each part ends with a selection of questions for discussion. While it is recommended that the parts and chapters be read and studied in the order presented, it is perfectly feasible to vary from this, using the index, summaries and signposting in the text to help navigation. An alternative strategy might be to read Parts I and II and then to choose topics from Parts III and IV depending on experience and interest.

Part I is mainly concerned with introductions, basic definitions, models and frameworks. It also gives a flavour of the business vocabulary (e.g. such terms as 'stakeholder') which provides a bridge between general ethical theories and their application in a business context.

Part II gives a basic exposition of many of the principal ethical theories derived from philosophy. In all instances these are contextualised into an organisational setting. Reference is also made to scientific and political ideas which add a distinctive flavour to business ethics.

Parts III and IV have similar objectives, basically to apply the previously mentioned theories into business contexts using a mixture of topics and cases. However, in order to simplify a very complex set of issues, a distinction has been made as follows. Part III consists of six chapters which include a range of generally applicable topics while Part IV reflects the main ethical concerns in a range of business functions.

It should also be noted that Chapters 1 and 11 are distinctive in that while introducing some ethical ideas and arguments, they also include sections of practical advice. Chapter 1 makes comments on how to approach texts on business ethics and why writing is an important way to explore and structure one's thoughts. Chapter 11 gives advice on how to work with case studies and how to conduct ethical research. Much of this advice is of value beyond studying business ethics.

Structure of each chapter

The purpose of this section is to describe how each chapter is structured, so you will know what to expect and be able to navigate around
the text in order to meet your needs.

Chapters 1–10 (Parts I and II) contain an introduction to the language,
concepts and models of business ethics. Chapters 11–22 (Parts III and
IV) apply these ideas to a range of contexts topics, cases and exercises.
Each of these chapters begins with a short statement of purpose and
a concise set of learning objectives. Underlying all this is the overall
objective of developing an integrated knowledge of business ethics and
improving your skills in ethical evaluation. The learning objectives are
followed by a brief introduction to the chapter in question. The intention in these introductions is to show the purpose of the material
included in the chapter as well as to describe its contents.

The body of each chapter is made up of a mixture of topics, cases
and exercises as appropriate. The topics may be descriptions of ethical
theories or may relate to specific business and organisational problems.
The sections labelled as 'cases' aim to show ethical problems as they may
appear in a business context. It should be noted that the text contains
many other descriptions of ethics in business contexts besides those
specifically called cases. We say a little more about the cases later. The
exercises usually also relate directly to real business situations and are
intended to be used mainly in the context of group discussion. In
addition to exercises which occur in the main body of text, separate
sets of exercises are included at the ends of the separate parts. These
exercises are intended to provide fresh challenges rather than routine
checks on learning. For this reason they introduce new problems and
situations and should be regarded as a resource to be utilised to the full.

Each chapter ends with a summary and some include a note on
sources of reference. The summaries are not intended as simply repeat-
ing the chapter materials in a briefer format. They continue the debate
and arguments in a way intended to draw together the key points
which have occurred earlier. The 'references and further reading' sections
of some chapters give examples of texts and other materials which you
might find useful if you wish to continue further in exploring some
topic or situation. At the end of the book all the references, along
with some further materials, are gathered together in an Annotated
bibliography.

In Chapters 1–10 the emphasis is on outlining basic concepts and ethical theories. However, a considerable amount of time is spent on situating this discussion in business practice and in showing ways in which the application of the theories of ethics to organisational life differ from other applications. Business ethics provides some specific challenges in addition to the application of the ideas of ethics to every-day life. These relate mainly to the competitive business environment and the complexity of organisational practices.

Chapters 11–16 (Part III) are concerned with specific topics and issues in business practice and Chapters 17–22 (Part IV) are structured mainly round a functional view of business ethics. You may be sur-prised to find out just how much has been written on the ethics of business and organisational life in books and journals over the past few years. This book explores a range of topics at an introductory level, with some topics developed to a greater extent. This is still, however, only a fraction of the material which could have been presented. It should be noted that some further models and theories relating to spe-cific business situations are introduced in these later chapters.

One thing which will rapidly become obvious is that a large number of ethical ideas and principles are introduced and a large number of business situations explored. As any of the theories might be relevant to any of the situations, we have a potentially confusing task ahead of us in arriving at a clear view of ethics in business. This is, however, a reflection of the reality of using business ethics as a practical disci-pline. We cannot avoid this degree of complexity but we can improve our skills in navigating through it!

Cases and exercises

If you have been studying business for any length of time you will have noted the considerable use made of 'cases' and the variety of situ-ational descriptions included under this heading. In an elementary text a case may be a simple exercise relating to an imagined or commonly occurring situation. At an advanced level of study, cases may be extremely lengthy descriptions of a particular organisation at a given point in time, based on a great amount of research. In this latter context, case study analysis skills will have been taught prior to the use of such material.

An important issue, particularly in the context of business ethics, is the extent to which a case study is, or ever can be, a truly objective description of a situation. The fact that certain events have been included in the case, that particular employees' views have been reported and that a language which reflects underlying values and beliefs has been used must be taken into account in evaluating the ethical merits of actions taken and reasons given. It is all too easy to write a case study which reflects a predetermined ethical position. In Chapter 12 we briefly explore this difficulty through some alternative descriptions of a situation.

With these concerns in mind, the parts of this book labelled 'case study' or 'case exercise' are reasonably short descriptions of situations intended to present ethical issues and dilemmas. They are based either on standard issues or on the author's experience but have been made anonymous except where widely reported events (such as the Bhopal tragedy) have been used. In Chapter 11 we set out some explicit guidance in case analysis which is partly intended to expose hidden bias. The intention is that the key ethical dilemmas may readily be made clear in order to facilitate analysis. Exploring the ethical concerns underlying major case study descriptions is a task beyond the scope of this book, though one which you may feel ready to take on as a next stage in understanding business ethics.

Part I   What is business ethics?

Introduction

The purpose of this part of the book is to lay some foundations for studying business ethics as follows:

- ► to introduce some basic concepts and definitions;
- ► to give some advice on studying business ethics;
- ► to introduce some key organisational concepts (such as 'stakeholder') which are useful in relating ethical theory to organisational practice;
- ► to show some ways in which organisations approach moral decision-making.

Chapter contents

In the introduction to each part of the book is included a brief description of the chapter contents for that part. You may, of course, also consult the 'Introduction' to each chapter for similar information.

Chapter 1 begins the study of business ethics in earnest by outlining some basic principles and ideas. As you will see it is not a straightforward task to say exactly what 'business ethics' actually is! We also make the point that the approach taken here (as in most similar texts) is based on a particular view of philosophical ethics and rational debate. As noted above, this chapter also contains some practical advice on studying business ethics.

Chapter 2 continues this theme with further models and ideas which underlie business ethics in totality. After reading the first two chapters you may wish to browse through later chapters to gain some first impressions of the actual issues which we will be addressing.

Chapter 3 focusses on two key themes. The first is the use of the term 'stakeholder'. While the use of this word is now widespread in business studies there are a number of serious problems which must be addressed, particularly as concepts such as universality and moral distance are fundamental to business ethics. The second theme, which is of considerable current interest in business research and practice, is that of Corporate Social Responsibility.

In Chapter 4 we introduce some ideas from descriptive business ethics which are indicative of a different approach to the mainly prescriptive theories of philosophical ethics we will meet in Part II. Such descriptive theories provide links to other forms of organisational research, such as those based on organisational psychology and theories of social behaviour.

The final chapter in each part of the book contains some questions for discussion relating to the part as a whole.

1 An introduction to business ethics

Purpose and learning outcomes

The purpose of this chapter is to provide an introduction to the study of ethics in an organisational context and to provide some useful resources for the study of business ethics.

You will be able to

► understand the purpose of business ethics;
► appreciate some of the challenges in studying business ethics.

Introduction

Our main work in introducing and exploring the discipline of business ethics begins in Chapter 2. The purpose of Chapter 1 is to clarify the purpose of business ethics as a discipline and to include some general notes and resources which set the scene and guide you through the complexity of this subject.

We begin by outlining the various approaches to ethics, in particular the difference between philosophical, normative, practical and descriptive ethics. These terms may be applied in a variety of contexts (e.g. politics, bioethics, everyday behaviour, etc.) and therefore our next task is to introduce the specific business and organisational settings which will be of concern to us. This section is of particular importance as the term 'business ethics' can be used in two different ways and should also be seen as different from, say, organisational ethics.

The next section has the provocative title 'Why read a book on business ethics?'! This is an important point as many introductory books on business and management are largely descriptive and technique oriented. While this book must start with some ideas, it quickly leads on to techniques of ethical evaluation and description of contexts where dubious practice has been seen. Business ethics must not be seen as merely a negative subject, telling managers what they should not do with little understanding of the pressures they face. Ethical evaluation can make a positive contribution to organisational life and the well-being of stakeholders. We then move on to a section offering some practical advice, mainly relating to reading texts on ethics and writing.

You may wish to read all the material in this chapter before moving on to Chapter 2. An alternative strategy might be to quickly familiarise yourself with this work and then continually return to it when the need arises.

What is ethics?

You might expect, at this point, a simple definition of 'ethics' or 'morality'. Unfortunately, any such definition will almost certainly be restricted and misleading and it is safer if we assume a common-sense understanding of what is meant by these terms, and refine this understanding as we work through the book. For simplicity we will use the terms interchangeably and assume that our use of them follows the tradition and arguments of Western philosophy (see in p. 7) rather than being based on a particular ideology or belief system, though phrases such as 'Protestant work ethic' show us that beliefs and traditions will inevitably affect ethical language and discussion.

We begin by asking the basic questions, 'what is ethics?' and 'what is business ethics?'. If you look at a textbook on 'ethics' as seen as a branch of philosophy you will see a number of differences from a text on 'business ethics'. The most obvious is that it will presume some knowledge of the general ideas, concepts and language which have been developed in the discipline of philosophy over the last 2500 years. That is assuming, of course, that we are speaking within the tradition of Western philosophy developed in Europe and the USA, which puts great emphasis on analysis of fundamental concepts and logic. Of course there are divisions within this large body of work, for example texts on post-modern philosophy (or on 'continental' philosophy) will sound very different from the writings, say, of Russell or Ayer, to pick two influential writers in the 20th century who wrote books for a wider readership than their professional peers. Even if one chooses a book by a philosopher who specialises in ethics you will become very aware that they are not only trying to communicate with non-philosophers but are writing within a community which uses words and ideas in very precise and particular ways. It can often seem that one is eavesdropping on a very sophisticated conversation!

Even beginners' textbooks on 'philosophical ethics' will inevitably assume some knowledge of (or at least some interest in) general ideas within philosophy. Though such texts may well introduce everyday examples and dilemmas to illustrate typical problems, the focus will be on the nature of ethics as a way of using language, say, rather than practical advice on how to handle a particular situation. Indeed, any business situation introduced will seem very simple, often no more than a caricature of the complexities of a real case, and can therefore be very misleading as a prescription for action. Therefore it is important to remember, if you read such a book, that these examples are often introduced either as motivation for the reader to engage with philosophical ideas or as intentional simplification designed to bring a philosophical issue into sharp focus.

To help you navigate through this sort of potential confusion we will use a simple model to differentiate between five 'types of ethical investigation'. Of course, philosophy being what it is, this model could itself be a subject of endless debate: Is it valid to use the word 'ethics' in these ways? What are the precise boundaries between the different 'types'? When you have used this model (and the others presented in this section) for a while you might like to reflect on these points.

Philosophical ethics

This is also referred to as 'meta-ethics', the prefix 'meta' showing we are talking about ethics itself as a discipline rather than working within the discipline to solve ethical problems. We are asking such things as 'what is ethics?', 'what is moral language?', 'are words used within this discipline in ways which are different from ordinary conversation?'. These questions are very difficult to answer, if they can be given any final answer at all! For example, one answer to 'what is ethics?' might be that it is a complete fraud; a vacuous use of words left over from discarded religious beliefs and a confusion in attempting to answer what are really just practical questions. A debate on whether this is true would be meta-ethical in nature. You might like to think how you would set about analysing this view rather than just giving an unconsidered reaction. This is a very difficult task to undertake with honesty and intellectual rigour.

A key question in meta-ethics is related to the authority of moral claims. If we state, for example, that 'stealing is wrong' then we must be able to give the grounds for this assertion. To take some examples:

► Is it based on a profoundly held belief? Yet beliefs differ and moral prohibitions are not constant over all belief systems. The philosophy of religion addresses issues of comparative religion and some religious traditions have a well-developed vocabulary including such words as 'sin' and 'evil'.
► Is it based on the accumulation of experience regarding what it takes to make a society work? If so we must ask whose experience counts, and how is it accumulated? The philosophy of science looks at issues of the validity of general statements built up in some way from particular observations.
► Does a society choose its own standards, for example through the processes of formulating laws? Laws often follow on from a sense of what people accept as right, as any government attempting to impose an unpopular law will soon discover. So how does a society arrive at, and agree, standards of behaviour?
► Is it simply something which is intuitively obvious to us? Then how do criminals view this? Do they lack this intuition, or do they think that stealing is wrong, but so what?
► Is it always true or is it conditional on other factors? In particular in an organisational context are some forms of stealing just so trivial that they escape this prohibition (e.g. using a biro or some notepaper from work at home) or are some forms of stealing (e.g. wasting office time) not really stealing at all? The idea that one should look at all behaviour in context is very appealing but does this make sense? Philosophical ethics quite naturally tends to search for fundamental principles which apply in all cases in order to provide some bedrock for further analysis.

As you can see, philosophical ethics is fascinating but do not expect it to tell you how to carry out business negotiations in another country (to choose a prosaic but useful problem area). We have spent a little time illustrating some of its attraction above as it cannot be the main concern of this book and will not be dealt with at length below.

Normative ethics

Normative ethics is also of considerable interest to philosophers in establishing and exploring the ethical theories that can be built on the foundations of meta-ethics. Of course, the subject did not develop historically in this way; theories were developed in what seemed to be a common-sense fashion at the time and became part of prolonged discussion over long periods of time, argued about from different perspectives, with meta-ethics then being based on the revealed grounds for disagreement and concern. Thus normative ethics covers a variety of theories which at one time or another were considered by key writers as the only sensible approach to ethics. The main theories which have survived overlap in some ways and are strongly differentiated in others. Together they provide a substantial resource and are explored systematically in Chapters 5–9 under such headings as 'virtue ethics', 'utilitarianism', 'Kantian ethics', 'theories of rights' and so forth.

In very general terms, normative ethical theories attempt to prescribe the best way to live, including how to resolve the dilemmas which may arise when making difficult decisions. They try to show what general rules and guidelines we should follow, how we should distinguish between right and wrong and what virtues we should develop. What they tend not to do is describe how people in practice act, how they develop moral codes or how this work relates to other disciplined approaches to understanding human affairs. Historically the social sciences have paid considerable attention to issues of moral behaviour. The early economist Adam Smith wrote a book on morality. Concerns relating to the ethics of money are strongly and often distinctively reflected in economic theory. Sociology, anthropology and similar disciplines have both described the behaviour of individuals using terms based both on their own discipline and on ethics, and have also described social institutions, such as religions.

Practical ethics

Whilst being closer to everyday situations, the theories of normative ethics are still expressed in ways which are not specific to context and may require considerable interpretation and development before they capture the particularities of such contexts. In addition, such areas as biotechnology throw up new challenges in the use of standard theories. Therefore, one of the major developments in ethics as a totality over the past few years has been the development of context-specific areas of theory, such as medical ethics and business ethics, along with the emerging role of the 'ethicist' as a professional able to contribute towards the resolution of difficult dilemmas.

Obviously, in this book we are focussing on business and organisational ethics. We are looking at questions of behaviour in the many and varied situations of organisational life. General questions we might raise in an ethical debate (e.g. is it ever right to tell a lie?) are still applicable as in other contexts but may now also have original twists, for example how do you behave in business situations where lying seems to be the norm and telling the truth is not seen as effective competitive behaviour?

Business ethics also overlaps with other areas of practical ethics, such as environmental ethics (e.g. the rights of financial stakeholders may be set against a proactive approach to 'green' issues), medical ethics (e.g. is a pharmaceutical company under any obligations to sell products, developed at great cost, at low prices in developing countries where need is great and financial resources limited?), the ethics of journalism and the ethics of politics or even the latter two together (noting the issues which arise when the communications industry's interests clash with those of governments around the world).

Descriptive ethics

A quite different approach often found in texts on business ethics but frequently completely lacking in philosophical texts is descriptive ethics. This approach looks at how individuals, groups and organisations approach ethical evaluation and decision-making in practice. It is an empirical methodology, often carried out as part of social science projects and using research methods commonly seen in sociology and psychology. It treats 'ethics' in just the same way as any other social construct and investigates its properties. Its outputs are descriptions and explan-ations, sometimes borrowing a technical language from the social sciences but also sometimes couched in everyday business language.

Thus while normative ethics begins with what are thought to be gener-ally applicable principles and moves towards prescriptions for ethical behaviour, descriptive ethics begins with observations of how people behave and attempts to provide explanations, integrated with social science and practical views of the world. One problem with descriptive ethics is the language it uses, which may borrow terms from philosophy or everyday language and use them in uncritical ways. It would therefore appear that normative and descriptive ethics may be complementary in providing insights into ethics in practice. In this book we will approach descriptive ethics in this positive way. Chapter 4 outlines some approaches to descriptive ethics and other examples occur throughout the book, in particular in Chapter 15 (which deals with other cultures) and Chapter 19, where the idea of moral distance is used in a variety of case examples.

Role of ethics in business

Thus there are several different roles to be played by business ethics, which may be summarised as follows:

▶ to describe and categorise (that is, provide a language for) the process of value formation in organisations and in the free market economy;
▶ to describe and categorise, as moral or otherwise, how decisions are made in organisations;
▶ to provide a critique of the process of value formation in organisations and in the free market economy. Some writers (see Chapter 2) argue that business ethics has become far too 'owned' by the business community to be incisively critical;
▶ to prescribe the values which should hold in organisations, presumably in combination with experience and the findings of the social sciences. It should be noted that this presumption is not obvious in some approaches;
▶ to prescribe how decisions should be made in line with sound moral principles (and with the above presumption).

It is obvious that the above are linked together in a variety of ways. To describe how decisions are made implicitly describes the underlying values of the decision maker; similarly with prescriptions. A key point made above is that ethics is not the only player in the game, hence the reference to the social sciences. Underlying this are meta-ethics and the various ethical theories seen in the literature. However, the whole point of business ethics is usually seen as the implementation of this body of theory in the specific field of organisations.

There is another intriguing possibility. The world of business and organisation has a number of unusual features, such as:

▶ the hierarchical nature of responsibility and authority;
▶ uncertainty management and risk taking;

- ▶ the complex chains of cause and effect;
- ▶ the key role of information flow and asymmetry;
- ▶ the size and interconnectivity of the systems under consideration.

Is it possible that consideration of these features of a system will suggest new approaches to ethical theory as a whole, or at least bring into the foreground ideas such as moral luck (an existing concept in normative ethics)?

Organisational contexts

Though we are using the generic title 'business ethics' to cover the material in this book, it is useful to use some more precise nomenclature in order to subdivide the organisational contexts under consideration. In discussing the following terms you should note that the definitions given below are not necessarily consistently used by all writers in this area.

Organisational ethics

This very broad title applies to the ethics of working in an organisation, that is the individual actions, duties, roles and responsibilities of people working together within a formal structure which itself has owners, stakeholders and objectives. This title is used independently of the environment within which the organisation operates (e.g. competitive business markets, public service, voluntary sector, etc.) and is therefore used for situations which are independent of that context. For that reason it tends to be associated with a primarily inward-looking perspective.

Management ethics

In practice, much of organisational ethics is about the process of management, the relationships between managers and the relationships between managers and other employees. One curiosity of the management profession is that the title 'manager' may be widely used in one organisation to include, say, supervisors and team leaders while in another organisation a very flat structure (i.e. few levels in the 'hierarchy' and many individuals reporting to one team leader) may mean that few people have the title 'manager'. Indeed in some organisations with a strong professional base, the only 'manager' may be an administrator with little if any supervisory responsibilities. It is also possible that some senior and highly paid employees will have no responsibility for the management of others but have considerable effect on how the organisation works and relates to its environment. For these reasons we will tend to use the phrase 'organisational ethics' unless we wish to draw particular attention to the issues involved in managing people and systems.

Business ethics

Unfortunately this widely used phrase has two meanings which are related but which can lead to confusion. The first meaning is simply the area of work we have called 'organisational ethics' but with the added stipulation of a competitive market environment, that is we are referring to the ethics of people working within a 'business' in the accepted sense of the word. Where the issues to be discussed are common to competitive and non-competitive contexts, it is more useful to talk about organisational ethics. If we are talking about ethical dilemmas which only arise within a competitive environment, then we can signal this by using the phrase 'business ethics'.

The other use of 'business ethics' is to refer to the business itself, as a distinct entity, acting competitively. Indeed the phrase is used by some writers in discussions of the ethical problems of doing business in general, though, perhaps, 'market ethics' might be more helpful in referring to a competitive market-based economic system. Obviously in reality all the actions of the 'business as an entity' are actions of individual entrepreneurs, managers and employees. Therefore provided we are aware of any possible confusion, it can be very useful to talk about 'business ethics' if the environment is competitive and we wish to balance a consideration of inward- and outward-looking approaches.

In a similar fashion we might also wish to refer to 'public sector ethics', 'voluntary sector ethics', the 'ethics of health care' and so forth if we wish to signal a focus on issues which are specific to these environments. In particular it is worth remembering that much public sector work is carried out in partnership with private sector organisations (e.g. construction projects) and hence even terms such as 'partnership ethics' might be useful, though are not used in this book.

Corporate Social Responsibility

Corporate Social Responsibility (CSR) is increasingly being used as a term to refer to the discharging of responsibilities by organisations, acting as corporate entities, to society as a whole (similar to the second sense of 'business ethics' above). An issue of some theoretical interest is whether the concepts and tools of analysis used within philosophical ethics can really be directly applied to an agent which is a legal entity (such as a business) rather than a person. We will take the conservative view that ethics directly relates to people, though we may use words like 'duty' and 'values' in relation to organisations when these have been defined in some way. For example, as people we have fundamental duties (see Chapter 7) and characteristics referred to as virtues (see Chapter 9). Organisations may also have legally defined duties and it may be useful to refer to organisational characteristics such as culture, capabilities and even virtues, provided we bear in mind the context and think carefully about what this might mean in practice. We say more about CSR in the next chapter.

Functional or professional ethics

Just as we can differentiate by environmental context, it may also be useful to consider the ethical problems which tend to arise within specific functional areas of an organisation. 'Accounting ethics' is important for all organisations as the audit, control and reporting aspects of financial management must be carried out with a high degree of probity and transparency; many examples of organisational malpractice arise when this is not the case and therefore accountants are bound by strict ethical codes of practice. 'Marketing ethics' is another obvious area of concern due to the consumer's perceptions of misleading advertisements and aggressive selling used by some businesses, most recently through the use of the Internet. Whilst this more visibly applies within business-to-consumer contexts, many issues can arise within business-to-business interactions (say, during negotiations or in supply chain management) or in public sector situations where clients have rightly come to expect high standards of information and service. Human Resource Management (HRM) is another key area where a consideration of ethical practice is essential, perhaps to such an extent that it is difficult to differentiate from organisational ethics as a whole, that is the overall management of people within an organisation may be broader than the traditional area of 'personnel and welfare', and strategic HRM may be defined very broadly by its practitioners and advocates.

Why read a book on business ethics?

What do you, as a reader, expect from a book on business ethics?

The first point to make relates to the diversity of your needs, managerial experience and educational background. Every reader of any book starts from a different position. If the book intends to teach technical material, then background knowledge and related skills will be the most relevant attributes you will bring to the experience of reading and learning. However, applied ethics is different. The potential contribution to the learning experience coming from your own knowledge and experience is very great. With this in mind, one might see a business ethics text as a dialogue, though a printed book is not always the easiest format to use if this is the case.

I would like to suggest some reasons why you might (or in some cases might not) find this or any other book on business ethics to be useful:

It gives a set of moral rules to guide conduct when working in an organisation
This would be a nice, straightforward outcome: the 10 commandments (more like a 100!) to be a moral manager. Now, is this the same as being a 'good' manager in the other sense of the word, that is being effective and successful, or are there another set of commandments for that? Management theory shows us that there is no one unique way to be a successful manager; there is room for creativity, leadership and style, and the need to respond to people and events in original and thoughtful ways. We might also argue that being a moral, though ineffective, manager is pointless except in the exceptional circumstances of, say, a thoroughly corrupt organisation. There might be occasions when one has to stand up against immoral policies, working cultures and individuals but we will take as a starting point that being moral as well as effective is normally possible. This view can be challenged by radical critiques of management and business in general, but that would be a different book.

A further complication is that the theory of ethics does not provide one agreed set of guidelines for action. Ethics is better seen as a process of argument and exploration which has been continuing in various guises and cultures for around 2500 years. This had the advantage that most obvious approaches have been explored in depth; the bar-room philosopher's pearls of wisdom on how business should be run will not be original!

So, in total, ethics does not produce unique recommendations, and prescriptions for moral management must also be seen in the light of effective management. There is much guidance but no hard and fast rules.

It is an attack on the immorality of the business system as a whole
As we hinted above, a number of writers have used examples of immoral practices in business as part of an argument that the system as a whole is irretrievably corrupt. Quite simply, this is a different way of approaching the subject and we take a more optimistic stance. This should not, however, be confused with complacency; the argument that unregulated, free-market competition based on an egoist ethics (see Chapter 5) is a valid way of characterising the business world provides a worthwhile challenge for ethical evaluation.

It is an introduction to the language and ideas of ethics as applied to business
This is far closer to the view adopted here, but a number of texts on applied ethics would do the same job. Hence...

It is an introduction to the language and ideas of ethics as applied to business, but emphasising the particular features of the business world which make business ethics different from other branches of applied ethics
A long description but closer to our intention, though see below for some additional features.

It is an introduction to the skills of ethical analysis of business situations
Yes, though expect to spend your entire career in honing those skills!

It is a summary of the main ideas in business ethics which may help you complete assignments and pass exams
Well yes, though I have made no effort to write the text as an exam guide. A health warning might be appropriate here. I have chosen material from a very large literature and illustrated this with cases and my own experiences of management. The intention is to show how ethics can be applied to business and management rather than reproduce a set syllabus. Other teachers will use some different materials and may have different expectations, as summarised in the learning outcomes of particular modules. To repeat a very old piece of advice, answer the question as set rather than reproduce the bit of your notes which is nearest!

It provides guidance in terms of life skills and moral development
One of the reasons why business ethics is valuable to us at a personal level is that we all at some times face considerable pressure to act in

ways that might be unethical, we may be unsure how to act, or we may need to summon up the determination to oppose others who we are sure are acting unethically. Reading widely, discussing our difficulties with others and taking advice on how to proceed may all be valuable in this context. Beyond that, it is up to you!

Practical advice for students of business ethics

In this section we introduce a number of ideas linked with some practical advice relating to studying business ethics either as part of a programme in business or some other discipline or as a topic in itself. Of particular importance is the development of good technique in crafting and communicating a compelling argument.

The above is particularly true of experienced managers who, after overcoming a natural resistance to the feeling that some fundamental ways in which they behave and relate to their world of work are being questioned, can become very forceful in debate and introduce new and exciting challenges to received ideas in ethics. Managers who have to deal with the politics and uncertainties of organisational life on a day-to-day basis may well find the prescriptions of ethics apparently simplistic and even unfair. If you are dealing with disciplinary issues of, say, email or Internet misuse, harassment and petty expense claims fiddling within an organisational culture where aggressive selling is seen as the route to survival, and where a questioning of this assumption is viewed as disloyal, then Aristotle and Kant may seem remote. However, employees in such situations need all the support they can get, whether from a sound grasp of the methods of ethical argument or the bolstering of their self-belief that moral behaviour is the best approach in the long term. In my experience, managers welcome this debate, but may not be as effective as we all would wish in formally analysing situations and constructing arguments. Yet this is exactly what change agents who wish to combine ethics with effective political action in organisation must be able to do (see Chapter 10).

How to read a business ethics text?

No one book or writer should ever be taken as definitive in addressing an issue in philosophy or ethics. However much you empathise with a text, it is essential to read around it, including the work of writers from different disciplines who may be antagonistic to an approach you like. This can be hard work and personally unsettling, but it must be done. In particular challenge introductory texts (such as this one) and collections of readings; even if the topics included in a basic introduction seem inevitable, constructing such texts involved decisions about what is relevant and what is not.

If you wish to refer to original philosophical resources you must be aware of the fact that some philosophical writing is very hard to understand. This is partly because philosophers often write in response to previous work and some modern writings are simply unintelligible without a good knowledge of the background debate. Some philosophers, such as Hegel, are extremely demanding, to say nothing of some 'continental' or post-modern writers whose dense style can seem obscure. Also it is important to realise, in order to maintain one's own self-confidence, that some topics are intrinsically difficult. For example logic, beyond an introductory level, is either extremely subtle (as in philosophical logic) or akin to studying advanced mathematics. In view of the above, particularly if you are not specialising in philosophy, it is important to do a reality check and ask yourself on a regular basis 'what am I getting out of this work?' and adapt your approach accordingly.

There is a constant tension in business and management writing between theory and its application in reality, as also reflected in this book. Theories are often best if kept as simple and intelligible as possible while the reality to which they apply is endlessly rich and complex. This tension cannot easily be solved by including large numbers of factors in our theories or ignoring most of the complexity in reality! It does mean that one needs a different mindset when reading and coming to terms with an elegant theory (which clarifies some points but is essentially limited) as opposed to a case study or description of reality (or our perception of a real situation) which attempts to capture a wide range of factors. However, both are important and at some point we have to be able to bring them together.

How to write (or why write?)

No doubt a student response to this strange question is that writing (or, preferably, typing) is a painful activity that takes place in class or as assignments or in exams. Traditionally many managers made a point of not writing, preferring dictation and the occasional signature. Technology has increased the need for 'keyboard skills', reminding us that for many people 'copy and paste' is at least as important as text generation.

Unfortunately 'cut and paste' may not do justice to our own thoughts and arguments. One of the main reasons for writing is to find out what we know! This was part of a number of good points made at a seminar on academic writing I attended some time ago and immediately accepted by those in the room as an interesting and practical way of looking at this strange and difficult process. It obviously does not refer to copying (even from memory!) but to sorting out the often forgotten or unrecognised jumble in our heads. It requires practice and confidence, and also assumes previous experiences and other inputs as well as a capacity to reflect on them.

This advice can also be extended to the notion of conversation and discussion as a way of finding out what we know, as well as what others know, though this is perhaps more obvious to most people. At first sight it may seem to run counter to ideas of careful planning, outlining and structuring written work but is best seen as complementary to them. The idea is that we type, write, jot and scribble text of various kinds as often as possible in order to explore and structure our thoughts. It is not intended that this becomes the finished article for our report or assignment, but with practice it may be close to it.

Then a second piece of advice is to rewrite until we (singular or group) are entirely satisfied with the finished product, in content as well as presentation. The real advantage of word processing now becomes evident. Perhaps one of the more miserable academic duties is marking a group assignment where we see a group of five students producing five sections, each obviously a first draft written by a different student with no obvious consultation or reading of the final offering. The workplace equivalent is the report similarly cut and pasted, though in this case the signature at the bottom may signify some acceptance of responsibility.

Summary

In this chapter we have outlined some ideas on the nature of ethics and business ethics. We have also provided some practical discussion to help with the study of business ethics. Chapter 11 is similar in providing support in case analysis and research. Unlike other chapters, this one does not have a set of references and further reading.

2 Concepts and models in business ethics

Purpose and learning outcomes

The purpose of this chapter is to introduce some of the basic language, concepts and models of business and organisational ethics to readers with no prior knowledge of this subject.

You will be able to

▶ see how some basic classifications are useful in understanding ethical theories;
▶ understand the difference between legal and ethical perspectives.

Introduction

This chapter consists of five sections of text giving some basic information and terminology, as well as a flavour of the arguments and issues typical of the rest of the book. Like the earlier chapter, the emphasis is on basic language and concepts rather than demonstrating examples of ethical analysis in action. A brief indication of the purpose and content of each section is given below:

▶ *Intentions, actions and consequences*: introducing a classification of ethical theories which underpins the remainder of the book and is intended to show the differing ways in which ethical theories work.
▶ *Other 'dimensions' of ethical theory*: providing some further classifications while gradually introducing more ideas of ethics.
▶ *Wesley Cragg model*: contrasts an 'ethics of doing' (i.e. action based) with an 'ethics of being' (related to moral development) and an 'ethics of perception'.
▶ *Ethics and the law*: is obeying the law all there is to being ethical in business? Some categorisations and comments.
▶ *A radical challenge*: is business ethics as an academic subject up to the task of providing a real critique of the business system?

It is suggested that the material in this chapter is read before attempting other chapters, even if you have some familiarity with business ethics. You may then find it valuable to refer back to it regularly as the subject as a whole begins to take shape through working with the theories and cases in later chapters.

Intentions, actions and consequences

If we look at the broad range of normative ethical theories available, it is useful to classify them in order to simplify their application and also see how they relate to each other. The simple model we will use here is shown below:

$$\text{Intentions} \rightarrow \text{Actions} \rightarrow \text{Consequences}$$

The idea we will try to capture is that the primary focus of a theory, or of a general approach (such as consequentialism) which covers a number of related theories, is one of the above. We also can see that intentions (along with a number of other inputs) inform our actions which (once again, along with other factors) produce consequences.

Intentions

Under this heading we include, in Chapter 9, ethical theories which give a prominent role to character and moral development. Particularly important here are the group of approaches under the heading of 'Virtue Theory'. Some of the earliest moral theories are those seen in the writings of Aristotle, who was concerned with how a life should be led in order to achieve its full potential and who argued for the cultivation of a range of personal virtues (each characterised as intermediate between more extreme and undesirable features). Thus courage was seen as a virtue to be cultivated whilst avoiding the extremes of rashness and cowardice. This approach was taken up by medieval Christian writers but then languished until becoming a major ingredient in normative ethics (and business ethics in particular) in the late 20th century.

Moral development is a subject of interest to psychologists as well as philosophers, leading to some controversial models (e.g. that of Kohlberg; see Chapter 4) with elements of description and prescription. Of obvious interest to criminologists, such models also have application in the human resource development (HRD) aspects of organisational theory.

Actions

Perhaps the most obvious approach to promoting morality in a society is through the prohibition of certain actions – you must not kill people! Banning actions which are visible and generally accepted as undesirable, making such prohibitions clear through the statement of laws, policing the situation so people who break such laws are caught and applying punishments is a well-established form of social control. You will notice that the reasons why something is prohibited may lie in the consequences of the action (if everyone evades tax, public spending crumbles) and the punishment itself is a consequence. However, the main focus is on the action itself. The theories underlying this approach are dealt with in Chapters 7 and 8.

There is a considerable literature on rights and duties which obviously also concentrates on actions, in this case possibly on things which should be done, rather than prohibitions. 'Deontology' is the term given to the study of moral obligations and this is usually contrasted with consequentialism as described below. A key writer in this area is Immanuel Kant who formulated a general prescription of how we should always act, the Categorical Imperative.

Theories which focus on actions can sound as if an assumption is being made that the agent, that is, the moral actor in a given context, has a free choice in decision-making. In a business context, however, we are more likely to be in a situation of drastically constrained action. For example, consider a telephone salesperson calling a prospective customer. This individual will probably be working to a script (usually obvious to the receiver of the call) and will have been trained in the responses they can make. The sales-talk and the decisions have been pre-packaged by the designer of the system who must therefore be at least jointly to blame if the sales pitch being adopted is dubious in some way. Thus we should also consider the 'action' of designing the sales pitch in our moral analysis, along with the strategic decision of marketing in this way. The ladder of responsibility therefore goes up to senior management. An interesting question, therefore, is the moral responsibility of the constrained and monitored individual at the bottom of the ladder who is in direct contact with the customer and may, in a very real sense, be delivering a product or service which is unethical. This issue is further considered in Chapter 19.

Consequences

Many business people consider themselves to be results orientated, thus putting the emphasis firmly on the consequences of their actions. The idea that 'the ends justify the means' has always been considered morally dubious, if only because it may be only too convenient to deflect attention from a current unethical course of action towards a promised good result in the future. However, the reality in the world of practical affairs is that many actions remain invisible while the results eventually come to light. This refers not only to financial performance (hopefully audited in a fair and transparent manner) but also to the less desirable consequences for other stakeholders.

This leads us to a key question in considering moral evaluation based on consequences: Which ones are relevant? From the mass of consequences of any action we take, which should enter our analysis and whose consequences are of primary importance? The most extreme case is when the decision maker considers only the consequences for themselves, an approach we term 'egoism'. In practice at least a family or other small social group is considered as relevant. In a business context shareholders (and other financial bodies, including the Inland Revenue) have a right to have the consequences for them given due attention (as they provide the capital) but a stakeholder approach will consider consequences for a wider group, including employees, suppliers, customers and the local community. However, if we continue this line of logic, as Environmental Audits actually attempt to do, we can see ripples of cause and effect spreading out in the future to wider populations. For example, we may decide to make a car out of a new material. Consequences may include the environmental effects of mining and producing that material and the eventual costs of disposing of it when the car is scrapped. Determining the consequences of all our actions is very demanding. In Chapters 5 and 6 (where consequence-related theories are considered) we argue it may well be impossibly demanding.

The theory which has the broadest view of the impact of decisions on wide populations is termed 'Utilitarianism' and has been the focus of much debate. The simple view that we must act so as to create the greatest happiness for the greatest number is fraught with problems of a theoretical and practical nature. At the very least our actions must also be constrained by laws to some extent, else would killing people be a moral option provided enough other people benefited as a result? We might say 'of course not', unless embarking on a highly dangerous construction project, typical of many undertaken in 19th century Britain and USA, which put the lives of workers at considerable risk, was considered as being equivalent to planning a murder!

More sophisticated versions of Utilitarianism can be defended, particularly those referred to as 'Rule Utilitarianism' (as opposed to 'Act Utilitarianism'), which attempts to overcome the difficulties of predicting every consequence through the development of robust decision rules (or heuristics) which can be relied upon to normally lead to appropriate consequences. Though this once again seems to put the focus back on controlling actions, the emphasis is still sufficiently on moral evaluation through consequences for our classification of rule utilitarianism as consequentialist to remain relevant.

Other 'dimensions' of ethical theory

While the 'intentions, actions and consequences' framework described above is of particular value in differentiating between different approaches to ethics, there are a number of other useful classification schemes, some of which we briefly outline below.

Scope of primary concern

When describing consequentialist theories above, it will be noted that our primary concern may be very narrow (the decision maker), broad (everyone) or some population in-between these extremes (a family, organisation, group of stakeholders...). This is not to say that we ignore individuals not within our focus, but there is a difference between, say, on the one hand considering ourselves to have ethical responsibility for a large group or alternatively having our focus only on our own well-being and considering our effect on the larger group in case it affects our personal well-being.

In Chapter 3 we develop this concept of moral scope in the context of 'stakeholder' terminology and in Chapter 19 the idea of 'moral distance' is briefly explored, with a number of case examples. The general idea we are reflecting is whether a group boundary is seen to exist where those within the group are worthy of ethical consideration whilst those outside are in some way treated differently. It should immediately be said that though some descriptive models seem to show that this is indeed how many view ethical decision-making (see Chapter 15 in particular), other theories of ethics are resolutely universalistic in application, arguing that we cannot pick and choose for our own convenience those individuals for whom we have ethical responsibility. In Chapter 7 we will see how Kantian ethics approaches this situation in a different way.

You will note that the above paragraphs contain a number of references to other chapters in this book. In fact, almost all the other chapters could have been referred to, as what I have called 'scope' is a fundamental concern.

Multiplicity of ethical theories

Many original writings on ethics will argue for a single and coherent approach for ethical evaluation and decision-making. However, no single approach has found universal favour. It has even been argued that particular approaches, and the technical languages in which they are expressed, will reflect the historical circumstances in which they were written. Indeed the meaning of words such as 'ethical' and 'moral' are hard if not impossible to pin down outside a given context. This argument can also be used to support the idea that a market-based business system is a unique social construction and therefore business ethics may produce different rules for behaviour than other contexts.

Without accepting this latter point in its entirety (i.e. business and organisational life do seem to present unusual ethical challenges but surely are not completely different from other human activity systems!), we have assumed in this book (in common with many others) that a number of different theoretical approaches to ethics have something to offer business ethics. It does appear that different theories do have the ability to highlight different aspects of the same problem context and therefore are of potential value.

This acceptance of the practical merit of using differing ethical approaches, together or as appropriate, itself reflects a theoretical position which not all would accept but most texts on business and organisational ethics do in fact deal with a range of theories even if they eventually favour a particular approach. In this text we will not argue for the primacy of any one approach and indeed encourage the exposure of any given case context to as wide a range of approaches as possible.

The organisation as a moral agent

Though firms and other organisations may be seen as legal entities (depending on the legal framework applying in a given country) there is a difference of opinion on whether an organisation itself can be seen as having moral responsibility. Obviously owners, directors, managers and other employees must accept moral responsibility in given contexts, defined perhaps by the law or by commonly accepted norms of social behaviour. To illustrate the latter point, a malicious gossip may cause considerable harm without falling foul of the law on libel, but be generally seen as having acted in a morally reprehensible fashion.

We may casually speak of an organisation being immoral but should this be taken as a shorthand way of saying its managers are acting unethically? It is common now to speak of an 'organisational culture' but can we say that an organisation has an immoral culture? There have been attempts to argue that an organisation can be viewed as a moral agent, in particular in the context of an environmental disaster when managers held culpable may wish to argue that they had been following traditional and accepted forms of behaviour. This might facilitate legal action taken against a firm. However, we will assume in this book that we can, strictly speaking, only use moral language when referring to individual people. We may refer to groups or an organisation as 'unethical' but this will be a figure of speech and used only when it carries a clear meaning. Legal language may refer to the rights and duties of individuals or firms as appropriate.

Wesley Cragg model

A different characterisation of the role of ethics in business is given in Cragg (1997), in particular his Appendix 8. This contrasts an 'ethics of doing' with an 'ethics of being', the latter being similar in scope and objectives to what we will term 'virtue ethics'. However, Cragg interposes a further dimension related to our perceptions of the world and this seems to be a useful focus in bringing to our attention the importance of how we see the world and other moral actors within it.

Thus we may interpret and extend our characterisation of the Cragg model as follows:

▶ *Dimension 1: An ethics of doing.* The focus here may be on actions (deontology) or on results (consequentialism). Typically proponents of such an ethic see their prescriptions as overriding other value systems and being capable of defining a personal goal of correct moral behaviour in a range of situations. The decision-making process is rational and explicit and we arrive at the values we adopt by choice. We are motivated by rational argument, whether internal or from our environment.

► *Dimension 2: An ethics of perception, vision, awareness and insight.* The focus in this case is on how we see the world and the language we use to describe and explain what we see. This is essential to any view of ethics which emphasises diagnosis and sensitive debate and is complementary to other views. It assumes a personal aim of broadening understanding through interaction with the environment and careful consideration of the inputs we receive, thus informing a process of personal value formation, decision and action.

► *Dimension 3: An ethics of being.* Here the focus is on the development of character and self-knowledge, sometimes referred to as virtues. This is driven by our internally recognised need to grow and develop as moral persons through interaction and reflection.

We may summarise the above in a slightly different way. In an 'ethics of doing' the goal is correct behaviour, while in an 'ethics of awareness' it is broadening our understanding and in an 'ethics of being' it is self-development and self-knowledge.

In an 'ethics of doing' we choose our values by rational argument, while in an 'ethics of awareness' we recognise the need for education and a searching of the environment for further insights and sources of meaning. An 'ethics of being' follows a similar path but with greater emphasis on reflection and the internalisation of values as part of our normal behaviour. The virtues reflect what we do as well as how we see ourselves.

Ethics and the law

The relationship between ethics and the law is something we will always have to bear in mind from a theoretical as well as a practical point of view. The philosophy of law, jurisprudence, is a large area of study with a considerable overlap with applied ethics, but which also addresses a number of issues we cannot deal with here. Both ethics (including business ethics) and the legal system in a given country evolve over time. If we see the law as the operationalisation of a moral code then we may note the following:

► There are actions which are legal but may be considered unethical by some individuals in a society.

▶ There are actions which may be illegal but have no specific ethical content (except, of course, that one should obey the law!). Typically this may include minor infringements of laws which are intended as administrational or where arbitrary limits have been set. This is not to say that such laws can be broken but that extensive ethical analysis may not be useful.

▶ Some non-deontological approaches to ethics relate to character development or to maximising social benefit which are simply not addressed by the law, except as they relate to resulting actions. It is not illegal to wish someone harm unless you do (or perhaps say) something about it, though this does not show a high level of moral development! Similarly, it is hard to see how a law could operationalise the utilitarian objective of maximising happiness!

Another key issue in political and social debate is the freedom of individuals in a society. An underpinning assumption in a market economy is that consumers have freedom of choice, if only for the practical reason that this is how a market works. There is also an ongoing theme in the history of ethics and political theory, in the Western tradition at least, of the importance of the liberty of the individual (see the section on utilitarianism in Chapter 6 and on human rights in Chapter 7). Some economic theories relating to business ethics translate this as an injunction to maximise the freedom of the individual through reducing rules, regulations and the influence of the state.

It should be obvious that many ethical theories prescribe limitations and constraints on the action of the individual or an organisation, often enforced by the law. One of the challenges facing utilitarianism (as opposed to egoism) is the constraint it places on the objectives to be pursued by ethical agents. Theories which propound various human rights automatically impose duties on other individuals and governments to respect and promote such rights. The balance between ethics, liberty and the law is therefore something which should always be borne in mind. At a simple level an organisation has to decide whether it operates through a large number of rules and regulations or whether it trusts appropriately trained individuals to act ethically in the absence of such rules. A danger is that when things go wrong, senior management can be vulnerable in the absence of internal rules and procedures, hence such devices may be imposed to protect individuals' backs rather than promote real ethical behaviour (see the section in Chapter 16 on the responsibility of senior executives when accidents occur).

A further point to note in the discussion above is the role played by politics and political institutions in a society. Thus the simple model we are suggesting of factors to be borne in mind here is a balance of the following:

- Ethics
- Law
- Liberty
- Politics.

It is important to remember that organisations really are diverse in their approach to legality and fairness to customers. Television programmes such as 'Watchdog' and some of the stories which appear in the financial pages of the press continue to portray the criminal world which adjoins the world of legitimate business dealings. Most business ethics literature is not concerned with outright criminal activity, simply because there is no ethical dilemma present in, say, the ethical assessment of a bogus organisation set up as a front for money laundering; this is obviously wrong and against the law! Business ethics is primarily concerned with such ambiguous and difficult boundaries as where legitimate business may have unfortunate consequences for some stakeholders, or where an entrepreneur crosses the line into shady dealings to protect the interests of stakeholders, or when new legislation shows previously accepted business practice as now being wrong.

It is quite useful at this point to look at a simple listing of some types of business and see how they relate to crime, noting that we are mainly concerned here with private sector businesses rather than public sector organisations:

- genuine businesses which intend to operate well within the law, though may inevitably include isolated examples of petty crime;
- genuine businesses which nonetheless have an operating culture which condones expense account 'inaccuracies' and minor thefts;
- businesses which pride themselves in testing out the edges of legally admissible practice;
- businesses which profess to work in the best interests of shareholders but which have a cavalier approach which frequently 'crosses the line', often for the personal benefit of managers;

- amoral businesses which will break the law provided a cost–benefit analysis of punishment and reward are in their favour;
- businesses which carry out some genuine trading but also condone criminal activity;
- businesses which are set up as a front for systematic criminal activity;
- businesses where the core activity (e.g. running fraudulent pyramid selling schemes) is illegal.

The value of such a list is to draw attention to some key points:

- There is a distinction between the core activity or culture of a business being dubious and the situation where a normal business contains parts with different ethical standards. It can be a mistake when conducting ethical evaluation to assume a business is ethically homogeneous.
- Many well-meaning organisations have issues of communication and control, though one may suspect that where, for example, low-level expense account cheating is rife, employees may be following the (perceived) poor example of their senior colleagues.
- There is a difference of intention between a business set up for criminal activity and one which sees breaking the law as a means to a more acceptable end. Unfortunately, doing the wrong thing for the right reason can become a bad habit.
- Some unethical, though in earlier times condoned, practices such as discrimination, bullying, deceiving the customer about their rights and so forth eventually may become illegal.

It is not too difficult to infer similar lists and arguments relating to public sector organisations, often with the added complication of political involvement.

It might finally be remembered that as the media contain many stories of immoral and illegal organisational activity this may simply reflect the large number and range of organisations which exist in our society and, as they deal with large amounts of cash, they provide a tempting setting for criminal activity. The prevalence of new technology in organisational life has brought both new means of control and new opportunities for crime, both within and against organisations. Modern organisations (public and private) are, however, some of the most highly audited and regulated social institutions that have ever existed.

A radical challenge to business ethics

It is sometimes useful to see a radically different characterisation of a subject. With this in mind, note the quotations from the opening of Parker (1998) given below:

> Ethics? I suppose the most common definition of ethics is the attempt to build a systematic set of normative prescriptions about human behaviour, codes to govern everyday morals and morality. . . . If in doubt about our conduct, we could refer to a comprehensive dictionary of ethics, a code book, to discover what we should do, to whom and why. Otherwise, what would be the point of all this thinking, talking and writing? . . . However, the project of ethics . . . seems to have spent an awful lot of time going nowhere . . . the idea of foundational ethics is one that cannot (and perhaps should not) be taken very seriously.

This is not a casual attempt to rubbish the idea of business ethics, as one might find in some proponents of an 'anything goes' philosophy of life. It is the beginning of a serious challenge by a number of writers (in an edited volume, though Martin Parker is the author of the quotes given above and of the similarly provocative 'Against Management', Parker [2002]) on the effectiveness of 'business ethics' in providing a critique of what are seen as a number of problems in organisational life.

It might be useful to see this discussion in the light of the following comments from Baldwin (2001), a survey of recent Western philosophy:

> moral practice and reflection have an iterative structure whereby simple systems of rules, responsibilities and virtues are progressively qualified and enhanced as human cultures become more complicated, self-conscious and self-critical, finding value in their own moral practices and institutions . . . it is vain to hope for a complete account of morality.

Following this view, we might see Parker *et al.*'s contributions as developments in ethical thought rather than an 'alternative product' (though see Parker [2002] on this!). This is the approach taken in this book where material from Parker (1998) is used as part of the business ethics debate.

Therefore we will view the first two sentences quoted from Parker (1998) above as an unsatisfactory (though not uncommon) characterisation of business ethics. Whether the 2500-year 'ethics project' has delivered the goods (or any goods) is a matter for discussion, though Baldwin's comments on the evolution of value systems seem useful, if somewhat guarded.

Summary and next steps

This chapter has ranged over a set of concepts and simple models which are essential background to studying business ethics. As we noted at the start, this material should be re-read when progress has been made in coming to terms with the later chapters in this book as the points made here will come into clearer perspective. It is also important to develop the habit of looking at current examples of reported unethical behaviour in the media, as well as experiences within organisations, in terms of the language and models of business ethics. As well as aiding the development of knowledge and understanding of business ethics as an academic discipline, such research and reflection make the subject real and far more interesting.

References and further reading

Specific references in this chapter, as in others chapters, may be followed up in the Annotated bibliography.

As an extra feature in this introductory chapter, included below are details of some elementary texts on ethics as well as on business ethics. These have not been specifically mentioned in Chapter 2. If you wish to explore this more general background you would be advised to browse through some of the texts below in order to find material consistent with your level of current knowledge. An Annotated bibliography is given at the end of the book. This includes comments on the texts listed below.

Baggini, J. and Fosl, P.S. (2003), *The Philosopher's Toolkit: A Compendium of Philosophical Concepts and Methods*, Blackwell, Oxford.
Baldwin, T. (2001), *Contemporary Philosophy*, OUP, Oxford.
Benn, P. (1998), *Ethics*, UCL Press, London.
Blackburn, S. (2001), *Being Good: A Short Introduction to Ethics*, OUP, Oxford.
Cohen, M. (2003), *101 Ethical Dilemmas*, Routledge, London.
Cottingham, J. (1998), *Philosophy and the Good Life*, CUP, Cambridge.
Frederick, R.E. (ed.) (1999), *A Companion to Business Ethics*, Blackwell, Oxford.
Gensler, H.J. (1998), *Ethics: A Contemporary Introduction*, Routledge, London.
Glover, J. (1999), *Humanity: A Moral History of the Twentieth Century*, Jonathan Cape, London.

LaFollette, H. (ed.) (2000), *The Blackwell Guide to Ethical Theory*, Blackwell, Oxford.

Norman, R. (1998), *The Moral Philosophers: An Introduction to Ethics* (2nd edn), OUP, Oxford.

Riddall, J.G. (1999), *Jurisprudence* (2nd edn), Butterworths, London.

Singer, P. (ed.) (1993), *A Companion to Ethics*, Blackwell, Oxford.

Singer, P. (1997), *How are We to Live: Ethics in an Age of Self-interest*, OUP, Oxford.

Thompson, M. (1999), *Ethical Theory*, Hodder and Stoughton, London.

Vardy, P. and Grosch, P. (1994), *The Puzzle of Ethics*, HarperCollins, London.

3 Stakeholders and Corporate Social Responsibility

Purpose and learning outcomes

The purpose of this chapter is to introduce two key concepts in business ethics. These are the use of the word 'stakeholder' and the idea of Corporate Social Responsibility (CSR). The ideas given here are an important part of the foundation on which a number of other ideas in business ethics depend.

You will be able to

▶ effectively use the idea of stakeholders in an ethical discussion;
▶ show an understanding of the concept of CSR and its basic variants.

Introduction

The use of the term 'stakeholder', originally introduced into management theory as a contrast to 'shareholder', indicates a willingness to consider an organisation as having moral responsibility towards a potentially wide range of individuals and organisations. The word 'stakeholder' is also used extensively in strategic management as a practical way of referring to agents who may affect, or be affected by, an organisation. In this chapter we show how valuable this concept can be in ethical analysis and note how it relates to the idea of moral distance which occurs with some frequency in later chapters.

The second major section in this chapter introduces the idea of CSR which, in effect, considers the ethical role of an organisation as a whole in its environment. It has been noted that business owners and managers may feel uncomfortable with some uses of moral language as applied to their areas of responsibility. This may result from a perception that ethical theories may be idealistic and excessively demanding when applied by outsiders with little experience of the pressures and demands of practical business management. There is therefore some merit in the development of ethical models of behaviour by business specialists and CSR is an example of this trend. However, it may be regarded by the 'outsiders' as yet another example of industry's use of public relations in pursuit of basically economic objectives! The discussion in Chapter 14 on moral muteness is also of some relevance to arguments relating to the language resources for discussing ethical issues in business.

Included within this section is a brief note on ethical investment – financial funds where investment decisions depend partly on the ethical nature of the companies and sectors involved. It is not always clear why some forms of commercial activity are considered ethical while others are not. Some of the cases in this book seem to suggest that a greater range of organisations operate with doubtful ethics than we would hope to be the case.

The stakeholder concept

Even if you have only a brief acquaintance with management theory you are likely to have come across the term 'stakeholders'. Though only developed in the later part of the 20th century this word seems to have struck a chord with both practitioners and management theorists. Broadly speaking, the stakeholders of an organisation are the individuals, groups or other organisations which are affected by, or can affect, the organisation in pursuit of its goals. A typical list of stakeholder categories for a business might be:

► Employees
► Customers
► Suppliers
► Shareholders
► Other suppliers of capital
► Local communities
► Government
► Pressure groups
► Competitors.

This may seem a long list but it barely scratches the surface of the potential complexity of a network of stakeholders. For example, it may be necessary to define sub-categories of 'employees' as the effect of company policy on shop-floor workers may be quite different from the effect on management and on board members, particularly in a large, multinational firm with a complex organisational structure or at a time of organisational upheaval. This broad category might also include Trade Unions and Professional Institutes who represent various employee groups or establish codes of practice of professional behaviour. Another example is 'pressure groups', which are likely to have a stronger influence in some industries (e.g. those involved in animal research) rather than others.

It should also be obvious, once one begins to seriously explore stakeholder groups in a specific context, that more complex network effects are important. Union action may affect all companies in a sector, that is a given firm's competitors, and government policy will likewise have effects on the full range of stakeholders. If a firm enters into a joint venture partnership with a supplier then the supplier's employees, its own (i.e. second tier) suppliers will be affected and so forth. This latter point leads to the idea that a network model relating to interacting stakeholders in a supply chain might yield more valuable insights than any model focussing only on direct stakeholder influences.

If one alternatively considers stakeholders in a public service context, for example local government or the health service, not only does the complexity increase but also the ambiguity of who exactly qualifies as a stakeholder. It is easy to argue in many cases that everyone (individual or corporate) is a stakeholder in some way! Whilst it is important to remember from an ethical standpoint that one's actions may affect such a wide range of people, it can also lead to the abandonment of any idea of systematic stakeholder consultation and analysis as impractical. This practical point should not be forgotten if effective ethical action is intended. Care and judgement is required even in this very basic stage of deciding who is really affected in a given context.

One approach, of course, is simply to note what legal and contractual duties exist with respect to other individuals and draw the stakeholder boundaries for ethical analysis with this in mind. A strategic use of stakeholder concepts is likely to draw different boundaries; customers are likely to be of greater importance to the survival of an enterprise than a purely legalistic view of the world will show. This illustrates an important point that the development of a 'stakeholder model' must depend on its purpose; different models are likely to have practical value in different decision-making contexts. In this book we adopt a pluralistic view of business ethics and therefore a narrow, legalistic approach to drawing stakeholder boundaries will not support many of the approaches we explore. It would also be of some concern if 'ethical analysis' became a narrow and defensive activity. Surely it is more valuable to consider the ethical implications of different uses of the stakeholder model, that is if we use stakeholder ideas in strategic market planning we need to reflect ethical concerns in this context.

The language we have used so far appears to strongly link stakeholder theory with a consequentialist view of ethics (see Chapter 2) and even a utilitarian perspective (see Chapter 6). The discussion in Chapter 6 on the limitations of applying consequentialist thinking to a wide population should be noted, as should the difficulties mentioned in Chapter 21 of environmental analysis, where long and diffuse chains of cause and effect are evident. We should also note that stakeholder ethical analysis can be conducted in terms of rights and duties (see Chapter 7), social contract theory (see Chapter 8) and discourse ethics (see Chapter 9). Indeed some limited notion of stakeholders may be seen to underpin the idea of a moral community, limited only because of the practical difficulties mentioned above.

Though the use of the term 'stakeholders' is generally seen as a major improvement on a narrow conception of 'shareholders' as the source of an organisation's objectives, there are some further problems in its definition and use. One can imagine a meeting of a company's executives, local politicians and environmental activists having a discussion on the company's plans for the future where each person uses the word 'stakeholder' but means something different. The executives will talk about paying attention to the needs of all stakeholders and the other participants may feel reassured, but the executives may be using a tight, legalistic view of their duties in terms of consultation and action. Rather than expose the differences between those involved, the term 'stakeholder' may hide them. This may be intentional, particularly on the part of the company, or may simply be a misunderstanding.

Of course, the non-company participants will eventually discover if they have been ignored and feel cheated and resistant to any further proposals the company may make. If the executives intended to mislead and see 'stakeholder' as just another weapon in the political arsenal of communicational 'spin' then they may have succeeded in the short term, though at a cost to long-term reputation. However, if all partici-pants were simply naïve and sloppy in their use of words then the loss of trust, as well as misplaced confidence that agreed actions were really appropriate for all parties, is highly unfortunate.

There is a substantial management literature which attempts to untangle the possible uses and meanings of the term 'stakeholder'. The optimistic view is that either a comprehensive definition can be found or that the sense of the word revealed by common usage is non-problematic. We noted above that a definition on the lines of 'all agents affected by the action of an organisation', though sounding reasonable at the level of elementary theory, is difficult to use in a practical context. We might then wonder if the term 'stakeholder' is vacuous and should be avoided? A compromise, typical of introductory textbooks, is to list some obvious examples of people associated with an organisation (as in the list at the beginning of this section) and leave the rest to common sense.

This all rather ignores the major role which the stakeholder concept plays in consequentialist forms of business ethics. For example, for utilitarianism to make any sense we have to be able to say whose utility counts in the 'calculus'. Assuming we agree that including 'everyone' would be hard to operationalise and 'shareholders' is hardly in the spirit of utilitarianism then we have a problem! Perhaps the only way forward is to explicitly and openly agree who counts in a given instance. In this case the focus of our ethical analysis turns to the process of deciding who counts and how their utility is to be taken into account.

Within a deontological framework, legal definitions of duties, obligations and so forth must obviously include some specification of who is involved. It is worth reflecting on whether the more utopian conceptions of human rights are entirely clear on such matters (see Chapter 7). Contractarian and discourse ethics must obviously also pay considerable attention to the specification of who is involved.

It should come as no surprise that this very basic concern of who is involved in ethical discussion and whose rights, needs and utility are to be explicitly taken into account is of critical importance. As we discuss elsewhere (e.g. in marketing ethics in Chapter 19) pla-cing individuals outside the scope of our ethical consideration may be a dubious move if it leads to their being stigmatised as ripe for exploitation or simply ignored as unimportant or 'nothing to do with us'!

Corporate Social Responsibility

One of the hot topics in modern management theory, usually termed 'Corporate Social Responsibility', is of particular and obvious interest to us in our introductory survey of business ethics. It should be said immediately that a large number of Web-based resources and published papers and reports relate to this area of work and these should be used to develop the ideas presented here. This is also an area of direct concern to all organisations and the professions which contribute to management and therefore much material is available in the forms of Codes of Practice and down-to-earth advice for senior managers.

Over the past few years we have become accustomed to seeing business as an essentially international, or even 'global', activity. An unsophisticated use of such language ignores the path of international trade and exploitation (in all senses of the word) that ambitious nations have followed throughout history. The Chinese, early in the Ming Dynasty (16th century), were unusual in that having sent a large exploration fleet round the world subsequently decided, based on a perception of superiority, not to bother with further trading ventures! Most Western nations embraced trade as an economic and political imperative, as China discovered to its cost in the 19th century.

In searching for a more useful characterisation of globalisation, Crane and Matten (2004) emphasise the technological and political nature of recent trends leading to a definition of globalisation as '...the progressive eroding of the relevance of territorial bases for social, economic and political activities, processes and relations' (see their book for detailed argument and references leading to this definition).

This definition appears useful in also drawing our attention to cultural issues (see Chapter 15), the differing legal frameworks within which business activity may take place (and thus becoming an important parameter in location decisions) and related issues of accountability and governmental control.

An associated concept is 'sustainability', or 'sustainable development', which has the following widely known, if controversial, definition '...development that meets the needs of the present without compromising the ability of future generations to meet their own needs'. While neatly capturing an idea usually referred to as 'intergenerational equity', with obvious relevance to the green environment, it can only leave unanswered the considerable doubts related to what this means in practical terms. It appears that even the most cautious practical approach to environmental management and business activity uses some non-renewable resources, creates some waste and involves potentially damaging technologies. Can we really relate present causes to future effects in order to guarantee sustainability? At even a basic level, there is surely a moral imperative that we should seriously address this issue and this is why the notion of sustainability, however vague, is an important component of business ethics. An implication of the acceptance of sustainability as a corporate objective is the importance of environmental and social measures of performance in addition to the usual economic ones. We return to these ideas in Chapter 21.

The question of whether a firm has 'social responsibilities' as well as economic ones has been debated with increasing vigour in recent times. As so often is the case, the idea that entrepreneurs and factory owners have social responsibilities to their workers, suppliers and customers has a long if somewhat patchy history. Some prominent industrialists of the past (e.g. Cadbury and Wedgwood) saw a moral duty in their relationships with all individuals and acted accordingly, often demonstrating that successful business can draw on apparently altruistic roots. We may, of course, merely characterise this as a cunning form of capitalism with an eye to long-term economic achievement and indeed it can often be difficult to extract a sense of the real motivation underlying such forms of socially aware action. More systematic debate in the latter half of the 20th century has led to the notion of CSR, typically defined as covering a comprehensive set of economic, legal, ethical and even philanthropic expectations. While the first two are fairly obvious the latter will need some explanation.

Ethical responsibility, over and above meeting legal requirements and satisfying the objectives of the owners of a business, relates to the broader expectations of society as to the way a firm and its employees should behave. This is often merely the anticipation of legislation, for example in areas such as unfair discrimination, access, environmentally friendly packaging and so forth. It may have the practical advantages of attracting good publicity or giving an organisation the opportunity to discover in advance the most effective way to meet legislation which is seen as inevitable. Thus ethical responsibility may be seen as long-term economic good sense. There is, as we mention elsewhere, an alternative argument that there are ethical duties, beyond the provision of the current law and any future legislation. We can easily see that such acceptance of ethical responsibility is the opposite approach to the firm which actively seeks to locate in countries with the most permissive legislation, for example, on the protection of workers rights and safety.

The idea that organisations should engage in philanthropic activities such as charitable donations and community action is an extension of the above discussion. Typically no future legislation is being anticipated but a similar debate applies in that such activity may have long-term economic goals. It can even be argued that all organisations should not engage in pure philanthropy (i.e. activities beyond their core mission and objectives). This is most forcefully put forward for businesses using the argument that philanthropy robs the shareholders, but can lead to subtle distinctions when applied to public sector organisations, voluntary sector bodies and charities. This debate is inextricably linked to the debate on the ethical nature of a corporation; of course, individual people can behave philanthropically and may see themselves as having moral duties beyond the law but can the same be said of an organisation?

Crane and Matten argue that the above characterisation of CSR is somewhat ineffective and put forward some alternatives:

▶ *Corporate Social Responsiveness (CSR renamed and made strategic)* – '...the capacity of a corporation to respond to social pressures'. This nicely reflects the view that social responsibility mainly relates to being strategically proactive, for example, by anticipating future legislation and social expectations.
▶ *Corporate Citizenship (CC)* – this covers a range of positions, some equivalent to those outlined above. The 'extended view' is perhaps most interesting as it addresses the political role of a corporation in championing citizenship rights (e.g. equality, a safe environment, etc.). As these will differ between countries, this addresses a key concern in the operation of the multinational corporation, where stakeholders will be drawn from different societies, legal environments and political contexts. It also relates to the debate on sustainability, that is through addressing the rights of future citizens.

Two points should be noted in this context. The word 'political' in the above paragraph relates to its common meaning of politics in a national context rather than the sense of 'organisational politics' as explored in

Chapter 10. Secondly, Crane and Matten (2004), as part of an extended discussion on the evolution of the various strands of CSR, note that practitioners from industry tend to dislike terms such as 'business ethics' and 'social responsibility' as they seem to infer a failure on the part of industry to behave responsibly. Hence 'corporate citizenship' could be seen as signalling a new and more positive start to the debate, with good behaviour appearing as a natural part of business thinking. This is in complete contrast to the radical analyses (see Chapter 2) which see business ethics as a tame concept, now lacking critical edge and in need of replacement with something tougher and more challenging!

Whether business ethics really is too soft for the radicals and too censorious for practitioners is something you will no doubt form a view on as you increase your knowledge of its concepts and application. Re-branding it under a different name seems a pointless exercise unless the new conception can uniquely capture some important and previously omitted facet of moral behaviour.

Having now explored some issues of theory and definition we now turn to some issues relating to current views of CSR and related concepts. A typical list of the concerns included within CSR are as follows:

▶ Corporate Governance, relating to top-level decision-making, accountability, risk management and the remuneration of executives (see Chapter 22);
▶ environmental management and the concept of sustainability (see Chapter 21);
▶ treating employees fairly (see Chapters 8, 13 and 17 for examples);
▶ operating ethically in the marketplace, in terms of suppliers and customers (see Chapters 18, 19 and 20);
▶ ethical investment and social reporting.

To begin at the top, one of the longest-running debates in management and organisation theory is about the effects of the separation between the ownership of a company and its management. While in a small company ownership and control may rest in the hands of a small number of highly involved entrepreneurs, the picture often changes dramatically when the company grows. Even a cursory glance at the business news sections of newspapers will show cases where the shareholders, often financial institutions (banks, insurance companies, pension funds and the like), are in dispute with strong-minded chief executives over major decisions relating to mergers, board membership and directors pay. Such has been the concern at the antics of some senior managers that a number of recent reports have laid down ethical conditions for managing organisations at the highest level (see Chapter 22). This area is usually seen as a key part of the finance and accounting function of an organisation, though the issues may well encompass all the functions in an organisation.

Environmental management may concentrate at the operational level, in terms of waste management, energy consumption, facilities management and so forth (i.e. with an emphasis on cost reduction and operational risk management). It may draw functions together, for example in terms of product and process design, and thus have an important role in integrating organisational activities, as seen in the use of such methodologies as the 'Business Excellence' model. It may also be concerned with compliance to legislation, both current and forthcoming. These activities, as we describe in Chapter 21, may be linked with the ideal of sustainability and more profound models of interaction with the natural world.

Much of the concern in management and organisational ethics is with the fair treatment of employees, perhaps driven by legislation (e.g. relating to unfair discrimination), by current ideas of motivation or even by some more direct reference to ethical norms. Whilst fairness may seem an obviously desirable objective, the pressures of competition, cost-cutting as well as organisational politics may reduce the practical management of an organisation to a battle-field where individual survival (or generous severance) becomes the goal.

All organisations operate in a variety of marketplaces. In terms of material supply, particularly at an international level, notions of fair trade are increasingly seen as being important. This provides a series of sharp dilemmas for many organisations, for example relating to the sourcing of material supply and manufacture or service provision in areas of the world with lower costs, and in some cases scandalous working conditions. The loss of jobs in the 'home country' can be considerable, as can be the benefits to emerging economies. It can also provide dilemmas for consumers in terms of the purchase of relatively expensive goods from small farmers and suppliers.

Ethical investment may relate to the above, but the term is often used in the context of investment fund management, that is the extent to which shares are only purchased in companies which meet certain criteria of ethical operation. Such criteria may be positive (in terms of the areas listed above, for example) or negative, that is involve not investing in companies of industrial sectors such as the arms trade, tobacco and suchlike. In a report on the structure of the share portfolios of 21 major UK-based 'ethical funds' (see the *Sunday Telegraph* 19 October 2003 for details), it was noted that the following sectors were avoided by such funds (number of funds avoiding the sector given in brackets):

► Alcohol production and sale (14 out of 21)
► Animal testing (20 out of 21)
► Armaments (All 21)
► Environmental damage (19 out of 21)
► Gambling services (16 out of 21)
► Nuclear power (19 out of 21)
► Oppressive regimes (17 out of 21)
► Pornography (18 out of 21)
► Tobacco production and sale (All 21).

Of the 21 funds listed, 10 avoided all the above sectors. The 21 funds have combined assets of around £2.5bn, that is around 1 per cent of the total market. It is interesting to ask what it is about 'armaments' and 'tobacco' which make these sectors universally avoided by funds wishing to attract the 'ethical' label, while 'oppressive regimes' and 'alcohol' have a more mixed response. The two funds not avoiding 'nuclear power' are not the same as the two not avoiding 'environmental damage'. So exactly how is the 'moral worthiness' of an industrial sector decided by an investment fund?

Finally, some companies expend considerable energy in carrying out internal social audits of their policies and operations and in reporting on this to stakeholders in, say, their annual report and accounts. While it may be good public relations to openly demonstrate the areas of your organisation which can boast good social policies, it will necessarily also show areas of concern. However, if these are matched to effective action plans and continuous improvement is shown from year to year, then this form of reporting can provide sound publicity as well as internal motivation and planning for continuous improvement and occasional more dramatic changes.

Summary

The stakeholder concept is of obvious value and underlies much discussion as our exploration of business ethics continues. Similarly CSR includes ideas which are central to an understanding of business ethics. You will have noticed that the above discussion shows that there is a certain amount of disagreement over the right way to introduce ethical consideration into management. There are a number of specialist texts which cover these topics in particular (see Annotated bibliography).

4 Descriptive ethics

Purpose and learning outcomes

The purpose of this chapter is to introduce some models and concepts of descriptive ethics, in particular relating to models of decision-making, the factors which may influence ethical action and the possible stages of moral development for individuals and organisations.

You will be able to

▶ demonstrate a knowledge of a range of practical models which are helpful in using ethical ideas in a business context;
▶ appreciate some basic ideas of moral development;
▶ show an understanding of the ethical concerns of business practitioners.

Introduction

As we noted in Chapter 1, descriptive ethics is an alternative approach to our subject, where observations of how ethics is seen to affect decision-making is the starting point in arriving at explanations and practical prescriptions. The first model we introduce below builds on a theoretical idea and a practical observation. Whilst we may agree that there is potentially some ethical content in all management action, it may require imagination and a willingness to 'think outside the box' of accepted preconceptions and working culture to be aware of the many ways in which we may relate ethics to action, in a complex organisational setting. What really are the consequences of our actions? Whose rights are we ignoring? Are we willing to engage in rigorous questioning of our own motives in taking some course of action? Furthermore, even if we are thorough and conscientious in thinking through moral implications, are we willing and able to carry our judgement through into appropriate action? The area explored by this simple model illustrates very clearly how ideas and observations may usefully interact.

The next section pushes this idea further by embedding it in a popular model which can then be related to individual and situational factors which relate to ethical judgement and decision-making in an organisational context. This material is typical of a range of recent management research and can be seen in conjunction with the 'perspectives from other cultures' outlined in Chapter 15. We then include a brief note on the Kohlberg moral development model which has been highly influential in areas including and beyond business ethics.

We then mention some models and findings from the descriptive literature on corporate attitudes to moral development and the typical lists that mangers produce when asked what they consider to be the ethical issues arising in their jobs. We end the chapter with a final model of ethical organisational decision-making, which is slightly more ambitious in the factors it takes into account. In fact some highly complex models have been produced which seek to link many of the factors mentioned in this chapter. However, a balance has to be struck in model-building between simplicity and the inclusion of a comprehensive range of factors. The latter can easily lead to structures which are impressive on paper but of absolutely no use to practitioners. We have, therefore, kept to simple models, which is also appropriate in the context of an introductory text.

Awareness, judgement and action

In Chapter 2 we introduced a contrast between ethical theories based on intentions, on actions and on consequences. We can now pursue the link between intention and action in a different way by considering the following simple three-stage model of how we might move from awareness to action. The model is similar to others existing in the practical management literature, for example the Awareness, Intention, Decision, Action (AIDA) model in marketing.

▶ Moral awareness (i.e. recognition that there are ethical issues in a specific decision-making context)
▶ Moral judgement (i.e. deciding what is the 'right thing to do')
▶ Ethical behaviour (i.e. doing the 'right thing').

One strength of this model is that it draws attention to two very important points which are central to business ethics. The first is that we may lack moral awareness, that is we often simply do not see that

LIBRARY, UNIVERSITY OF CHESTER

an ethical perspective is needed in many decision-making contexts. In many cases we make a decision by looking to see how things were resolved in the past with an automatic, and often totally unjustified, assumption that previous behaviour was ethically satisfactory. This may not be the case or the situation may have changed. In particular, many management and working practices which were accepted in the past may now be considered quite unethical, for example in the areas of working conditions, the role of women in organisations or the need to promote diversity. A simple solution would be to develop the ability to look for an ethical dimension in the context of all decision-making. Certainly this looks reasonable for major and unusual decision contexts but most organisations have thousands of small decisions made every day at an operational level and it is in such areas, particularly when contact with customers and suppliers is involved, that vigilance may be needed.

The second point shown by the model is the distinction between deciding and doing. The gap which often exists between decision-making and implementation is a regularly occurring theme in the management literature. The decider may not be the doer, or may not fully communicate what needs to be done or may not monitor implementation. The decision maker may attempt to avoid the consequences of unethical implementation by blaming others, perhaps in another department or a supplier who cuts corners. The obvious point is that we must clarify issues of responsibility, that is a decision not only covers what should be done but also how this is communicated and the implementation controlled. It could be argued that when ethical decision-making is discussed in the literature, it is assumed that the decision-making process includes all three stages of this model. In an organisational context, this is a naïve assumption and this model draws attention to some of the potential problems.

However, one drawback of this model (hinted at above) is that it almost appears that only one agent (or a cohesive group) is doing the recognition, deciding and acting. Interesting points arise when we ask whether awareness is likely to differ in intensity in a less-homogenous group and how such differences are to be resolved. How does this relate to ideas of organisational culture and to accepted decision-making practices within large organisations? Once we begin to look at this model in an informed and critical way we can easily see ways in which it should be extended. This is typical of management models. The balance between simplicity (which makes a model memorable) and complexity (covering a larger range of factors) is always a matter of judgment. Feel free to experiment with model building as you gain an understanding of further aspects of this complex area.

Descriptive ethics – how do individuals actually make moral decisions in practice?

Based on similar ideas to those in the previous section but with an expansion of the 'action stage' which is of particular importance in an organisational setting, one of the simplest models of ethical organisational decision-making envisages four stages as follows:

1. recognition of a moral issue;
2. making a moral judgement regarding that issue;
3. establishing an intention to act on that judgement;
4. acting in line with the intentions.

This model is used as a framework in Crane and Matten (2004) (see this reference for more details of the factors mentioned in this section, in particular of the research which supports these findings), with links being made to individual and situational factors (see below) which appear to influence actual decision-making in practical organisational contexts. While this model is primarily prescriptive (i.e. there are few studies which show that individuals routinely follow such an approach) it is useful in structuring a consideration of the factors which may affect such decision-making in practice.

As we noted earlier, such models are valuable in emphasising first of all the need for recognising a moral issue – whether involving an individual's imagination and sensitivity to moral concerns or effective mechanisms in an organisation for alerting staff to ethical concerns relevant to the industry or profession in question. Moral development and education have an obvious part to play here. It is not clear, however, in this model whether 'making a moral judgement' is an individual or group concern. Perhaps some reference to the ideas of discourse ethics (see Chapter 9) might be of value in unravelling the complex group and individual psychological factors involved in forming and expressing moral concerns. In Chapter 14 we are concerned both with moral muteness (when moral concerns are not adequately articulated) as well as whistleblowing, which is often based on an employee's ethical judgement which is at odds with an organisation's policies and working culture.

The importance of establishing an intention to act rather than ignore an issue is of obvious importance – ethics is more than a spectator sport! This is at the core of Hume's approach, as briefly mentioned in Chapter 5. In an organisational context, where there are conflicting priorities and continuing competition for resources, establishing an intention to act may be difficult. Finally, even with all the best intentions, we still have to actually act according to these intentions or ethics becomes empty promises and vacuous posturing. This is an obvious point to make, though in many instances may be highly problematic. We explore this in the context of reputation and the internal politics of ethical action in Chapter 10.

It should also be noted that this simple linear model may be misleading, or perhaps even perceived as naïve, for a number of reasons. Recognition of a moral issue may well depend on our past experience, rewards and punishments as well as our observations of the actions of others as might our steady progression through the four stages of the model. Organisational and personal history is important, particularly if it promotes a culture where asking too many questions may lead to challenging an organisation's mission. This is a concern raised in Chapter 19, where ideas of moral distance in the context of selling dubious products is a useful concept in showing how some ill effects of an organisation's actions may become characterised as non-issues, beyond some mythical ethical boundary of relevance.

As so often in this book, and in management theory in general, models of decision-making are mainly useful as objects to be radically criticised and learnt from rather than converted into flow diagrams and pinned on the office wall. They do, however, remind us of issues to be addressed and this is of considerable importance in the busy world of targets, networks and problem solving.

The individual factors mentioned by most researchers include some factors where there is no decisive evidence of correlation with ethical actions (e.g. gender and education) though common sense might suggest otherwise. Also included are factors such as national culture and moral development which have been the subject of much research (see Chapter 15 on the former and the short note on the Kohlberg model of moral development). Moral imagination is also important in this context, as we mentioned above, though it is not easy to test its effect.

There are a large range of situational factors and sources which may in practice affect the ethical values we choose in business and organisational life. These may influence us in direct and obvious ways or be part of the ethical theories we are exploring in this book. Such factors can most easily be seen as a systems hierarchy as shown below:

▶ *Individuals* – the values and beliefs resulting from our personal histories and development.
▶ *Groups (away from work)* – family and social groups with their own histories, development and norms of behaviour.
▶ *Groups (at work)* – group norms and expectations of behaviour as well as plans, budgets and targets (i.e. the informal and the formal aspects of working relationships.
▶ *Organisations* – structure, systems, mission, culture.
▶ *Professions* – formal codes of practice (which may have legal backing) and informal norms and expectations of behaviour.
▶ *Industries* – competitive characteristics (including structure, relative power, economics, etc.), culture.
▶ *Nations* – history, characteristics and culture, social institutions, legal frameworks.
▶ *International situation* – power, economies, international law.
▶ *Universal norms of behaviour* – commonly accepted expectations and constraints, belief systems.

Such factors may reinforce each other or they may act against each other to produce the dilemmas typical of applied ethics.

Many of the situational factors which have been found relevant in describing ethical behaviour are organisation, profession or industry related; the pressures of 'how we do things here'. These are often characterised through descriptions of organisation culture, structure (responsibilities and roles), reward systems and the rhetoric of mission and goal statements. These are extensively addressed in studies of organisational behaviour. Crane and Matten (2004) draw attention to the notion of 'moral framing', a term which relates to our discussion of moral muteness and moral distance (see later). They also draw attention to an interesting range of factors under the heading of 'moral intensity', as shown below. These factors attempt to reflect the relative importance of the ethical issue in question in the given decision-making context:

▶ *Magnitude of the consequences*: the impact (positive or negative) of the decision on those affected. This is directly related to our discussion of Utilitarianism and its limitations in Chapter 6.

Moral intensity increases if the consequences for any stakeholder are dramatic.

▶ *Social consensus*: relates to agreement regarding the ethical import of a course of action. Moral intensity increases if some consider a proposed action unethical.

▶ *Probability of effect*: relates to the likelihood of effects, in particular negative consequences, actually occurring. Our Chapter 16 on managing risk relates to this issue.

▶ *Temporal immediacy*: the idea that moral intensity is likely to be greater if effects are sooner rather than later. As much of business appears to favour short-term results and fears short-term damage, this notion is important as a description of behaviour. However, it is useful to note the arguments in Chapter 15 relating to cultural differences and Japanese management as well as the discussion in Chapter 10 on reputation. The whole discussion on sustainability (see Chapters 3 and 21) shows the importance of time to ethical argument, though it is not clear whether 'temporal immediacy' is a satisfactory descriptive or prescriptive variable.

▶ *Proximity*: captures an idea similar to moral distance, which we explore in Chapter 19. If intensity is empirically seen to be greater with shorter (perceived) moral distance then we have a major social issue when management decisions affect individuals beyond some 'moral horizon'.

▶ *Concentration of effort*: this attempts to show the notion that a strong harmful effect on an individual, say, is more morally intense than an effect which is diffused over a large population. Hence cheating an insurance company may not be seen as being as bad as robbing an individual.

Thus to summarise, moral intensity is at its greatest when an action has consequences which are major, considered unethical by some, are likely to occur and to occur soon, are close to home and are concentrated on a few stakeholders. These consequences may be positive or negative in their effects on stakeholders, though substantial negative effects surely increase moral intensity. This set of ideas is obviously closely related to our later discussions, particularly on utilitarianism. While it usefully addresses some points it appears to ignore some other crucial issues (e.g. the balance of negative and positive effects on differing stakeholders) and therefore at best may be seen as complementary to more philosophically traditional analyses.

A key point we should note, however, in our present context on descriptive ethics is the reported empirical findings that moral intensity does indeed appear to go some way towards characterising some individuals' attitudes to decision-making. It should also be noted that such attitudes may be strongly affected by the surrounding norms of organisations and society, as we previously noted when mentioning the idea of moral framing. As we will see when summarising some ideas from normative ethics in Part II, there is a considerable tension between prescriptions of appropriate moral behaviour and those reported in empirical research as well as evident in everyday behaviour and media reportage. In a later section we reflect on how business executives themselves describe the moral context of business activity.

The Kohlberg model of moral development

This chapter is mainly concerned with attempts to describe how individuals and groups address moral concerns when making decisions in an organisational context. Models of such decision-making processes tend to assume a rational and thoughtful approach by the individuals concerned, who will nonetheless be affected by their social situation. It should also be noted that such individuals will have a history of moral learning and development, a dimension we have not so far addressed.

Lawrence Kohlberg is an American psychologist who developed a model of moral development in the early 1980s based on studies of the behaviour of boys. The model is briefly shown below in the form of a list. It is argued that an individual moves from Stage 1 upwards with increase in moral maturity.

Level one (pre-conventional); Stage 1
Right is determined by physical consequences.
Right action is taken to avoid punishment.

Level one (pre-conventional); Stage 2
Right is determined by what satisfies one's needs.
Right action is taken to serve one's own needs.

Level two (conventional); Stage 3
Right is determined by what gains approval from others.
Right action is taken to be seen as a good person.

Level two (conventional); Stage 4
Right is determined by what is legal.
Right action is taken to abide by the law.

Level three (post-conventional); Stage 5
Right is determined by respect for individual rights and social
   agreements.
Right action is taken to abide by social contracts.

Level three (post-conventional); Stage 6
Right is determined by universal principles.
Right action is taken in recognition of the principles of justice,
   fairness and universal human rights.

Some subsequent research amongst managers suggests that moral reasoning in an organisational context is often permanently located at around Stages 3 or 4, though it does vary depending on the specific case and dilemma. Limited evidence suggests that managers of small firms tend to reason at a higher stage than those in larger organisations, as do students. This latter point may simply reflect differences between an idealistic view of how one might act and a realistic assessment based on past actions. It is also not clear whether the stage of moral development might differ between work, home and social life for the same individual and also whether this is gender and age related. An interesting speculation is whether it can move down stages, for example when student idealism is replaced by conservative practicality!

An interesting extension of this model is given in Verstraeten (2000), where a 'worker perspective' is given to the above stages. For example, at Stage 2, punishment may be avoided by following orders and organisational rules while the goal is entirely the satisfaction of the worker's needs. In contrast at Stage 6, work is seen as an integral part of one's moral life. Similarly a 'corporate perspective' is also developed. While very interesting it is not clear if this defines a developmental path or is simply a classification of worker attitudes. It is very obvious that a worker's perception of what stage they are, or should be, currently occupying will be dependent on level in a hierarchy, acceptance of external professional codes of practice and the industry in question. A health care professional, for example, might well have a different view of the moral import of their work than a production line operative and it is not clear that either will follow a Kohlberg style developmental path.

Corporate moral development

So far in this chapter we have been describing the ethical decision-making context of the individual manager. By way of contrast we might attempt to describe the 'ethical (or unethical) organisation'. Now, we are all familiar with the typical 'tough' statements which are made about the nature of business practice in general. Based on Webley (1997), we can summarise some of these as follows:

'All's fair in love, war and business'
(an approach emphasizing the freedom of business executives to act and make money)

'Good business ethics is just good business'
(what works in practice is ethical by definition)

'We operate according to our clear rules – if you don't like it, go somewhere else'
(a legalistic and intolerant subculture)

There are two issues here which should be separated; the ethical norms publicly espoused by the organisation and the extent to which these actually do guide organisational decision-making and control. If pushed to give a more public statement of corporate ethics, many business executives would say something along the lines of 'we have obligations to our shareholders', or if they have been influenced by more current jargon (or are in the public sector) 'we have obligations to our stakeholders' or even 'we have obligations to society'. It is not always clear that such statements truly reflect underlying ethical attitudes within the organisations concerned. A public espousal of 'high-quality goods' may hide an internal preoccupation with high volume production and cost reduction.

Webley (1997) also quotes the Reidenbach and Robin model of corporate moral development, which suggests an organisation moves through a series of stages on the path towards improved ethical behaviour. These stages are characterised in the model as follows:

- ► *Amoral* – the only value is greed.
- ► *Legalistic* – if an action is legal, then it can be done.
- ► *Responsive* – decisions are guided by enlightened self-interest.

► *Emerging ethical* – we want to do the right thing.
► *Ethical* – we will do the right thing (i.e. actual implemented policies are based on core values).

It should be noted that the inferred definitions of such terms as 'amoral' and 'legalistic' in the above is somewhat crude, if clear and direct. Thus 'amoral' strictly relates to an absence of accepted guiding principles rather than an admission of greed as a driving force. However, the idea of a series of stages of increasing social responsibility is obvious.

We can see the above as an exercise in descriptive ethics as well as normative prescription. We might use the above list as a means of classifying organisations, we may believe they do actually follow such a route to improved ethical behaviour or we might even prescribe this route as a set of necessary stages in the improvement of organisational ethical behaviour. It is a matter of empirical investigation whether or not organisations do in fact follow such a path. This is a similar to controversial models of individual moral development such as that of Kohlberg (see above). It is by no means established that organisations, or individuals, actually follow such paths and we can find examples of newly formed organisations which attempt to base their business mission on being ethical.

If you are 'amoral' (and greedy), financial legal sanctions can push you towards 'legalistic'. If you are also concerned about your long-term reputation and financial well-being you may then become 'responsive'. We may, of course, argue that you are still really only 'amoral' but have become more cunning in how you act and present yourself to the world. It is not clear in this why one should become really 'responsive' or even move towards the 'ethical'. Much of business (and applied) ethics is about this fundamental issue. For example, among the standard writers from the history of ethics, Hume (see Chapter 5) would argue that we have natural sympathies beyond greed, while Kant (see Chapter 7) would argue that if we are really guided by reason we would recognise that we have duties derived from the Categorical Imperative, but more of this later!

However, as this is an introductory text, we will only suggest the above classification is used as a description of apparent organisational attitudes. If you wish to do further academic work on business ethics, researching the developmental route that organisations take is of considerable interest and practical value.

Examples of ethical issues faced by business executives

While much of this chapter has been theoretical in its approach to describing ethical decision-making in an organisational context, it is useful to occasionally remind ourselves of the moral issues in real business practice, or at least the perceptions of managers regarding the moral dilemmas that may occur. Fritzsche (1997) summarises a variety of research exploring ethical issues which business managers feel they face in their work. Drawing from this, and without indication of frequency, we arrive at the following illustrative (though certainly not exhaustive) list which we have put under four headings:

1. Relationships with suppliers and business partners:

    (a) Bribery and immoral entertainment
    (b) Discrimination between suppliers
    (c) Dishonesty in making and keeping contracts

2. Relationship with customers:

    (a) Unfair pricing
    (b) Cheating customers
    (c) Dishonest advertising
    (d) Research confidentiality

3. Relationship with employees:

    (a) Discrimination in hiring and treatment of employees

4. Management of financial resources:

    (a) Misuse of organisational funds
    (b) Tax evasion.

It is interesting to note some obvious themes in this list which recur a number of times in this book. The first is discrimination and a lack of fairness which may occur in a number of guises, in particular in our treatment of employees and of business partners, such as suppliers and customers. The second is a manipulation of information in negotiation, advertising and financial dealing. Where companies can obtain consumer information, issues exist in preserving confidentiality. Further themes include a misuse of resources and failure to do what an organisation says it is going to do.

This descriptive approach to business ethics can be useful in complementing the usual prescriptive approach through focussing the latter on observed business practice and the concerns of real managers. Brenkert (1999) reflects on empirical work relating to the actual 'observed' (or, at least, stated) values, beliefs and practices of marketing staff and how they differ between contexts.

Some key words which recur in discussions of ethical marketing, usually in the analysis of unethical marketing practice, are given below (with examples of unethical practice):

► Honesty (misleading claims about products and services).
► Confidentiality (use of customer data as market intelligence and to sell).
► Privacy (aggressive telephone selling to homes).
► Vulnerability (advertising to children).
► Freedom (manipulation of vulnerable minorities (young, elderly, sick, etc.) to sell products; large retailer use of supply chain power).
► Well-being (product safety).
► Justice (product pricing; use of cheap labour in developing countries).

Thus the relationship between a business and its customers (i.e. just one of the relationships mentioned earlier) can itself be the source of a wide range of ethical issues and potential problems. It is important to note here that an apparently tight focus on the relationship between retailers and customers is misleading. Marketing sees itself as applied to an increasingly wide area of human activity (i.e. not just traditional selling in a market economy), for example religion, political spin and relationships with a business' own employees. Whether we see such activities literally as 'marketing' or as the use of marketing concepts as appropriate tools and metaphors is less relevant than the obvious ways in which the problem areas listed above can carry over into a wide range of business situations.

Ethical decision-making

There are a large number of models which attempt to embody ethical concerns in management decision-making. We have demonstrated some of the problems inherent in using such models, whether as a description of actual managerial practice or as a prescriptive framework. We end this chapter with a slightly more complex model given in Brenkert (1999) in the context of marketing ethics, though we have made some adaptation of language to enable comparison with other models.

This model of ethical decision-making takes into account personal, organisational, industrial, professional and cultural variables in arriving at a set of steps in ethical decision-making. It also refers to some ideas we will meet in Part II and is therefore useful as a bridge between the essentially descriptive concerns of this chapter and the more prescriptive approach which will be adopted in the next few chapters. The stages of ethical decision-making are seen as follows:

1. awareness of an ethical problem, usually characterised as a dilemma;
2. identification of alternative actions and consequences. This requires experience and imagination and is not usually carried out in isolation from other decisions and agents, which does, of course, complicate the analysis;
3. deontological evaluation (rights and duties) and consequentialist evaluation (for a range of stakeholders);
4. reconciliation of rights and consequences ('rights' usually act as constraints in specific situations);
5. impact of ethical judgements on decision makers' preferences and intentions (what do I/we actually want to do here?);
6. control and power in an actual situation (what can I/we actually do here?).

Some texts include comprehensive flowcharts of elaborate ethical decision models which one doubts have ever been used in practice. The advantage of a simple list such as that above is that it is memorable. It should, however, be read in conjunction with accepted theories of organisational decision-making which show the real complexities of such processes.

Summary

This chapter has introduced a wide range of factors which may be of relevance in any specific context of ethical organisational decision-making. It is perhaps most useful to return to this collection of ideas when specific case contexts have been introduced later in the book.

In the next few chapters we will introduce a range of philosophical approaches to ethics which can be translated into normative prescriptions.

You will, I am sure, be becoming increasingly aware of the complexity of this subject. It is important to note that few people would even pretend to be able to hold all these ideas simultaneously in mind when carrying out ethical analysis. However, you will increasingly see that they form patterns of similar concepts and, with exposure to case examples and continual re-reading and use, will make sense eventually.

Questions for discussion – Part I

We have included in the last chapter of each part a series of questions which may be used to link real contexts, cases and exercises to the theoretical ideas in the book.

Note that the five discussion questions given below relate to material covered in Chapters 1–4 but may introduce new ideas and perspectives. These questions are meant to challenge rather than review basic learning of the material in the chapters in Part I.

Question 1

Why should you study business ethics? Some possible answers are given below:

▶ because you hope it will be useful for yourself and for the people you work with;
▶ because you have a duty to become informed, as part of being a management professional;
▶ as part of your personal development.

Expand the list as appropriate.

Question 2

A central question in business ethics is the following: Why should the powerful and advantaged not exploit the weak in order to survive in a competitive business world?

How would you respond to this challenge? Be sure you fully consider the logic and persuasiveness of any suggested answer.

Question 3

The Ancient Greek philosopher Socrates was a 'gadfly', executed for corrupting the youth of Athens with his dangerous ideas. Yet the Socratic approach is a useful antidote to pompousness. Ethics has now become a highly technical area. One could argue that it is of most value if it is acerbic and endlessly critical of business practice; challenging and irritating in new and innovative ways and at a fundamental level.

There is a real danger that business ethics becomes self-serving; it justifies its place in business talk by providing a language and set of concepts which can be used by the powerful to justify their actions and special position.

The other side of the coin, however, is that ethics becomes so aggressively confrontational and critical of the world of the practising manager that its pronouncements are treated as idealistic by its targets. A coping strategy results whereby managers feel threatened and ignore ethical prescriptions while taking refuge in accepted practice and common sense ('I'm no worse than anyone else, so why pick on me?'). By providing critiques with the benefit of hindsight, radical ethics offers no practical way forward for the manager operating in a context marked by current information overload and ambiguity, complex power politics, a confusing mixture of competition and co-operation and uncertainty.

Any critique of business practice must be matched with humanity, personal intellectual honesty ('would I have done any better?') and modesty.

Discuss.

Question 4

What are 'objective facts'? Do the personal values of individuals colour the language in which facts are expressed? If we have power, do we inevitably use it (particularly as managers) to shape the language and discussion of facts? If we have power, do we use it to influence the sources of information?

Does this apply to 'facts about ethical behaviour'? If so, should all descriptions of an ethical context be treated with care? (For example, our descriptions of what we consider to be ethical behaviour may be inevitably affected by our personal beliefs and values.)

Question 5

Managers are barbarians!

Discuss.
(*Hint*: see Chapter 10.)

Part II   Ethical theories in an organisational setting

Introduction

The purpose of Part II is to introduce a wide range of normative ethical theories, that is prescriptions of how individuals should behave. Many of these are directly based on the philosophical theorising which has been a feature of Western thought for 2500 years, though some have origins in recent organisational literature. All are relevant to modern organisational practice. The outline descriptions of theories given in this book must be seen at best as brief introductions to ideas which are capable of endless debate and elaboration when applied to complex social systems such as organisations and a market-driven business environment.

The six chapters in Part II are best read in sequence as there are a number of occasions where ideas carry over from one chapter to another. Care has been taken to provide a business or organisational context for concepts which are also of general application in society. However, actual case studies are not a feature of this part of the book. In Parts III and IV the discussion of business topics and functions provides a setting where cases can be related to theoretical perspectives.

Chapter contents

Chapters 5–10 each consider one or more major branches of applied ethical theory and relate these to the business world. In Chapters 5 and 6 we mainly look at theories where the evaluation of consequences is the key. This allows us to begin with the simple case where the only consequences the decision maker cares about are the ones affecting themselves and then widens the net to include other potential stakeholders. This set of theories has been chosen as a starting point because it has become a natural way for business people to think about decision-making. It has its problems, however, both in terms of practical application and in view of the acute criticisms which have been levelled against it by writers on ethics. In Chapter 5, which concentrates on the individual, we also include a brief introduction to the ideas of David Hume and make some generally applicable points about consistency.

We then move on, in Chapters 7 and 8, to considering theories where an evaluation of the actions of people is central to the debate. At its most basic level actions are constrained by laws and we may simply say that breaking laws is wrong. Whilst an important point, this does not answer the questions of why such actions are wrong or where the laws come from. The ensuing discussion covers a range of philosophical positions, many of which are quite hard to understand and harder to apply. It is important that the basics of this area of ethical theory are grasped as it affects large areas of application.

The idea of human rights is critically introduced in Chapter 7 and followed by a short, business-related example of some of the problems which may occur if we intensively use a vocabulary based on 'rights'. As much political and organisational debate uses such a language it would be impractical to ignore it! We follow this with a basic introduction to Kantian ethics, an approach which is demanding but also useful and interesting. Chapter 8 has the single focus of a debate on the application of the ideas of social contract theory in an organisational context.

Chapter 9 introduces topics which focus on the characteristics of the individual; in the jargon of the subject we become 'agent centred' rather than 'action centred'. We look at what are called the 'virtues', at moral development, at the ethics of care and the need for debate and discussion. This may be termed a 'softer' approach to ethics, though it is demanding in practice. It fits well with many modern conceptions of organisational behaviour and good 'people management'.

Most books on basic applied ethics will cover the theories outlined above. They have become considered as standard features in business and other applications. In Chapter 10 we depart from this line by looking at ideas of reputation and power which have become very fashionable and useful in modern management theory. This leads on to a consideration of the idea of personal and organisational integrity. These are recent developments in business ethics and of considerable interest and value. Chapter 10 ends with a set of discussion questions relating to Part II as a whole.

5 Egoism

Purpose and learning outcomes

The purpose of this chapter is first of all to introduce some theories of applied ethics where ethical evaluation centres on consequences for the decision maker and a small surrounding group of individuals. We then move on to considering some non-consequentialist theories which once again are focussed on the feelings of the decision maker. Finally we consider the logic underlying a range of subjective approaches.

You will be able to

► understand the basic concept of egoism and appreciate its limitations as a consequentialist theory in a business context;

► show an appreciation of how the concept of egoism can be extended to provide a description of some attitudes to moral action in business;

► show a basic understanding of a range of subjective approaches to ethical evaluation.

Introduction

This is the first of six chapters in which we consider a range of ethical theories which have been effectively applied to business and organisational systems. In Chapter 2 we met a classification of theories based on the distinction between intention, action and consequence. In this chapter we begin with a focus on some consequence-based theories, that is where ethical evaluation is mainly focussed on the results of actions. Our discussion of consequence-based theories continues in Chapter 6. We start with these theories mainly because of the intuitive simplicity of the ideas they contain when interpreted in a business context. It should, however, be noted that while such ideas underpin some social science theories (though usually applied in a highly sophisticated form, as in economics) they are also rejected by other philosophers as inadequate vehicles for the prescription of ethical behaviour. It would certainly be advisable, as we do in this book, to only consider them in conjunction with other approaches to ethics.

Therefore we begin this chapter with a consideration of a group of theories under the umbrella title of 'egoism'. At its most simple, egoism involves the decision maker acting entirely out of self-interest in optimising the personal consequences of actions. There are numerous problems with this approach, not least of which is that many would hardly call it ethical! It can, however, be developed by taking a longer-term view or by including the gains and losses of some other parties in the calculations, which is where the notion of stake-holders recurs. It might be possible to see egoism working in the context of basic entrepreneurial activity in a perfectly competitive market, but organisational ethics must be applied in far more complex contexts.

We then provide an interlude, before continuing with consequence-based theories in the next chapter, by including a short introduction to the ideas of the 18th century philosopher David Hume. His very distinctive approach puts an emphasis on our personal view of what constitutes an ethical action. The focus is our own feelings and intuitions. This is a view which has never completely lost favour, despite a con-centrated assault from those who wish to locate ethics in a more objective framework. Hume also drew attention to the important point that ethics is not only about having the right thoughts, opinions and arguments. These have to be carried forward into ethical action.

There are a number of approaches to ethics which are similar to Hume's theories and these are briefly summarised using a form of expression from Gensler (1998). You may well find you have considerable personal sympathy with one or more of these approaches, and therefore might be advised to note the problems each entails. We follow this with a brief section outlining Gensler's key point that consistency in belief, judgement and action is an essential characteristic of an ethical person, though it may not be easy to achieve.

Thus the defining characteristic of the theories we are considering in this chapter is a narrow focus on 'the self' as the source of moral evaluation. Though we might not wish to describe some of the the-ories included here as 'ethical', it is important to see their attraction as well as their faults. The final points about consistency are of particular importance.

An introduction to egoism

In this section we introduce an approach to ethical decision-making that many will view as the antithesis of 'ethical'. The amount of time we spend discussing this approach is partly due to the fact that some observers feel the defining quality of many business people is their determined pursuit of their own advantage but also due to the need to explore the logic underlying this position before developing other positions which will be readily identified as 'ethical'.

We might even feel that few of us need an introduction to egoism, which has a dictionary definition as 'an ethical theory that treats self-interest as the foundation of morality'. Our instinct for survival combined with the everyday objective of being happy would suggest that the pursuit of self-interest is a natural way to organise our lives. We might, however, be surprised to see this described as an 'ethical theory' – surely the role of morality is to act as a constraint on our more selfish and destructive acts?

It is important that we treat egoism seriously as an ethical theory and subject it to careful analysis, particularly in its application to the world of business and organisation. The idea that 'greed is good' (as proposed by a character in the film *Wall Street*) is a crude, if unoriginal, statement of the idea that if business people seek to act in their self-interest then the market will work efficiently to the advantage of the community as a whole. Yet even at this early stage we must begin to wonder whether the logic of this argument is sound. Will the market actually work efficiently if everyone acts in this way? This is the somewhat technical concern of economists addressing instances of market failure. We may also ask how long will it take for this ideal state of efficiency to occur and how many people will be severely disadvantaged along the way? Of course, if we really are egoists, then it is unlikely we will be concerned about this. Indeed we might use the inefficiency of markets as an opportunity for wealth creation, or simply argue that if the world is unfair then it is up to us to ruthlessly promote our own advantage – if we do not look after ourselves, then who will?

Simple egoism

So egoism is a consequentialist theory, where the only consequences of interest are those which affect the decision maker, that is, we define a decision rule that:

Each person ought to do whatever maximises their own self-interest, regardless of how this affects others.

This may be seen to be naïve and restrictive and hence we refer to it as simple or crude egoism. This limited form is where the consequences of interest are taken to be solely those directly affecting the decision maker. However, a practical point is obvious here, particularly in the business world where organisational roles and power can amplify our influence. Our actions may produce an array of results affecting ourselves and others. The effects on others may well rebound on us in a variety of ways which are hard to predict. Therefore even calculating consequences in a selfish way can be impossibly demanding in a complex network of cause and effect. This is, of course, a standard problem with consequentialist decision rules as we will see elsewhere. We may also add in for good measure practical issues of risk and the predictability of the results of any action. However, are there more fundamental objections to the crude version of egoism than these practical problems, which might even be overcome in many simple situations or which might be ignored when the selfish benefits are so great that risks are ignored and the rewards will compensate for any backlash from those hurt by our decisions?

Let us look at the above decision rule in another way, typical of the methods of analysis used in philosophy. We assume that we wish everyone to be consistent in applying this rule (i.e. everyone will apply it at all times) for otherwise this rule is only part of another larger decision rule covering all circumstances. This is the idea of 'universality' which is of key importance in philosophical ethics and is assumed to be desirable here (though will be explored more fully in Chapter 7). Therefore we must assume that everyone else follows their own self-interest, but this must be potentially damaging for our own individual interests. To assume otherwise would be hopelessly idealistic in general, and specifically illogical in a business world where we are competing in the use of resources. Therefore we are following a rule which if consistently applied encourages others to act against our interests, which is inconsistent with our wish to maximise our self-interest. Hence this simple form of egoism is self-defeating and therefore inconsistent.

By going through this argument in detail, we can see ways in which crude egoism might still have some attraction. If we consider ourselves to be different in some regard (more deserving, more talented or more powerful) then we might promote a rule which makes the most of our perceived social position. Thus a wealthy and clever individual might be happy to use a 'rule' which builds on their personal advantage on the assumption that they are immune to unfavourable consequences and retaliatory action. This gives us some insight into why Rawls (see Chapter 8) advocated rule-making in the context of a 'veil of ignorance', in particular that we should design rules independent of our initial position in the system in which the rules are to apply.

An alternative is to argue that such a rule is applied to ourselves (and a few favoured others) but not to the majority. As talented entrepreneurs, our selfish actions will benefit society as a whole! Weak support for this is the observation that special dispensation can be given, for example, to surgeons to cut people with a knife in spite of the general rule against such action. Of course this ignores the fact that they are doing this for the patient's benefit, even though they do gain themselves through payment! A more telling example is the unscrupulous politician who systematically denigrates whole populations as being of a lesser status than that of the favoured group in order to justify or even 'legalise' discrimination or persecution. If this seems to be an extreme example in a book on business ethics, one should note the comparisons made by some authors between marketing and the Nazi Holocaust (more of this in Chapter 19 when considering the concept of moral distance).

Altruism and psychological egoism

The above analysis shows the sort of territory we are getting into by following through the logic of egoism, which is nothing compared with the complexities of more sophisticated forms of consequentialism such as utilitarianism! We can, however, continue our exploration of egoism in some different ways, of which the first is to move towards 'descriptive ethics' and ask if people do behave in this way. Are salesmen actually willing to cause great distress to their clients in return for small personal gain, for example by the inappropriate selling of financial products (once more, see Chapter 19)? There seems to be considerable everyday evidence that behaviour of this type does occur, perhaps bolstered by organisational cultures which expect, encourage and reward such behaviour. We should also not forget the criminal subculture of the business world where egoism is the norm. It is for these sorts of reason that we cannot entirely ignore egoism in some form, in descriptive ethics at least.

One issue that those who wish to explain every form of behaviour as the product of egoism have to confront is the existence of altruism, that is concern for the well-being of others over and above one's own self-interest. Some might wish to dismiss altruism as calculated long-term advantage seeking or even self-delusion; we might say and even think we are working for others, but we are actually working to improve our own position in society, or our self-esteem or some other subtle personal benefit. Yet most of us can recognise behaviour, even if only within a family or close group of friends, which is directed towards the benefit of others. A considerable amount of money is also donated anonymously to charities and good causes. If it is argued that all such behaviour is simply a means of increasing our self-esteem, whether or not we accept or admit it, then we have an explanation of altruism which cannot be proved or disproved. Philosophers are adept at spotting such arguments and dismissing explanations which seem to cover every eventuality as simply an empty use of words.

A slight variation on this is sometimes referred to as 'psychological egoism', a term used to denote the view that we are all egoists in the sense that all our actions are really motivated by a concern for our own long-term best interest rather than any real feeling for the interests of others. Thus we might act to our short-term disadvantage but only in our long-term best interest. It is even argued that we are deceiving ourselves if we think we are acting in any other way! Once again, this is an empty explanation of behaviour because, with sufficient ingenuity, it can be applied in all cases. It would only have explanatory power if it could distinguish between cases and show how this self-deceiving was actually carried out, a difficult task as the unconscious calculation of long-term best interest would not be easy. A way round this would be to assume we had a 'survival instinct' which showed itself through unconscious calculation of personal best interest, or possibly group best interest if a more sociologically sophisticated approach was taken. Psychological egoism has a problem with extreme altruism, such as risking one's life to save that of another or when obeying a command in a war. This problem might be addressed as an instinct for group survival, whatever that might mean.

Another interesting line of enquiry is to delve into what is meant by 'self-interest'. Can I actually recognise, measure and quantify it? Do I really know how to act in ways that will reliably promote it? This is similar to the problems utilitarian theorists face with discussions of a 'hedonistic calculus' (i.e. quantifying pleasure and pain). Even if one identifies pleasure with money acquisition (as a means to an end, or simply miserliness!) then we have issues of whether to forego money in the short term for benefits in the longer term; time and risk are always important variables in such a calculus. From the outside, we may seek to infer what makes someone happy through their purchase actions; the 'revealed preferences' of economists and marketing professionals. However, these leave so many things unknown, in particular the reasons for a purchase at that time and the psychological context in which the purchase was made, quite apart from the obvious consideration of the availability of cash! Therefore, quite apart from the logical objections of philosophers to its prescription as a norm for behaviour, crude egoism appears to represent a naïve and inadequate description of how people actually bring their personal values to bear on decision-making in real and very complex social situations.

Beyond simple egoism?

You will note that the words 'simple' or even 'crude' has been appended to 'egoism' in the discussion so far. This is intended to summarise the idea of the intentional promotion of narrow self-interest without the constraint of worrying about the interests of others. Is it possible to put forward more sophisticated forms of egoism?

The first possibility is to follow the path, hinted at above, of including family, close friends and work colleagues within a concept of 'group-interest'. If this is done merely as a device to protect self-interest then we are still within a conceptually crude egoism, though with more sophisticated practice. To be genuinely concerned about, and to promote, the interest of the 'family' (even with its mafia connotations) at the expense of those outside is still within the spirit of egoism, though one might see considerable complications in decision-making where self-interests compete within the family. As an example, an organisation may wish to institute devices such as group bonuses in order to encourage co-operation, and much has been written about the advantages and problems of such management tools. I would argue that we are still firmly within the area of egoism and the principled objections to this are the same as to crude egoism. In contrast, utilitarianism (see next chapter) is the form of consequentialism which has, at least in theory and for human subjects, an open-ended acceptance of some moral responsibility.

A version of egoism which has some appeal (and many honest citizens would assume this is what is meant by egoism anyway) is egoism within the law, that is we pursue self-interest within the legal framework of the society within which we act. It may be taken as an over-riding principle that we accept this constraint, or it may be seen as a risk-avoidance measure within crude egoism, that is we assume that if we break the law, we will get caught and therefore we wish to avoid the punishment. The latter is poor logic as it stands, as the punishment (if it occurs) may be far less than the rewards gained. This is the economic calculus of the professional criminal as well as the individual who sees what has recently been called 'middle-class crime', such as fraudulent insurance claims, expenses fiddles and so forth, as a permissible way of life. This latter view is crude egoism, while the acceptance of the law as a constraint in principle is significantly different.

There are, however, some complications in this stance. Some minor forms of law breaking may be seen as acceptable (exceeding the road speed limit by a small margin being an obvious example) and business owners may feel they must 'bend' some more technical requirements of the law if the alternative is severe distress to employees and customers. There is also the problem of law breaking (e.g. direct action as part of an environmental campaign) where the objective is publicity rather than violence and damage; in such cases the interests of a community appear to be paramount as the individual campaigner incurs costs. Finally, laws vary between different countries and develop over time in response to public perceptions of what is right and the practical needs of public administration, such as tax collection. Thus a proposed business action may be constrained in one country and not in another, which may lead an organisation to pick and chose which laws it will be subject to through location decisions.

Science and egoism

At this point we should also mention the contribution initially made by the practical economists of the 18th century. 'Invisible hand' egoism is a pragmatic view developed in Adam Smith's *The Wealth of Nations* (1776). The argument is that if all entrepreneurs act freely in their own interest then society as a whole benefits. Whether or not this is true is a matter of fact to be investigated through empirical research as well as by theory and argument. As economists have shown, the facts are not decisively in favour of the invisible hand being entirely reliable, as seen by the large amount of legislation which seems to be necessary to constrain business decision-making and preserve free markets.

Other scientists have more recently developed interesting theories building on the observations of anthropologists as well as the key scientific explanatory principle of evolution. Thus a quite different approach to that of traditional moral argument is taken by scientific egoism, as shown in the work of evolutionary biologists and psychologists who argue that we have only evolved as a society because we have been successful in balancing self-interest with altruistic behaviour in order to ensure the survival of our genes. Exactly what this means in terms of human anthropology is explored in references such as Hinde (2002) and Ridley (1996). Part of the background to this work is the use of the mathematical theory of games to show how altruism is logical in a context of self-interest (see Chapter 6).

The ethics of David Hume

David Hume (1711–1776) was one of the leading figures of the Enlightenment in Scotland, perhaps best known to students of philosophy as part of the British trio of 'Locke, Berkeley and Hume'. His ideas on ethics and religion were part of his highly original approach to philosophy and much discussed by subsequent generations. As a man he was well liked and greatly respected, a friend of the founding economist Adam Smith and a contributor to the ideas and fashions of the time, even if his books on philosophy famously sold badly. A flavour of his writing can be found (with a modern introduction) in Hume (1998).

He is perhaps best known for the assertion, which sometimes bears the name 'Hume's Law', that you cannot derive a judgement of what you 'ought' to do (in the moral rather than the practical sense) from a series of 'is' statements. Reason relates to logic and to matters of fact. It can address practical questions about how you might achieve some objective you have decided upon but it cannot tell you what moral ends you should aim for. In many systems of thought the moral dimension is supplied by religion but Hume had strong reasons for not following this path. Indeed his writings on religion are highly sceptical, even atheist, and could only be published after his death.

In Hume's early writings the moral dimension comes from a fairly basic form of what is now called subjectivism, that is 'X is good' simply means 'I like X'. We are using the letter X here to stand for a moral principle, for example 'it is wrong to steal'. Our moral judgements are taken to be subjective, though Hume uses words like 'the passions' which can be misleading if taken in a modern context. Thus our moral inclinations are a matter of our conscience and feelings.

The difficulties in this are obvious (as they were to Hume) and can be summed up by the idea of moral immaturity. If I happen to like hurting other people then I appear to be saying that, for me, 'hurting people is good'. It would seem that my conscience and feelings are in some ways underdeveloped. More modern objections might use the language of psychology and talk of deviant behaviour and psychopaths. Hume, however, argued that there was in principle nowhere else to go, though his stated views were modified in his later work into what we might call the ideal observer view where 'X is good' means 'we would choose X if we were fully informed and impartial' (using the formulation in Gensler [1998] described below). If we really believe that aberrant behaviour is merely based on error and ignorance and that we can cure these through our moral development then this later formulation is an improvement. If, however, we see this as idealistic (i.e. what does 'being fully informed and impartial' actually mean?) then we are left with a somewhat limited view of morality unless we have considerable faith in human nature.

We may link these formulations of Hume's ideas with the previous section by asking whether we would personally want to substitute 'each person ought to do whatever maximises their own self-interest, regardless of how this affects others' (i.e. the formulation of simple egoism) for X in the various versions of 'X is good' (see below for further possibilities). We might also try this out for the more sophisticated consequentialist rules of behaviour. Do you believe your feelings on this matter to be widely shared by others, particularly when working in organisations?

There is a further, though related, aspect of Hume's thinking that I believe we can accept without too much concern. This is the distinction between having the right thoughts and good intentions on the one hand and actually doing the 'right thing' in practice. As morality is seen by society as largely about what we do and its consequences, this is a very important distinction in showing the limitations of reason. Hume draws our attention to the role of 'the passions' and the avoidance of pain in moving us to action, that is using modern business language we must pay attention to the motivation and the control of action as well as to good intentions and decisions. This emphasis on the need for motivation towards right action provides a useful counterbalance to any excessively analytical view of ethical evaluation and decision-making.

We can summarise this as follows ('right' and 'wrong' here referring to ethical content):

▶ *Wrong decision and wrong action* – consistent but ethically dubious.
▶ *Wrong decision but right action* – is it ethical to do the right thing for the wrong reason?
▶ *Right decision but wrong action* – failure to carry through the good intention.
▶ *Right decision and right action* – doing the right thing for the right reasons.

The fourth item in the list is obviously the ideal situation. You might like to consider for a moment why the second item in the list above is problematic!

The enduring influence of Hume's general position can be seen by its reflection in British philosophy in the early part of the 20th century. Value formation was seen as radically different from gaining knowledge of the social and physical world. A more sophisticated view of individual and group psychology underlies much recent theorising in organisational behaviour.

A comparison of subjective approaches

We can attempt to draw together some plausible approaches to the choice of moral principles by using a framework to be found in Gensler (1998). We have briefly mentioned this when looking at the philosophy of David Hume. Gensler surveys a number of approaches to ethical decision-making in terms of the underlying principles on which they are based. These are presented in a common format, of which a selection (adapted from Gensler 1998) is given below:

cross cultural

Cultural Relativism: 'Good' means 'socially approved'
That is you pick your moral principles by following the norms and behaviours that are approved by the society in which you live.

This approach is routinely attacked by writers on philosophical ethics as being totally inadequate, not least because societies can (currently and historically) be observed to have approved wildly different things, some of which we would find wholly unacceptable (e.g. persecution of minorities, slavery, differing rights for different groups in society, etc.). We might, however, note its descriptive power, both at the level of organisations and countries (see Chapter 15). Social approval and reference to peer groups can be seen as very influential in everyday decision-making. We may counter this way of thinking by asking if socially approved things are always good – it is not hard to find counter-examples! If socially approved actions are not always good, what is the extra feature which makes some 'socially approved' things good if some are not? It is highly likely that following this path will lead to the addition of factors from the other approaches given in ethics texts. An alternative line of argument is to try to find things which we accept as good but which are often not carried out in practice, thus showing inconsistency between social approval of what one should do and acceptance of non-conformance. These forms of argument may not be as watertight as the logic in the textbooks but they can start some interesting debates.

> Subjectivism: 'X is good' means 'I like X'
> That is you pick out your moral principles by following your feelings.

This is characteristic of Hume's original writings and can be criticised as shown above. However, once again this approach should not be ignored as it is a characteristic of the arguments people often use to defend their freedom to make up their own minds on moral issues.

> Ideal Observer: 'X is good' means 'We would desire X if we were fully informed and had impartial concerns for everyone'.
> That is you pick out your moral principles by trying to become as informed and impartial as possible and then seeing what you desire.

This is typical of Hume's later approach and probably a better description of the view of those people who take a serious view of morals as a matter of their personal conscience and decision. If one were to be cynical, one might wonder how hard individuals work in practice at becoming informed and impartial and also the extent to which they are in fact influenced by cultural norms, religion and other moral theories. Nonetheless, if part of a fully reflective personal philosophy which acknowledges the influences which surround us, this can be seen as an interesting, if demanding, approach.

> Emotivism: 'X is good' is an emotional exclamation (not a truth claim), and means 'Hurrah for X!'.
> That is pick out your moral principles by following your feelings

This is an extreme version of subjectivism that attempts to avoid the usual counter-arguments (see above) by making the claim that moral statements are an unusual use of words, similar to exclamations of support or dislike. The effect is to banish ethics from the rational debate of philosophy! It should be noted that ethics has at times been a minor part of the curriculum of philosophy and at other times has played a major role. Emotivism is not widely accepted at the moment but the idea that moral statements can be handled at the level of advertising slogans appears similar to the extreme cynicism of some business practitioners, at least in private or in unguarded public statements. For this reason it is useful to remember emotivism for its descriptive rather than prescriptive contribution to business ethics.

While the differences between the approaches shown above may appear, in practical terms at least, to be slight, they do provide us with a way of classifying some everyday attitudes towards business ethics. I suspect that the more cynical and world-weary business practitioners would find, upon reflection, that their 'practical' approach was some variant of the above with little appreciation of the underlying assumptions and inconsistencies. Gensler (1998) makes considerable use of the notion of consistency and it is useful to include his threefold characterisation of this apparently straightforward idea:

1. *Logicality* – avoidance of inconsistencies between the beliefs you hold. This is, in practice, very hard to achieve as we all tend to make general statements that can be inconsistent in specific cases.
2. *Conscientiousness* – avoidance of inconsistencies between your moral judgements and how you actually live.
3. *Impartiality* – avoidance of inconsistent evaluations of similar actions.

Gensler (1998) is a useful and 'user-friendly' source for exploring the somewhat forbidding world of Kantian ethics (which is the main focus of his approach) and it might be of value here to reflect some of the good, practical advice he gives before moving to a discussion of Kant in Chapter 7. I have expanded and contextualised this advice into a business setting.

▶ Be consistent (as shown above); obviously desirable but far from easy in practice. This is particularly important in the world of organisations where inconsistencies of treatment can become sources of grievance resulting in dysfunctional work performance or formal complaints.

- ▶ Be informed in terms of facts, possible consequences and the feelings and beliefs of others as well as ourselves.
- ▶ Be imaginative; it cannot be stressed too highly that imagination, both in the sense of appreciating others' points of view and creating new solutions to problems, is a crucially important feature of good management which can be lost in the drier and more legalistic and technical aspects of business ethics.
- ▶ Use your head; think for yourself rather than simply conform to the norms and culture of your organisation.
- ▶ Develop feelings which support rational principles; it is important to internalise the rational analysis which is central to this approach to ethics and make it a routine habit of thought rather than something which struggles against our inclinations.
- ▶ Communicate widely in your own and in other social groups; ethical benchmarking and networking is important so we can see how things are done elsewhere as well as try out our own ideas.
- ▶ Respect the rational arguments of others with more knowledge and experience; 'respect' does not mean blindly accept!
- ▶ Do not be dogmatic; always be prepared to change if convincing arguments and new facts or perspectives become available.

Summary

Consequentialist theories often take a back seat in books on ethical theory, reflecting their unpopularity with many specialists in philosophical ethics. Egoism may not even be dealt with as a separate issue and will almost certainly be dismissed as illogical. However, in business it is often said that 'results count' and the importance of the 'bottom line' (i.e. profits) is routinely emphasised. Hence the consequentialist views of ethics reflected in this chapter and the next must not be ignored.

The subjective approaches, including the ideas of Hume, are probably more often seen in philosophy texts than those of business ethics. This is unfortunate as they seem to encapsulate some common positions on the source of morality, particularly as expressed by the more entrepreneurial individuals who put great emphasis on personal liberty and see their individuality as key to their success. It might be remembered that Hume wrote during a great period of commercial expansion in the UK and had considerable influence on the development of the embryonic social sciences.

You may find it useful to compare the normative (or prescriptive) approach to ethical theorising found in this chapter with the 'descriptive ethics' of Chapter 4. Much of descriptive ethics applies to individual moral decision-making in situations which are far more complex and ambiguous than those seen in basic philosophical ethics texts where simple, everyday contexts are often used to clarify difficult conceptual points.

6 Utilitarianism

Purpose and learning outcomes

The purpose of this chapter is to continue our discussion of some theories of applied ethics where ethical evaluation centres on the importance of consequences for a range of individuals. In addition to ideas of utilitarianism, some modern 'scientific' concepts are mentioned in the context of showing difficulties in the application of the standard ethical theories.

You will be able to

▶ show an understanding of the background to utilitarianism and its place in organisational ethics;
▶ show an understanding of the limits of consequentialist theories in an organisational context;
▶ show an appreciation of the potential value of some recent scientific approaches to management in the context of ethical analysis.

Introduction

One of the major deficiencies of the type of consequentialist theory developed in Chapter 5 ('Egoism') was that the narrow focus appears to make this approach the very opposite of what many would think of as 'moral' behaviour. Surely, at the very least, we should be concerned by the effect our actions have on a wider set of stakeholders. We may even feel that there is no boundary of responsibility, that is any effect of our actions on people or the natural environment are our responsibility. If we now consider ourselves as acting in an organisational context, our ability to affect the environment is greatly increased and therefore any argument relating to a boundary of responsibility is made more critical. Utilitarianism assumes we have responsibility for the consequences of our actions with the widest possible scope and seeks to provide a practical methodology for balancing positive and negative effects.

Unfortunately, there are massive practical problems in basing our decisions on such a methodology. We explore these in the later part of the chapter and go on to speculate on the contribution of some modern scientific contributions to this debate. It should however, also be noted that utilitarianism has developed as a more complex doctrine than a simple aggregation of effects. The idea of 'rule utilitarianism' (basing our consequentialist calculus on general heuristics rather than specific decisions) goes some way towards meeting the practical objections and the implicit quantification of ethics fits well with much of economic theory. There is also within utilitarian theory a strong argument on the freedom of action necessary for moral decision-making, which is consistent with much management theory.

An introduction to utilitarianism

A discussion of utilitarianism can begin with Jeremy Bentham (1748– 1832), a social and political thinker who placed a particular emphasis on the reform of government and the penal system. Bentham, who graduated from Oxford University at the age of 16, was a decidedly eccentric character, even by the standards of 18th century England. An extremely shy recluse and atheist, he rejected conventional ideas of moral theory in favour of a strictly rational approach where concepts like 'good' and 'right' should be defined in terms of the greatest happiness of the greatest number of people. Happiness is defined in terms of the pursuit of pleasure and the avoidance of pain. He memorably referred to the idea of natural law as 'nonsense on stilts' (see the discussion in Chapter 7 on the Magna Carta).

Bentham suggested an impressive list of potential pleasures, including those of the senses, wealth, skill, power, imagination and expectation. It is recognised that some people gain pleasure from causing pain to others, though we may assume that the magnitude of the pain wipes out the positive standing of any such pleasure in any aggregative calculation (assuming sadomasochistic relationships are not relevant in a text on business ethics). Pains may result from a lack of necessities, disappointment, shyness and expectation of unpleasantness as well as the more obvious bodily and mental problems we would like to avoid.

We can all see that any act may produce consequences of pleasure and pain for a range of individuals. More ambitious is Bentham's view that we may attempt to aggregate these for a population and this is where the notion of utility becomes important. In order to add up pleasure and pain over a population he introduces what is termed a 'felicific calculus' where each instance of pleasure or pain is given a value or score referred to as its utility (positive for pleasure and negative for pain). If an act results in a positive overall utility score then it is seen as a good thing and moral decision-making is seen as choosing the actions which maximise utility over the population.

Therefore in its crudest form, utilitarianism has the following characteristics:

- *Consequentialist* – the rightness of actions is determined by consequences.
- *Hedonistic* – the pursuit of pleasure and the avoidance of pain are the characteristics of consequences that are measured.
- *Particularist* – the analysis refers to particular instances rather than general kinds of acts (e.g. to a particular instance of stealing rather than theft in general).
- *Universalistic* – is applicable at all times and places, to individuals and to groups.
- *Aggregative* – it should take into consideration all those affected and produce a utility score based on the total consequential effect.
- *Maximising* – it attempts to produce actions with the best consequences (as measured by utility) rather than merely adequate.
- *Impartial* – it does not give extra weight to the pleasures or pain of any one individual or group.

Of interest, also, is what utilitarianism does not do:

- It does not seek to pursue the self-interest of the decision maker.
- It does not consider motives or intentions.
- It rejects reason as a source of moral values. This sounds odd as the principle of utilitarianism is itself argued to be rational. However, the point is that it is not 'unreasonable' for one to consider doing something unpleasant to others but it may well be immoral. You may think this is an odd use of the word 'reason' but perhaps the point is clearer if we remember that clever people may be evil.
- Though the focus is on consequences, these are not seen as 'ends' (or inherent purposes) in the same way as early virtue theory and

natural law proponents suggest, for example, that the 'end' of a seed is to grow into a plant or the purpose of a human being is to increase their personal virtue and knowledge. Bentham is referring to the consequences of intentional acts, which are therefore far from inevitable and not desirable unless they maximise utility.

It should be obvious by now that there are a number of difficulties with this approach. The most obvious is an apparent lack of safeguards for minorities; provided enough people are made happy, are we allowed to contemplate extreme pain and perhaps death for minorities? A glance at the history of 'civilisation' will show that the persecution of minorities, slavery, war and so forth indicate that society has been all too willing to do exactly that! Ironically this is just the sort of state of affairs that Bentham was passionately opposed to, but it is not clear that his calculus by itself is adequate in providing a rationale for social change. A further objection is that this sort of calculated morality is exactly the opposite of the personal value systems that many people associate with 'goodness' in a person. This approach is in sharp contrast to the other moral theories explored in this book but its attempt at an objective ethics has some attraction to economic theory and business practice. How it links with these two areas is discussed in pp. 84–91.

At this point in our introduction we should also mention another great proponent of the utilitarian framework, John Stuart Mill (1806–1873), a child prodigy whose father worked with Bentham. Mill was drawn to this general theory but troubled by the possibility that such an approach is an encroachment on personal liberty and if applied at the level of the state could lead to totalitarianism.

One theme in Western culture has been the right of the individual to be free from the interference of others and the state. This refers to 'outer freedom', that is liberty, freedom from harm, freedom to have political opinions and freedom of religious observance. We also note the 'inner freedom' to adopt what beliefs and moral principles we would wish. Mill takes up this theme:

> The sole end for which mankind are warranted, individually or collectively, in interfering with the liberty of action of any of their number if self-protection. The only purpose for which power can be rightfully exercised over any member of a civilised community against his will, is to prevent harm to others. His own good, either physical or moral, is not a sufficient warrant ... over himself, over his own body and mind, the individual is sovereign. (Mill 1972)

This is a very fundamental statement which challenges over-organising tendencies of the state (even in the name of utility maximisation) as well as the human rights ideologies which place extensive duties on others. It provides a moral principle which has been influential in political theory and is a counterbalancing influence to the calculating consequentialism of the felicific calculus, even though Mill writes within the general framework of utilitarianism.

In recent ethical theory, more sophisticated forms of utilitarianism have been promoted as practical ways of addressing contemporary problems, though it should also be said that many moral philosophers entirely reject this approach as an adequate characterisation of ethics. In the sections that follow we explore some practical issues with the use of this framework in business decision-making whilst recognising that many managerial decisions are in fact taken on grounds of a cost–benefit analysis that looks suspiciously like utilitarianism applied within a more limited stakeholder model.

Some problems with the application of utilitarianism

Despite its obvious attractions as an objective way of operationalising moral decision-making in a business context, utilitarianism faces a number of practical challenges as outlined below and in the remaining sections of this chapter.

Pleasure and pain

Happiness and pain mean different things to different people and it is not clear how these key concepts can be used in a practical way which reflects our inward emotions and feelings. An alternative approach is to ignore these and base utility measurements on our observed actions, for example by observing our buying habits in a market context. This leads to the idea of revealed preferences.

For many people, moral worth is concerned with other things as well as happiness and pain. Indeed we often associate moral behaviour with some forms of self-denial for the benefit of others. Though the 'felicific calculus' may seem to handle this in a mechanical way it somehow seems to ignore the real value of altruism. Furthermore if we broaden the definition of utility to include concepts like personal safety, health and peace of mind we have real problems in connecting specific actions by individuals with these consequences. In fact, what do we include in measuring personal utility, quite apart from the difficult problems in comparing and aggregating this to include whole populations?

The impartiality assumption leads to an equal weighting of utility for members of a population. We may, however, believe that some should receive preferential treatment, perhaps due to need within a health care or social services context. Yet deciding on the weightings to be given to individuals is a daunting prospect. The interested reader might wish to pursue this through such topics as welfare economics, though they should be aware of the analytical difficulties which await them.

Some actions may be thought to be intrinsically wrong, independent of their apparent consequences in a given instance (i.e. apart from economic and legal consequences). Concepts such as natural justice and fairness are basic to the way we view the social world but seem to be ignored by, or even conflict with, strict utilitarianism. Can we accommodate them without losing the whole point of the utilitarian approach?

We also judge peoples' motives and intentions. We are suspicious when the 'right action' may have been carried out for the wrong reason, if only for the practical reason that future actions may be more in line with the frustrated intentions. Surely people are more than pleasure seekers and pain avoiders? What is the place of the decision maker's personal integrity in this apparently impersonal, automatic calculus of decision-making?

Scope and stakeholders

How broad is the set of potential stakeholders to be considered in a given situation? We can begin with shareholders, suppliers of capital and the Inland Revenue, and then continue with the usual set considered by corporate strategists (customers, employees, the local community, etc.). Environmentalists, however, will point the way to broader human and natural systems which may be disturbed by our actions. Do we consider all human life or include the pain inflicted on animals and possible damage to the natural world? If this seems extravagant consider the debates surrounding the impact of tourism on communities and sites round the world.

Even if we can find an acceptable list of stakeholders, how do we balance, in particular, the advantages gained by many people against severe disadvantages suffered by the few (typical business examples involve major projects which disrupt communities; business decisions which put a competitor out of business with severe loss of jobs and social upheaval, etc.). If we simply reply that all this is not our concern, that is we just play the business game by the accepted rules, then we can hardly be classed as utilitarians! Such action is surely an extended form of egoism.

Challenges for utilitarianism as a practical decision-making tool

To state the obvious, all consequences are in the future! Can we predict them with sufficient accuracy to be sure we are making moral decisions? This may be particularly problematic if the consequences are the results of our own and others' actions, in particular competitors. It is quite easy for mutually competitive action to get into a destructive spiral or to produce quite unexpected results.

An issue we mentioned above is how far must we trace the consequences of actions? This is a particular problem in environmental ethics where long chains of cause and effect are explored in an attempt to establish the potential environmental impact of decisions (see Chapter 21). Then we must also recognise that we are usually not sure of the consequences of our actions and must include forms of risk analysis which account for alternative futures (see Chapter 16). This not only increases the number of future alternatives to be considered but introduces the need for probability assessment of alternative impacts.

We may pretend that the above analysis can be carried out in an objective fashion but assessments of risk depend on our perceptions and cultural biases as well as objective probabilities. Thus a course of action (e.g. an immunisation programme or a change in the operations of a health system) may be objectively seen as carrying small risks but produce a dread within a population leading to major public anxiety and protest. The decision makers may be sure they did the right thing, and in terms of objectives measures of utility, such as mortality, may have done so, but the decisions may produce a great deal of unhappiness and uncertainty for a large number of people. This is a difficult paradox for the committed utilitarian; you genuinely think you know the best thing that should be done and you carry this out, but as a result are vilified and perhaps sacked for your actions. A simple response is to say, as politicians are prone to do, that you failed to communicate properly the reasons for your actions and its real benefits. Unfortunately in many competitive and politically sensitive situations things are not so easy, particularly if the decisions are being made by a group of people (as typically is the case in an organisation) who are not totally in agreement about means and ends.

Implicit in the above discussion is the assumption that we are engaging in 'act utilitarianism', that is we are attempting to assess the impact of a single decision. Judging all of one's actions in this way is impossibly demanding if we consider the number of small-scale decisions we may make in a day. Such operational decisions may well have considerable consequences, for example if we are allocating resources to projects (e.g. as a bank) or interviewing applicants for a job. The latter is a good example of a simple everyday decision which can have superb positive consequences for all concerned or lead to disaster for the individual and the organisation. We usually cope in such situation by the use of decision rules. These may be formal and even embedded in IT systems which automatically check data against objective criteria, though we should then remember that the moral decision-making has now been at least partly moved back to the choices made when setting up the system. Decision rules may also be informal as when we learn from experience (individually or as a group) and encapsulate the results in rules-of-thumb (or heuristics) which are consistently applied. These practices can be seen as applications of 'rule utilitarianism', where individual actions are controlled through rules and procedures in such a way that the aims of utilitarianism are conserved. It is useful to see the setting up and monitoring of sets of rules as an exercise in act utilitarianism, that is it is sensible to review procedures in terms of the aggregate consequences over a period of time.

An interesting point which will have occurred to those interested in research (whether academic or applied, such as market research) is that applying utilitarianism requires a search for information which may itself involve ethical decisions. We should ask if a search is intrusive and does it affect the perceptions of gain and risk amongst affected parties? Asking questions on sensitive topics (e.g. such as stress or management bullying) within an organisation can itself lead to consequences, whether intended (e.g. increased awareness) or not (e.g. resistance to proposed plans). This can be seen as a paradox in the use of utilitarianism:

1. Decisions are made with reference to predicted consequences for stakeholders
2. ...but we need data on the possible consequences.
3. Obtaining such data may need research involving the stakeholders
4. ...and this research may itself have negative consequences for all concerned!

Trying to do the right thing thus may lead to unexpected negative consequences! The only response to this is to recognise the need for skill, subtlety and professional integrity in applying any decision-making procedure in an organisational context. This in turn may lead us to consider the role of the positive personal qualities we refer to later as 'virtues' and to see the inter-connectedness of the moral approaches we are considering.

A general point to note here is that learning (individual and organisational) has an effect on decision-making and vice versa. It may even be the most valuable consequence for some stakeholders but not easily equated to pleasure or pain! It may even provide a more positive view of some projects which appear to have been unsuccessful (e.g. the launch of a speculative product) but which have provided valuable information and learning to support future projects.

However, a negative aspect of this line of thought is the situation where a decision maker may not pursue an information-gathering strategy because they do not want to learn, for example a design team may feel disinclined to carry out certain forms of product risk analysis because if they do and a potential fault is discovered then they will be obliged to do something about it! Alternatively if they test, find a potential fault and do not act then their liability is likely to be greater if legal action is taken against them. This may seem an extreme scenario but at a more everyday level, how often does a manager say 'I don't want to know' when offered a piece of information which may oblige them taking action they do not want to take, for example in a case of a minor breach of discipline.

A final point in this long and varied set of practical obstacles to the mechanical use of utilitarianism in organisational contexts is the recognition of inter-connectedness and feedback. Apparently separate decisions with different decision makers may interact thus affecting the consequences, for example, several firms invest in R&D thus lowering the expected profits of each and causing bankruptcies. In a complex, interactive human situation with feedback decision loops and multiple levels of learning, the consequences of a decision may be impossible to model. This line of thought is explored by specialists in the application of chaos theory to social and organisational contexts.

Chaos and complexity

Most people will be familiar with the arresting image used by chaos theorists to popularise their subject, namely the idea that a butterfly flapping its wings in one continent might affect the weather in another. It is, of course, a strange and paradoxical thought! Surely there are lots of butterflies and other creatures doing something similar and how could one ever connect a particular butterfly with a distant event except by intrusive measurements which would interfere with the effect. Perhaps you will feel that I am taking a beautiful picture too seriously, and what has all this to do with business ethics?

The answer to the last question is 'cause and effect', but first of all we must say something further about chaos theory and other ideas from the sciences which are relevant to our discussion. Chaos theory is strictly a branch of applied mathematics and its recent popularisation began with attempts to find mathematical models for predicting the behaviour of the weather. Using the large amounts of meteorological data collected regularly and the ability of computers to model the equations reflecting such variables as pressure, temperature and air movement in the atmosphere it is possible to predict the weather at a given location in the short term, that is we know roughly whether it will rain in Blackpool tomorrow, the uncertainty being increased if conditions are changing rapidly, for example due to a storm. We can also predict the weather a few days ahead in more general terms. We can also make long-term predictions of climate change, given assumption about global warming and other currently pressing topics. Unfortunately, however much current data we collect and computer power we use, there is a limit to the accuracy of prediction we can achieve, and the reasons for this have been explored in the mathematics of Chaos Theory. While 'chaos' is a catchy word to use, the real issue is the sensitivity of the predictive theories and equations to the inevitable inaccuracies in the initial data used. This type of sensitivity has been seen in other branches of the physical sciences and engineering. It can occur when only a few factors are at work but is obviously made worse when many factors are present and interact.

Situations where many factors are present and affect results independently are typically studied by statisticians through the use of probability models. The situation where many contributing factors interact in a network of influence is typical of contexts modelled by Complexity Theory. You may also have heard of Catastrophe Theory, which originated around 20 years ago and dealt with mathematical models of situations where a small change in some key input resulted in a major change in an output variable. The word 'catastrophe' was useful in bringing this area of mathematics to a wider audience, including the social sciences, where attempts were made to use it in predicting social and psychological events of a dramatic nature. A more recent idea is the notion of a 'tipping point' which applies to social phenomena such as crime and fashion where a particular behaviour (e.g. type of crime or demand for a specific consumer good) becomes widespread in a short space of time, that is situations which can be modelled as the diffusion of a behaviour within a large population (see Gladwell 2000).

This is by no means a complete list (see later for an introduction to Game Theory and Evolution) but the items mentioned have some particular features in common, that is they:

▶ relate to the development of mathematical models which can be applied to human behaviour;
▶ explore situations where unusual and apparently counter-intuitive behaviour can occur, which is important for making predictions;
▶ encourage us to think more clearly how our actions may lead to unintended consequences.

As a result they are increasingly being applied to social phenomena such as economics, stock markets, consumer behaviour, political analysis and business strategy. A typical example is the analysis of the behaviour of stock markets where a period of stability in share prices can suddenly end in abrupt rises or falls (see, for example, Cohen 1997). Common to many of these phenomena are changes in accepted opinions and beliefs which lead to sudden action on a large scale. This can be positive, as in massive demand for a consumer item, or negative as in a stock market collapse. Attempts have also been made to apply such ideas within an organisation, for example the use of ideas from Complexity Theory to explore differences between situations where styles of ordinary management apply and to change management contexts, the latter being characterised by turbulent times where major changes are intended and different approaches to management are needed.

If we move our attention now to the concepts and models of business ethics we can see how the above may affect our views. The most obvious set of problems occur if we adopt a utilitarian framework, that is we intend to take action to maximise positive outcomes for a wide range of individuals. To put it bluntly, we may simply not be able to do this as we cannot predict the results of our actions. Worst still, we may find that our well-meaning but ambitious policies backfire and produce the opposite results to those intended. We should also note that hiding behind our good intentions is not an adequate response to such disasters; there has long been an informal tradition (typically referred to as 'sod's law') that things often do not turn out as we intend and this is now reinforced by a number of theories and examples showing why this may occur. Ignorance is neither bliss nor a justification for moral ineptitude.

However, this cannot mean that we do nothing, itself an action and often morally inadequate. Our best approach may well be a combination of knowledge and morally sound analysis tempered with a large portion of modesty when considering our predictive abilities. Perhaps these should be added to the list of managerial virtues.

We cannot escape the above issues by adopting deontological rather than consequentialist approaches to organisational ethics. Even if we do not pretend to follow a utilitarian calculus we still need to take actions to fulfil our obligations and the appropriate action may not be certain. Perhaps we can see here why the Kantian ethics places so much emphasis on the idea of good will, though doing our duty may not always be a simple matter (see Chapter 7). The point we are reinforcing here is that good moral intentions must be matched with knowledge and understanding of the world we are operating in as well as the skills of analysis and implementation necessary to be effective.

Game theory and evolution

In the 1940s, economists began to explore what has now become known as 'Game Theory', an area of mathematics which attempts to model human decision-making in situations where outcomes depend on the choices of more than one agent, who may be acting co-operatively or competitively. This work has spawned a massive literature and the development of a number of very sophisticated mathematical theories which can be related to a wide range of practical situations as well as different branches of the social sciences. There are a number of elementary texts in this area, Hargreaves Heap and Varoufakis (1995) being interesting for our purposes as it relates these ideas to ethical theories. However, in this area of work 'elementary' should be interpreted as introducing the elements of the subject rather than being easy! Game Theory is very challenging, both technically and conceptually.

The 'Prisoners' Dilemma' is an example of a theoretical game which has itself generated much discussion and can be related to a range of practical situations. In this simplified competitive situation two opponents make decisions which involve either co-operation (with a small, positive outcome for each) or defection. If both opponents defect at the same time, both suffer a negative outcome. If only one defects, the defector receives a larger positive outcome and the opponent suffers a severe loss, for example as when one prisoner blames the other for a crime. The core concern being explored in such models is the nature of rational action, indeed, some would claim, of rationality itself, that is it is 'rational' to defect only if the other player does not do so! If such a challenge can be made, then it has considerable repercussions for the philosophical approaches to ethics which, like Kantianism, are based on the idea of rational decision-making rather than blind obedience to some external laws or our internal feelings and intuitions.

One very interesting development of 'Prisoners' Dilemma' type games is to assume that a series of games are played. In this case the reputation of the players becomes important, for example, if you renege on an agreement in an early game, other players might then make their decisions with this in mind, to your disadvantage. This obviously parallels business behaviour, as instanced by the prominence given to 'reputation' in some of the models in this book (see Chapter 10) as well as our common-sense understanding of its importance. This type of repeated game is hard to analyse but considerable progress was made in a classic set of experiments reported in Axelrod (1984). This involved game theory experts being invited to play repeated Prisoners' Dilemma games against each other using their preferred decision rules. These usually came down to specifying the situations in which a co-operative move is made rather than a defecting move. The 'winner' of this tournament was a rule called 'tit-for-tat' which was also the simplest rule suggested. This rule works as follows: the first move is co-operative and after this the programme simply copies the opponent. If the opponent continues to co-operate, then so does 'tit-for-tat' which is to both players continuing profit. If the opponent defects then so does 'tit-for-tat' in the next round but returns to co-operation if the opponent does.

This 'tit-for-tat' rule makes sense if translated into similar real-life situations, particularly if the threat of 'tit-for-tat' action can convincingly replace the need to actually retaliate. Thus co-operative, and profitable, behaviour in a group context can be seen to result from a believable threat. This poses a considerable challenge to ethical theory and gives support to the more 'political' models which include reference to power, influence and reputation.

An interesting side issue here is the problem (from a theoretical point of view) of altruism (see Chapter 5). A considerable challenge to the more egocentric views of human behaviour is the observed phenomena of altruistic behaviour, that is cases where people do things which are not in their own interests. A simple example may be anonymous charity donations while more dramatic instances are seen when someone loses their life to help others. One can make attempts to explain such actions as ultimately selfish or as the result of social pressure but we may also wonder if such actions demonstrate genuinely ethical behaviour, that is they are examples of doing one's duty or acting for the benefit of the greatest number. This difficult area, along with game theory, evolution and many other matters, is dealt with in Ridley (1996). In a similar vein, Hinde (2002) explores the evolution of ethical behaviour, working from a scientific perspective. Hollis (1994) introduces the philosophy of the social sciences with considerable reference to game theory and to ethical concepts while Hollis (1998) deals with the notion of 'trust' in a similar way.

Texts on business and organisational ethics seldom explicitly relate in any systematic way to the above 'scientific' theories but we can see that there may be considerable value in using these insights in a constructive way. This does not mean discarding the language and concepts of ethics but understanding them in new ways. In particular such theories attempt to address issues such as the evolution of ethical behaviour in co-operative social groups and in competitive situations and allow discussion of ideas such as reputation. The difficulties inherent in such areas of theory should not be underestimated, however.

Summary

The importance of the utilitarian approach is shown by the high degree of influence of economic theory on the understanding of market systems and on business practice. Many techniques and models in business and management, particularly when quantified, have an origin in economic theory. Examples are to be found both in the private and public sectors as well as public policy relating to such things as the regulation of markets and taxation. Much economic theory inevitably reflects some variant of utilitarian thinking, if in highly sophisticated disguise.

We have therefore spent some time in outlining the problems inherent in basing moral decision-making on forecasts of results for some appropriate group of stakeholders. In fairness it should be noted that the alternative theories outlined in the next few chapters have their share of problems and therefore the potential value of conse-quentialist approaches as one component in a varied strategy of ethical evaluation should not be dismissed. If the survival of an organisation is seen to be a worthy moral objective, then results will count.

You will have noted a fair amount of 'signposting' in the above text to other chapters in this book. In fact the ideas in this chapter can be linked in some way with almost all subsequent chapters, as can the remaining 'theory' chapters in Part II. This inter-relatedness is a feature of business ethics that you will gradually get used to; it is counter-productive to compartmentalise the ideas and concepts of ethics as applied to organisations.

7 Human rights and Kantian ethics

Purpose and learning outcomes

The purpose of this chapter is to introduce some established 'action-based' models of applied ethics, with a particular emphasis on ideas of human rights and on Kantian ethics.

You will be able to

▶ understand the appeal and the limitations of the idea of 'rights' in a business context;
▶ demonstrate a basic understanding of Kantian ethics in a business context.

Introduction

In this chapter we introduce a number of non-consequentialist views of ethics. As we mentioned earlier, this is not to say that consequences are of no importance in applying these theories but the focus of ethical evaluation will be on actions rather than results. The chapter is divided into three main sections. The first two deal with some basic ideas of human rights. The final section on the Kantian approach introduces what many readers will find to be difficult material. Prior to reading this section it might be advisable to look back at the material on 'consistency' in the final section of Chapter 5.

We begin with some discussion on human rights, a way of approaching ethics which may have considerable appeal for individuals and groups who are unfairly discriminated against or who wish to find articulate support for political action and change in the law and society's attitudes. Unfortunately it is not difficult to generate long lists of rights without consideration of the resources needed to fulfil the resulting obligations or the priority rules which have to be used if rights are inconsistent with each other. We continue this theme with some more down-to-earth examples of the problems which occur when rights, obligations, agreements and promises are mixed together in unhelpful ways.

The next stage is a consideration of Kantian ethics, which can only be a brief introduction to one of the most sophisticated and debateable ways of viewing ethics. These ideas are further developed in Chapter 8.

Human rights

Deontological theories in ethics are those which assert that some actions are right or wrong in themselves, quite apart from their consequences. This usually leads to some consideration of rights, duties and obligations. Thus deontological approaches to moral decision-making are based on rules and principles which encourage or constrain actions rather than focussing on consequences. Laws usually act in this way.

While sympathetic to the revolutionary movements of the time, Bentham argued that lists of 'the rights of man' were arbitrary and dependant on context. We can see this if we examine the list of demands in the Magna Carta, very much a reflection of the political concerns of the more prominent subjects of King John in 1215. Here the obviously important 'To no one will we sell, to no one will we refuse or delay, right or justice' is seen alongside 'All fish-weirs for the future shall be removed altogether from the Thames and Medway, and throughout all England, except upon the sea shore'. Whilst the latter quoted sentence was no doubt of crucial economic importance to many people, the injunction that 'No one shall be arrested or imprisoned upon the appeal of a woman, for the death of any other than her husband' is more distinctive to the social norms of the time! The quotations above are from Stroud (1980), which gives a translation of the Magna Carta with comments.

Modern considerations of the inherent rights of all people have moved on a long way from the above. Human rights are general statements which are meant to apply to all people, independent of the legal system operating within a particular country. The United Nations Universal Declaration of Human Rights (adopted in 1948) is one of the best-known examples of a set of such statements. The articles in this declaration are often very broad, for example:

Article 1
All human beings are born free and equal in dignity and rights. They are endowed with reason and conscience and should act towards one another in a spirit of brotherhood.

One might hope that most people would agree with the underlying sentiment of such a statement and reflect this in their actions. It is, however, not too difficult to raise issues of definition and application, for example:

► This is a statement relating to the recognition by humans of the rights of other humans. How does it relate to the unborn (either a specific foetus or future generations in general), the dead, other living organisms or even the ecosystem of the world? We may simply reply that this article is not meant to address such issues.
► Are all humans actually endowed with reason and conscience? As a statement of fact this appears to ignore some individuals who appear to lack the latter and against whom society needs to protect its members.
► Whilst acting in a spirit of brotherhood is fundamental to some religions and an aspiration to many individuals, the competitive environment we explore in this book seems at odds with this or at least is very selective as to who is to be regarded as a 'brother' (e.g. stakeholders).
► This, and many other articles appear to be addressed to governments and can easily be read as 'things the government should do for me' rather than a guide for individual action. This debate therefore appears to be within the sphere of politics rather than individual ethics.

The latter point can be countered by considering the influence which business in general has on governments and also on the international aspects of business ethics considered in Chapter 15 and elsewhere.

A useful exercise is to reconsider these articles as if referring directly to organisations, for example:

Article 19
Everyone has the right to freedom of opinion and expression; this right includes freedom to hold opinions without interference and to seek, receive and impart information and ideas through any media and regardless of frontiers.

I suspect that many office workers would like to pin this up over their desk or send an anonymous copy to their manager! Not all organisational cultures promote such freedom of expression, in principle or in practice. We may also ask how this relates to whistleblowing, in particular, and this is something we will consider later in Chapter 14.

Article 24
Everyone has the right to rest and leisure, including reasonable limitation of working hours and periodic holidays with pay.

This more obviously relates to organisational practice and raises the interesting issue of the extent to which such a right can be over-ridden in specific circumstances (e.g. emergencies) or can be 'bought out' with overtime payments and bonuses, that is where the individual freely exercises a right to choose their working conditions. We will leave it to the reader to imaginatively explore other ways in which these articles can be contextualised to business situations.

Some general points must be made here. The fact that I have a right to free speech, say, also implies a duty not to violate the rights of other individuals to similar freedom of expression. However, do I not also have the right to use reason and judgement in deciding what may or may not be appropriate comments to be made by myself and others in a specific situation? The 'right to manage' (self and others) may not be enshrined in the UN Declaration but it is implicit in carrying out the role of a manager.

Similarly, granting appropriate working hours to others may impact adversely on my own quality of working life or the survival of my business and hence the jobs of others. Consequences cannot simply be ignored, though there is a counter-argument that management can easily use the fear of bad consequences to over-ride employee rights while not sharing the data sources on which the prediction of gloom has been made.

As so often is the case, we find that simple statements of rights, like the use of simplistic theories and models, are inadequate in dealing with the complexity of real practical situations in large systems such as those typical in business and politics. There are too many inter-connected actors, each with their rights, and too much uncertainty. But we need simple models and ideas in order to make sense of the world, so the language of rights may be useful provided we do not expect it to encapsulate all issues in the business world. Unfortunately many individuals, such as irate customers and disillusioned employees, may wish to approach complex situations with simple issues in mind – the supposed violation of their presumed rights. Even the word 'violation' (with its connotation of violence) is unhelpful! Perhaps it was extreme for Bentham to refer to the discussion of rights as 'nonsense on stilts' but one can see his point (see Chapter 6).

Rights, loyalty and compromise – a practical digression

In order to provide a break in ethical theorising, this short section explores some of the problems we can get ourselves into in a business context when we take the idea of 'my rights' very seriously. It also introduces some of the problems associated with the notion of loyalty. This theme will be revisited in Chapter 15 (relating to Japanese management) and Chapter 14 (in the context of whistleblowing).

> 'I have my rights and I will not back down in demands based on those rights.'
> 'I have principles which I will never compromise.'
> 'I will never break a promise.'

If we have ever made statements such as those above, it is likely we will eventually land ourselves in a problem. The difficulty is less to do with having rights and principles and making promises than with the absolute certainty with which we hold to them. Consider the following situations:

> I have an agreement with my family never to travel abroad or to be away for more than a couple of days. This is due to the pressing need to care for a seriously ill dependent. My firm urgently needs me to travel overseas for a week to rescue a contract negotiation which is at a difficult point and where my particular expertise is essential. What should I do?

Let us suppose that I have always been straightforward with my firm and made this constraint on my travel well known for some time and this has always been accepted by management. It would then appear that I am morally right in not going. Furthermore it would seem wrong for the firm to ask me to go and for my fellow workers to be resentful with me if my position causes them problems and a loss to the firm as a whole. We all had an agreement and kept to it! It might have been only natural for my colleagues to be unhappy with my behaviour if keeping an agreement had been the only reason for refusal. Even if keeping the agreement was the basis for the decision, the plight of my relative provides some sort of justification for the action.

However, it is tempting in such a case to weigh the conflicting demands in terms of the needs of those involved. In this case if I say to my firm I will not travel abroad, then describing the reason may well elicit sympathy and understanding. My family situation acts as an explanation of the rationality of my decision. Let us, therefore change the situation as follows:

> I have an agreement with my family never to travel abroad or to be away for more than a couple of days. My firm urgently needs me to travel overseas for a week to rescue a contract negotiation which is at a difficult point and where my particular expertise is essential. What should I do?

The balance between my promise to my family, presented as an agreement with no supporting rationale, and my loyalty to the organisation is now seen in a stark form. If my decision is still not to go, now based on promises and agreements, then it might be admitted I was in the right but had hardly acted as a team member. If we took this further we might have:

> I have an agreement with my family never to travel abroad or to be away for more than a couple of days. My firm urgently needs me to travel overseas for a week to rescue a contract negotiation which is at a difficult point and where my particular expertise is essential. Failure to achieve agreement is likely to lead to severe job losses, including my own. What should I do?

Perhaps I can now use the firm's crisis to explain to my family why I should go back on my promise and travel overseas. Of course, we could make the situation especially difficult as follows:

> I have an agreement with my family never to travel abroad or to be away for more than a couple of days. This is due to the pressing need to care for a seriously ill dependent. My firm urgently needs me to travel overseas for a week to rescue a contract negotiation which is at a difficult point and where my particular expertise is essential. Failure to achieve agreement is likely to lead to severe job losses, including my own. What should I do?

Difficult factors now weigh on both sides and we could continue to imagine situations where the balance is ever finer. Where real harm may be done to different persons by my decision either way we have a moral dilemma. Can we address this simply by quoting rights, agreements and promises, even if bolstered by consequences?

We can bring further factors into play here by considering the consistency of my actions over a period of time. Am I similarly willing to respect the rights of others? Do I always keep my promises? Should not my willingly accepted role as a member of this moral community (i.e. my firm) lead to me being willing to seek compromises when difficulties arise?

Another line of argument here is to pursue the perspective of the firm. Should the firm ask me to do this? A more subtle position would be if the firm had made every effort to exhaust other ways of rescuing the contract, even at considerable expense and time to other staff, and now came to me as a fully justified last resort. This seems to give them more 'moral leverage', whatever that means!

We might also wonder if the firm was sensible to allow this agreement to exist. Perhaps it would be prudent to always agree to working practices only if normal conditions apply. This would be typical of a situation in the armed services where exceptional situations may lead to an overturning of normal working routines. The problem now is that almost anything can be requested as 'exceptional'!

It is also important that we do not overrate our ability to see into the future, both as individuals and as managers. The danger with promises and tight agreements is that circumstances change, a perpetual difficulty when contracts are used in situations of uncertainty and long timescales.

It can be argued that in many real working situations, the choice is not between right and wrong but between competing rights (using the other sense of the word 'right', of course). In a world of rights, contracts, obligations, promises and agreements we will always have conflict and the only way forward is debate, compromise and further provisional agreements. Perhaps this is one of the best arguments for seeing moral debate in the context of a committed community and recognising the role played by power, information and persuasion. See Chapter 9 on ethical debate in a community and also Chapter 15 in order to appreciate how other cultures may handle this issue of maintaining work relationships through compromise. The idea of reputation, explored in Chapter 10, is also relevant here.

Kantian ethics

One of the greatest philosophers within the Western tradition is Immanuel Kant (1724–1804). Kant's writings demonstrate an analysis of the major issues in philosophy approached very firmly through the careful use of reason but with an attention to the practical implications of his theoretical analysis. He lived the whole of his life in the German town of Konigsberg where he worked as an academic. Unlike Hume, he was not an atheist but was determined to base his philosophical analysis on reasoned argument rather than any appeal to religious faith. The resulting work remains a staple ingredient of many courses in philosophy both for its own merits and to help the understanding of the many authors who have used his work as a base for further development.

Kant produced what is, in effect, a classical statement of deontological ethics, where right actions conform to basic rational principles summarised in the various alternative statements of the 'Categorical Imperative' (or 'Moral Law'). Part of Kant's stated reason for developing this approach was a fundamental disagreement with Hume's approach. Kant simply did not accept that moral actions followed from one's feelings or desires. Indeed, quite the opposite; we do what is right because it is our duty to do so rather than our inclination. Unfortunately, this attention to reason results in a somewhat abstract principle, which is not easy to relate to many practical situations, and to an idea of duty which some people may find at odds with notions of moral development and motivation. Some immediate support, however, can be found in what is sometimes called the Golden Rule:

> Treat others only as you consent to being treated in the same situation.

This idea of reciprocal action is historically found within a number of belief systems and forms the basis of much common-sense thinking about practical ethics. Kant's basic rule, the Categorical Imperative, sounds fairly similar but should not be confused with the Golden Rule as it avoids some problems of the Golden Rule as well as the latter's narrow focus.

There are three different formulations of Kant's rule, and here we are following a recent text which relates these to business practice (Bowie 1999). A derivation of these rules is beyond the scope of this book but further details can be found in Gensler (1998) and in Kant (1998) (a modern edition with useful notes). A good introduction to the philosophical issues in this area are Chapters 4 and 5 of Benn (1998).

The Categorical Imperative or Formula of Universal Law

> Act only in accordance with the maxim through which you can at
> the same time will that it be a universal law.

Briefly, if we are considering whether a particular action is morally
right we should imagine that this action becomes an instance of a
general rule which is adopted by everyone at all times. We should then
logically assess the repercussions of such a situation and ask whether
this is viable. For example, suppose we are considering making a promise
which we know we will not keep. If we apply the above rule, we must
imagine that all promises are made with no intention to keep them.
This is obviously not a viable situation as the very nature of a promise
is undermined; the whole point of promises is that they are kept (at
least unless some subsequent event occurs which might make a given
promise impossible to keep). Therefore we reject the idea of making
a false promise, not because we have bad feelings about it but because
it is illogical when applied universally.

It can be seen that the Golden Rule is a restricted version of the
Categorical Imperative. It should be noted that this approach is not
consequentialist, though the results of actions will be in our minds
when deciding if we would wish maxims to be universally applied. The
primary focus is on actions.

Another idea of Kant's we should introduce at this time is the
centrality of the notion of 'duty'. In Kant's view (and for reasons he
refers to at length) the only motive which can confer moral value is
duty; we do what is right because it is our duty. We may also be motivated by feelings of sympathy or fear of retribution, but an action is
not seen as free if it is caused by such things. Moral worth is attached
to actions which we freely decide to perform because it is our duty to
do so. This idea has been criticised as harsh and difficult to relate to
how we usually act. It should be said that Kant does not despise
sympathy and feelings but simply detaches them from assessment of
moral worth. It is good to empathise with another person but this is
not the same thing as assessing the moral worth of an action to help
them. In a Kantian framework, the latter should be based on a rationally
derived notion of duty.

A further idea which should be mentioned even in a brief introduction
to Kant's ethics is the idea of 'good will', a willingness to do one's duty
for duty's sake. Good will is the only thing which is good in itself,
without qualification. We can make sense of this by realising that the

other virtues (e.g. intelligence, courage and so forth (see Chapter 9)) can be put to immoral purpose.

The Formula of Humanity or Formula of the End in Itself

Act so that you use humanity, whether in your own person or in the person of any other, always at the same time as an end, never merely as a means.

This formula reflects Kant's view of the dignity of human beings and the basic need to respect this in all situations. It can be seen as equivalent to the Formula of Universal Law if we argue this implies that other agents have the right to use their own reason and show moral worth through their own actions freely undertaken as their duty. We are allowing others the fundamental liberty we have assumed for ourselves, of having the means to demonstrate moral worth.

As we will see later, this formula is readily applicable to many organisational situations. Indeed, it strikes directly against the crude managerial approach where employees and customers are merely seen in terms of their effect on the financial results of a company, that is merely as a means to shareholder (and managerial) wealth, and are manipulated as a means to that end. However, if our actions recognise the 'ends' of others (i.e. their goals and ambitions) and we seek ways to balance the meeting of our objectives with allowing them autonomy, in particular freedom to act and demonstrate moral worth, then we may meet Kant's strict view. This very interesting idea that we should not attempt to 'bypass' the rationality and moral autonomy of another person may not always be compatible with a manager's felt need to exert control over his environment.

Autonomy and the Kingdom of Ends

We should so act that we may think of ourselves as legislating universal laws through our maxims.

The laws of the kingdom of ends are the laws of freedom, both because it is the mark of free citizens to make their own laws, and because the content of those laws directs us to respect each citizen's free use of his or her own reason.

This version of the categorical imperative is in some ways one of the easiest to relate to, particularly as it mentions the word 'legislate' and therefore reminds us of lawmaking in the traditional sense of the role of the state. If we relate it to organisations as moral communities of purpose, then the second quote reminds us of the freedom and autonomy of the 'citizens' of this community.

We will return several times to the implications of these rules in work contexts. However, it is perhaps important at this stage to reflect on some of the general problems which have been found when using this framework to guide moral decision-making in a practical context. Kant is hard to translate from the original German and hard to understand as the arguments he presents are highly sophisticated and interwoven with his more general theories.

The major problem is that the categorical imperative defines a theoretical process rather than actually telling you what to do in a given situation. When it can be used to derive rules for behaviour these must, by definition, be universally applicable, which can in turn make them insensitive to special cases. It may also lead to conflicting obligations. Kant also insists that we act out of a sense of duty, rather than feelings of warmth or sympathy for the conditions of others. This can all sound rather cold and legalistic even if the alternative formulations, emphasising respect for the dignity and freedom of others, provide something of a counterbalance.

One development of the Kantian framework we might consider here is that due to W.D. Ross, who attempts to overcome some of the problems mentioned above, therefore putting some flesh on the Kantian bones. This is done through the idea of a list of 'prima facie duties', that is duties which can be overridden, unlike Kant's categorical imperative. There are seven of these, as listed below:

1. Fidelity (keep your promises)
2. Reparation (make up for harm you have done to others)
3. Gratitude (return good to those who have done good to you)
4. Justice (upset distributions of utility that do not accord with merit)
5. Beneficence (do good to others)
6. Self-improvement (in terms of virtue and knowledge)
7. Nonmaleficence (do not harm others).

At first sight, this is a rather odd list, combining fairly obvious statements like 'don't hurt people' with ideas of justice, a difficult concept as shown by even a quick reading of the literature on jurisprudence, criminology, politics or economics. The list is then rounded off with some nice notions of beneficence and self-improvement. Perhaps there is no easy way to reconcile the rigours of Kantian thought with 'easy to follow', practical advice for managers. (See Norman [1998] for a clear explanation of Ross and the idea of a duty.)

Now another problem which arises within the Kantian framework is given the catchy title 'moral luck' in the literature, though Kant would presumably deny that 'luck' enters into it! Benn (1998) is a useful general introduction (with case examples) to the problems we outline below.

As we mention a number of times in this book, we cannot always be sure that our actions will lead to the intended results. Other factors, including the actions of other agents, may intervene. In reality other factors will always be present and will have some effect on results in all but the most trivial cases. This presents a couple of difficult problems for the Kantian ethicist:

▶ Are actions justified by actual or intended results?
▶ Are judgements of our moral character dependent on things beyond our control?

These are issues of cause and effect, of the information sources available when we do things and of the often unintended consequences of actions in competitive situations (see the sections on Chaos and Complexity and on Game Theory in Chapter 6).

Consider a routine industrial situation where a common working practice leads to an accident on one, unfortunate occasion. As the manager it could be argued that on this occasion we were negligent. However, would we have been equally negligent on all the other occasions when this accident could have happened, both before and after its actual occurrence? After all, our actions were the same in each instance. From a Kantian point of view, this latter situation does indeed appear to be the case, which leaves us all to carry the blame on countless occasions of non-accidents! Now this may be reasonable for occasions after the accident, as we had the extra information of the occurrence of the accident to prompt us. However, suppose the accident never happened and it never occurred to anyone that a danger was present. We now seem to be in a situation where we are doing something wrong but nobody will ever realise this is the case and blame will never occur.

One way round this in a practical sense is to refer to a continuing duty of care and vigilance. We should continually carry out safety audits and seek to improve our knowledge of systems and risk. If we benchmark ourselves against the best practice, can we still be negligent? This is, of course, a common defence when something nasty occurs and the finger of blame is pointed.

Another connected issue arises if we try to assess the moral character of an individual who has been subjected, voluntarily or otherwise, to an intensive programme of training. Can he then be expected to make free moral decisions? Is the trainee now exempt from moral evaluation? We might associate such situations with extreme forms of brainwashing. Benn (1998) uses the example of torture sponsored by a totalitarian regime in considering the moral position of the highly indoctrinated torturers but much management development has a goal of some behaviour modification down to the level of habits and attitudes (see Chapter 17).

As with the other theoretical approaches, our explorations in the area of Kantian ethics have raised more problems than they have solved. Provided the language and concepts we have used have helped us express and think about problems and issues in business and management, this is to be welcomed! Kantian ethics does not provide a calculus for solving ethical problems. The more you explore this area, the greater will be your awareness of the difficulties of moral evaluation and decision-making in an organisational context.

Summary

The material presented in this chapter is often dealt with in a number of chapters of ethics books or even in separate texts! There is no escaping the intrinsic difficulty of many of the concepts introduced, nor the practical problems of using these ideas in a business and organisational context. However, much writing on business ethics depends on these ideas and some familiarity with them is necessary.

The notion of human rights might be seen in contrast to the Industrial Revolution's emphasis on individual freedom and self-promotion but is in fact part of the same development in social thinking. The reconciliation of individual rights with the duties placed on society and organisations is a major continuing theme, as evidenced by legislation to protect the employment and consumer rights of minorities. This is, of course, linked to notions of fairness and impartiality in a society.

While the concept of human rights is probably seen as accessible by most readers, Kantian ethics can appear abstract and difficult. This is unfortunate and the section on Kant above has been written in order to explain these ideas in a business context without losing the whole point of this rigorous approach. For further reading, Bowie (1999) is recommended as a detailed application of Kant's approach to a business context. Gensler (1998) also works very hard to make Kant understandable to non-specialist readers, though his book does not specifically deal with the world of business and organisations.

8   Social contract theories

Purpose and learning outcomes

The purpose of this chapter is to introduce some concepts of social contract theory which readily apply to organisational contexts.
  You will be able to

▶ understand the importance of the concept of a 'social contract' in modern business ethics;
▶ appreciate the advantages and challenges inherent in attempting to produce practical ethical working agreements.

Introduction

The Kantian concepts introduced in the previous chapter are elegant but difficult to directly apply to business situations. One way to move forward in developing an 'action-based' ethics is to incorporate ideas based on a social contract. This notion has been an important part of political theory for some time and many business practitioners find the idea that the 'rules of the game' (complementing the legal system) result from agreement between experienced 'players'. Unfortunately it is not always easy to arrive at a process for deciding such rules.

After outlining some of the ideas underlying a contract-based ethics, we include a discussion of what is meant, or not meant, by distributive justice and fairness. From this we lead on to a consideration of what is termed the 'contractarian view' of how we reach agreement in a society on what is right and wrong. This involves an introduction to the innovative ideas of Rawls. The idea that ethics is based on an agreement within a social group has found considerable support within the world of business organisations. These approaches will repay considerable further reading and examination by anyone who is seriously concerned with the practical grounds of ethical decision-making in organisations.

We end this chapter with a short exposition of an explicit model of rule formation based on the social contract approach. This is of particular value in considering issues in international business where differing legal systems may produce apparent inconsistencies and ethical dilemmas.

An introduction to contractualism

A development within action-based ethical theories which has considerable intuitive appeal is variously referred to as contractualism or the contractarian approach. Historically it links to the notion in political theory of a 'social contract'. The intention when applied to a nation-state is to use the idea that social organisation is founded on agreement between citizens. This agreement may not originate in a specific event but may be seen as based on an implied agreement, for example to accept the leadership of a monarch or a ruling elite in order to preserve social order.

If we apply this to other situations we have the idea that moral obligation is based on an agreement between the parties concerned, hence the idea of a 'contract', though perhaps not within a legal framework. This obviously raises a number of questions, in particular how this agreement might come about in practice and whether the agreement is in any way constrained, that is how do we agree and can we agree to anything! We also have to address what happens when someone reneges on the agreement; how are sanctions arrived at and justified?

The latter problem is explored by the mathematically based 'Game Theory' (see Chapter 6), for instance through such models as the 'Prisoner's Dilemma'. We all know situations where it is in everyone's interests to keep an agreement but where there is great temptation to break it. Another example from Game Theory is sometimes called the 'tragedy of the commons', based on the idea of an asset (such as common land) kept aside for everyone's benefit but which could be the source of a quick profit by an individual who breaks the agreement. A typical business example might be a price-fixing arrangement, assuming a context where this is legal. Though it may be in everyone's interest to keep the agreement in the long term, thus providing reasonable profits, it may be tempting to be the first to break the agreement and make a quick profit by price cutting.

The sanction, here, might be the threat of a price war. It might also be a loss of reputation as someone who can be trusted. Thus the agreement breaker may not be considered as a suitable future partner. Building on this line of logic we can see that to become a prospective partner it is useful to have a solid reputation as being co-operative and reliable. This is not dissimilar to a 'virtue' (in the sense used in Virtue Theory, see Chapter 9 and also Chapter 10), that is a habitual way of doing things as 'second nature'.

While this may give us some ideas on how agreements may be brokered, to have any chance of arriving at an agreement which is likely to be kept by all parties, some ground rules need to be in place. Typically the agreement must be freely entered into by rational agents who respect the moral autonomy of others. This provides a link with Kantian ethics. It is also likely that the agreement addresses some fundamental purpose, for example providing a stable basis for doing business, without limiting the freedom of action of the participating agents in any way they cannot accept. This may be quite difficult to manage; we may wish for freedom of action ourselves but fear the consequences of other agents' freedom of action. We would also wish all agreement to be fair, though this is not easy to define.

One way forward was developed by John Rawls (see Rawls [1972], though a brief summary such as that found in Benn [1998] may be more useful in order to gain an appreciation of this complex set of ideas). This is based on the idea of a hypothetical 'original position', where rational agents reach an agreement while behind a 'veil of ignorance'. The idea here is that the agents might have acted in a self-interested way if they knew where their advantage lay. So it is assumed that in the original position they do not know what pattern of rules in the agreement would be to their advantage.

Hence they will have to assent to an agreement while allowing for the possibility that it will not build on their, as yet unknown, strengths. As a 'thought experiment' this is an imaginative way of ensuring that an agreement takes into reasonable account effects on the weaker members of the group, as each party is aware that they might be in such a position. The underlying idea is that this will promote fair rules and impartiality.

While Rawls' ideas have entered the vocabulary of applied ethics, it is difficult to see how it can be directly operationalised, even if this was ever intended. How would one actually work behind a veil of ignorance? How can one discount one's strengths and attitudes, for example, to risk avoidance? If this is thought as being too literal an interpretation of the theory, then what is actually being suggested beyond the Kantian ideal of respecting the moral autonomy of others?

One rather limited possibility is that this apparatus simply draws attention to the importance of agreeing the 'rules of the game' before engaging on any joint venture. If we want the agreement to be viable, it should surely be fair and take account of the perspective of all the agents involved. This seems reasonable, though without addressing many 'ethical' concerns, such as the effects on anyone else!

Justice and fairness

Rawls' ideas may be placed in the context of a theory of distributive justice. The word 'justice' has a variety of connotations, some relating to punishment following a crime and to compensation for victims of crime or accident. However, another form of justice of particular interest to politicians, social theorists and economists, as well as the population at large, is the idea of distributive justice. This addresses the vexed question of how economic goods (e.g. land, wealth, natural resources, etc.) should be distributed. This debate is obviously at the heart of fundamental differences, say, between open market economies and state ownership and control. Even within market economies there are many issues of taxation, regulation of industry and the control of public services which involve some notion of distributive justice. Obvious examples (currently in the UK) include the tension between public and private health provision and the funding of higher education. Health and education are resources of fundamental value to all members of a society but the issues of 'who pays' and 'who benefits' are not easy to resolve.

Underlying this debate is some notion of fairness. This may apply to an actual distribution of income, wealth and other resources as when a population looks at the assets of a billionaire or the income of a celebrity and comes to a consensus that this is fair or otherwise. In practice, of course, a consensus is highly unlikely and individuals will be bringing different criteria and information to their assessments of what is or is not fair. Remembering that we are all born with different assets and talents we might soon come to realise that life is not fair!

An alternative way of looking at fairness is through the processes of resource allocation rather than the results. Whilst a revolutionary might wish to change a perceived unfair distribution by force or punitive taxation, most economists and practical legislators are likely to be concerned with ensuring that resource allocation mechanisms in a country are fair and reasonable. Examples of public policies with this aim in mind include taxation, public expenditure and devices for ensuring that business is conducted in a fair manner. Examples of the latter include action against monopolies and unfair trading practices.

The work of Rawls explicitly addresses how a society develops policies and procedures to ensure, or at least promote, distributive justice. Part of this must be to arrive at some consensus on what distributive justice looks like in practice in a given situation. We can easily see how the idea of a social contract is relevant here, that is as society agrees on the ground rules of economic justice through democratic processes. We can also see the attraction of such devices as the 'veil of ignorance' to combat, in theory at least, the effects of individuals' current economic situation on their views of how a future economic system might work. The wealthy and the economically deprived may find it difficult to arrive at an objective view of economic policy and even harder to agree to policies which would act to their personal disadvantage.

Though we have linked Rawls' writings to the idea of distributive justice, it should be noted that this is a highly contested area of political and economic theory as well as moral debate. Rawls' work is often contrasted with that of Robert Nozick, whose theory of economic justice is based on ideas of entitlement, that is ownership in everyday language. This approach, going back to the 17th century English philosopher John Locke, asserts that people are morally entitled to what they have produced. As one might expect, this view of economic activity strongly emphasises individual liberty and the minimum interference by the state in the action of markets. It also provides support for the idea that the 'superstars' in our society (e.g. in the worlds of sport and entertainment as well as business entrepreneurs) deserve their large incomes and wealth if they have as individuals generated such income by their own efforts. For example, it is argued that if the success of a football team does depend to a disproportionate extent on an individual and if the number of supporters watching a match is increased if that individual is playing, then they are entitled to their large salary. Exactly how their personal effect is separated from other team members, the coaching staff and other club resources is not clear!

Whether we are convinced by the rhetoric of the political right or left, some idea of a policy being applied in a way which is fair is inescapable. If a policy entails the redistribution of resources, fairness may reflect some notion of society at large (i.e. 'we are all in this together'), long-term personal advantage (e.g. a policy will benefit your children and future generations) or simply ask people to put themselves in another's position. However, it is unlikely that such appeals will be conclusive and totally persuasive. They are more likely to be part of a debate than an economic calculus. We can see this in Chapter 13, where we discuss unfair discrimination and diversity. Our views will hopefully be well informed, carefully argued and sensitive to the views of others but are likely to rest on our intuitions of fairness and justice.

In the running of an organisation, the concept of fairness is of importance. However much we may wish to regulate the activities of staff, and the organisation as a whole, by rules and regulations we will always have to be sensitive to the need to exercise judgement in difficult situations based on some agreed idea of fairness and reasonableness, often taking previous and similar situations into account. In all the everyday routines of staff management, for example task allocation, remuneration, development, discipline and grievance handling, we must be aware of the need to take a fair and even-handed approach. This may be seen as a moral imperative or as a practical necessity, the latter due to the tendency of staff to share information on management actions and perhaps the possibility of appeal to a higher level of management or an external body such as an employment tribunal. Whatever the motivation, judgements of fairness and reasonableness seem inescapable.

Thus in practice the idea of 'fairness' seems inescapable. It is interesting to note that it tends to be avoided by ethical theory, with such notions as distributive justice put in its place, though this only explores one aspect of the everyday use of the word 'fair'. In Chapter 9 we consider ethics in a different way, as the development of personal virtues. Perhaps we might look at our personal ability to be fair-minded in our judgements as a virtue, allied to the other virtues of personal moral development.

Social contract theory in a business context

One approach to the development of moral norms of behaviour in a community emphasises the community's freedom to decide such things for itself through the agreement of its members. This idea of members of a group or society being free to draw up their own rules is central to many writers, in particular Rawls and Donaldson and Dunfee (see next section for their integrative social contracts model). This idea can be defended on practical as well as theoretical grounds. Such a group will be aware of local conditions and constraints as well as the skills and aptitudes of its members. A group may feel better motivated to implement rules they have freely agreed as well as monitor the performance of other group members. The emphasis on freedom and autonomy is consistent with the views common in many societies that the preservation of individual freedom is a paramount objective, provided some mechanisms are in place to arbitrate the effects of such freedoms; my free actions may constrain yours or in some way hurt you unless safeguards exist.

Though early social contract theory relates to a country as the system within which norms are to be decided (and legislative processes do exactly that), there is an interest in transnational social contracts (e.g. internationally recognised human rights and trade agreements). Business theorists have also picked up the idea of the organisation as the unit of analysis and it is this line of thought which will concern us most in our use of social contract theory. An adjacent issue to this is the moral norms which apply when engaged in international business, thus combining organisational and transnational perspectives.

Unfortunately this whole approach appears to be walking straight into the problems of cultural relativism. For a social contracts model to be even remotely feasible it must specify processes which preserve an appropriate measure of freedom while arriving at a workable moral system. In particular the following appear to be necessary:

▶ universal norms – an acceptance of some universally recognised features of a moral system which must be reflected in the social contract;
▶ a mechanism for arriving at, reviewing and updating the agreement;
▶ mechanisms for reaching agreement at the boundaries of different groups or in the case of membership of multiple groups;
▶ ways of dealing with differences in the power and influence of group members.

Before going on to describe a specific model (see next section) we will here briefly discuss some of the issues in this approach. The first is whether this in fact provides a model of business ethics at all or is, in fact, really concerned with practical management, rules, procedures and conventions. If you read books on, say, selling in other countries you will find lots of practical advice on how one should greet people in other parts of the world, how one should expect negotiations to proceed and so forth. It is obvious that much of this material relates to social conventions, whose breach may cause great offence and difficulty but which do not appear to be matters of moral concern. In fact, this may be short-sighted as such conventions are often tied to ideas of personal dignity, respect and mutual obligation, for example in giving and receiving token gifts. More seriously, we may well come up against issues of whether the payment of a large commission to an official is bribery or an accepted practice in that community. I believe we can accept that conventional ethics enters this debate in terms of the universal norms and also as a critique of the whole process in delivering the freedom and autonomy which it promises.

A positive aspect of this approach, from the point of view of the management theorist, is the attention paid to systems, their boundaries and their interactions. Much writing in ethics takes such a strong universalist perspective that differences between groups are either ignored or left as implicit. Yet much of management is concerned with the particular and the differences between organisational systems. This can be seen in the widespread use of the method of case study analysis as a teaching vehicle, thus emphasising the need to develop skills of diagnosis and analysis relevant to specific contexts and to arrive at recommendations which are appropriate to the particularities of a situation in terms of the history of a system, its environment at that time and the people involved. One theme of this book is that business ethics as a discipline should pay more attention to management theories and practice and this is one context in which a synergy of approaches could be demonstrated.

A further point to note is that some approaches (e.g. that of Rawls) consider an initial situation in which a social contract is drawn up. Now this may simply be considered as a theoretical, or even a rhetorical, device to make some basic point about social contracts, for example how differences in the initial position and power of individuals should be handled. However, most systems do not begin in this way with a clean slate, though in fairness one should note that some business start-up situations have been imaginatively handled to produce social systems with unusual approaches to human relationships in the workplace. Most business systems have some history, their members have experience of other comparable situations, legislation exists (e.g. health and safety) as do professional codes of practice. In total a considerable amount of cultural baggage is brought to a new system. More to the point, we may often be considering the norms and values within existing systems in an attempt to describe their ethical culture. An evolutionary model may be more appropriate than even a theoretical 'big bang' approach to the determination of a micro social contract.

Similarly few if any organisational systems exist in isolation. They interact and influence each other in useful as well as counterproductive ways, individuals change membership and larger systems can impose norms against the wishes of members. As a description of how systems work, social contract theory models seem limited, though more down to earth than some ethical theories. As a prescription (which is, after all, the point of ethics as a normative discipline) there is some possibility that the insights of this approach may contribute to organisational change and development.

Integrative social contracts theory

A typically Western response to the tension between universal and situational ethics (see Chapter 15) is the development of an integrative model which mixes the two. The Donaldson and Dunfee model described below builds on the contractarian framework introduced above and we are here following the description of the model given in Fritzsche (1997). This model envisages a hierarchy of systems each developing appropriate social contracts within the freedom of action allowed by higher level systems.

The motivation behind this work is to provide a practical 'social contract' style model of ethical behaviour across different cultures. The intention, therefore, is to be sensitive to local differences while allowing mechanisms for the arbitration of conflict between local areas. Thus while the models we briefly introduce in Chapter 15 are descriptive, and possibly explanatory to the extent that they link behavioural variables into clusters, this model is prescriptive in structure (hypernorms and rules) while allowing for agreed local differences of action. Of course, there is a world of difference between agreeing a social contract within a group and reaching agreement between groups, as international agencies and political institutions discovered during the 20th century.

Hypernorms

Essential to the operation of this model are several universally accepted 'hypernorms' (in contrast to the locally generated norms which are specific to a given sub-system). These are listed below:

▶ Personal freedom
▶ Physical security and well-being

- Political participation
- Informed consent
- Ownership of property
- Right to subsistence
- Equal dignity to each human person.

These hypernorms are taken within this model to be obvious and in no need of justification. They do, of course, include such things as 'ownership of property' which is not in fact universal to all possible political systems. The hypernorms are not, therefore, universal in the sense of Kant's categorical imperative. They define a political and social background which is likely to be acceptable to a global, free-market business system.

Macro social contract

At the next level down, the macro social contract defines the rules of the game in which micro social contracts are to be formed, that is they provide a minimum set of conditions necessary for the social contract model to work.

- Local economic communities are to be allowed moral free space to generate ethical norms for their members through micro social contracts.
- Norm-generating micro social contracts must be based on consent, with an absolute right to exit.
- In order to be obligatory for members of the community, a micro social contract norm must be compatible with hypernorms.
- Priority rules compatible with the above must be employed to resolve conflicts among competing, mutually exclusive micro social contract norms.

It is not entirely clear at what level, and by whom, the macro social contract is guaranteed; who defines and enforces the priority rules? The assumption must be that the above are considered as obviously valid by the parties involved.

Micro social contracts

A wide range of systems may develop micro social contracts, of which the list below gives some examples. It will readily be seen that some of those below are sub-systems of others. The higher level systems must abide by the rules given above, of which the first should be noted in particular. Higher level systems should not be too prescriptive.

Economic communities creating micro social contracts may include:

- Informal groups within organisations
- Formal groups within organisations
- Firms
- Industries
- Professional Associations
- National organisations
- International organisations
- Countries.

At this stage of the description of the model, the reader might be losing sight of the end product, that is the actual norms to be developed as part of a micro social contract Examples of specific norms might include:

- Don't lie in contracts
- Don't break contracts
- Provide a safe workplace
- Give employment preference to local staff
- Give contract preference to local suppliers.

We have mentioned the priority rules which must exist to arbitrate at the boundaries between the operation of the norms of particular micro systems. An example might be when an international company is considering the working practices within its factories in different countries. The suggested priority rules are as follows:

1. Transactions solely within a single community, which do not have significant adverse effects on other humans or communities, should be governed by the host community's norms.
2. Community norms for resolving priority should be applied, so long as they do not have significant adverse effects on other humans or communities.
3. The more extensive or more global the community which is the source of the norm, the greater the priority which should be given to the norm.
4. Norms essential to the maintenance of the economic environment in which the transactions occur should have priority over norms potentially damaging to that environment.

5. Where multiple conflicting norms are involved, patterns of consistency among the alternative norms provide a basis for prioritisation.
6. Well-defined norms should ordinarily have priority over more general, less precise norms.

As will be seen above, these norms are vague and potentially divisive. For example, the third one in the list seems to suggest that the norms of a large organisation or a dominant country will have precedence. This is, perhaps, more acceptable in some parts of the world than in others. Once again, this model does seem to reflect an underlying political and economic agenda rather than reflecting a genuine inter-cultural consensus.

Summary

The social contract approach dealt with in this chapter appears to have considerable appeal to business and organisational specialists, both academic and practical. It should be noted, however, that such an approach needs a foundation in order to avoid degenerating into cultural relativism, that is actions being considered moral simply because a group agree that they are. Rawls' work builds on a Kantian perspective though the other theories mentioned in this book could also be called into service. Even at a basic level, it is a considerable achievement if a social contract is consistent, and this is an important point to bear in mind if we seek to interpret an organisation's rules and working culture as a social contract.

9 Virtue ethics and the moral community

Purpose and learning outcomes

The purpose of this chapter is to complete the introduction of theoretical perspectives based on philosophical ethics through a consideration of virtue ethics, an ethics of care and some guidance on the operation of a moral community.

You will be able to

▶ demonstrate a basic understanding of virtue ethics and the ethics of care in business;
▶ understand the importance of language and argument in practical ethics.

Introduction

This is the last of five chapters introducing the standard ethical theories based specifically on the philosophical literature which has had a major impact on business ethics. The next chapter, the final one in Part II of the book, deals with some theories and concepts from the business literature.

The first part of the chapter is devoted to a cluster of ideas which have come to be known as 'virtue ethics'. Despite their origin with the ancient Greek philosophers, these have become an important part of modern writings on business values. Some business writers have been explicit in using Aristotle as a source of organisational ethical inspiration, as we show in a summary of Solomon's six corporate virtues. We next move to a brief consideration of what is sometimes called an 'ethics of care'; a more helpful title than 'feminist ethics' in that it isolates the key feature of this approach from the broader agenda surrounding women in organisations.

We then consider a quite different way of looking at ethical ideas in a business context. Rather than focus on a standard theory we look at some ideas surrounding the use and misuse of language in an organisational context. We note the value of a search for shared meaning in a group, thus leading on to the idea of discourse ethics. The final section aims to expand our understanding of the implications of the concept of a moral community by suggesting some guiding principles based on a Kantian ethical framework.

Virtue ethics

The approaches we have been looking at so far may be termed 'principle-based ethics', as their focus is on abstract principles which are meant to guide us towards moral actions. Hume is perhaps the exception here with his emphasis on feelings as the root of ethical behaviour but in general the theories so far dealt with do not relate to personal moral development and an 'ethical life' in its totality. Attention has been concentrated on a piecemeal consideration of individual actions and their consequences.

It may then be somewhat of a surprise for the reader to realise that one of the first comprehensive texts on ethics, written by the great Athenian philosopher, Aristotle (384–322 BCE), puts the development of individual virtues as a key ingredient. This work, called the *Nicomachean Ethics* (see Aristotle [2000] for one of a number of recent translations and introductions), was probably dictated to Aristotle's son and is, in effect, a set of lecture notes to set alongside discussions on politics and other explorations of the natural and social world. Aristotle was born on the island of Stagira, in Macedonia, and came to Athens to study at the Academy, the school set up by Plato. Aristotle at a later time set up his own school, the Lyceum, and was a tutor to the son of the Macedonian ruler who, as Alexander the Great, conquered large amounts of land adjoining the eastern Mediterranean and beyond.

Plato and Aristotle lived in a thriving centre of trade and culture and wrote within a tradition of thought in which very basic ideas of knowledge and behaviour were explored. One of Plato's central themes was that ideas like 'goodness' existed as separate entities in a world of forms. Aristotle, with a penchant for listing and classifying ideas, took a different path, as we will see below. Both philosophers have had a massive influence on subsequent Western philosophy and are still carefully studied today as at least providing a foundation for rigorous debate. This was particularly seen in the Middle Ages in Europe when their works were gradually rediscovered and became an important influence on developments in theology at that time. Therefore it is possible for the general reader to confuse what Aristotle said with the Christian theology developed by, say, Thomas Aquinas.

While the influence of this style of ethical writing diminished with the Renaissance, it has strongly reappeared in the late 20th century as part of 'virtue ethics', an approach to ethical writing which has been seen to have considerable relevance to business ethics. A collection of readings on this general approach is Statman (1997). Particularly influential in the general debate on virtue ethics have been the writings of Alistair MacIntyre (see MacIntyre 1985). A business writer who has contextualised these themes is Robert Solomon (see Chapter 9 in Statman [1997] and the summary below).

Incidentally, the writings of Plato and Aristotle are highly readable, in translation of course! Yet it has to be remembered that these men were part of an aristocratic minority in a society based on slavery and the aggressive promotion of trade by warfare. Women are almost invisible in these works and the social unit referred to is likely to be the city state rather than a commercial organisation. These points inevitably have an effect on the choice of 'virtues' listed by Aristotle so it is a considerable surprise that the material does still have an immediacy and relevance.

Aristotle's ethical theory is teleological, which means that a basic assumption is that human beings have a 'telos' (i.e. goal, aim or purpose) which is summarised in the development of 'eudaimonia', which can be translated as happiness but one should be careful to avoid too close a comparison with utilitarian theories which also use the word 'happiness'. The basic idea is not one of the temporary or occasional satisfaction of desires but a life-long development of 'well-being' in its most fundamental sense. It should also be noted that this is not seen as a goal that we may choose from amongst a set of alternatives but as the right objective for a human life.

To make sense of this, one should also be aware that Aristotle sees a man (inevitably in this context an adult, male, free and politically active citizen of a small state) in the context of his society, that is the need to fit into this society and excel as part of this social group is essential. The qualities which make the individual achieve 'eudaimonia' also lead to a successful society. In many ways it is easiest to start by considering the characteristics of the roles to be played out in a successful social group and then project these onto the individual who is to achieve well-being as part of that group.

So the virtues are the characteristics of the individual which should be developed in order to achieve eudaimonia within a society. We can usefully compare this with the Japanese notion of 'kaizen', continuous improvement in a social context. We also note that the social context could be taken as an organisation, which explains the recent interests in these ideas as an early 'pursuit of excellence'.

We must also note at this point another idea usually referred to as the doctrine of the 'Golden Mean'. The idea here is that each virtue is set between two vices. It is perhaps best if we quote some examples from *Aristotle's Ethics* to show how this works. If we take the general area of confidence, Aristotle characterises courage (the virtue to be developed) as the mean between rashness (which shows an excess of confidence) and cowardice (which shows a deficiency). He takes temperance as the mean between licentiousness (too much pleasure) and insensibility (too little). Another example in the area of assertiveness (to use a modern term) is patience which is seen as a mean between irascibility (too much anger) and a lack of spirit (i.e. a 'couldn't care less' attitude).

Thus we can see that despite the unusual terminology (this being a translation from a text written 2500 years ago) and context, the resulting virtues are recognisable as having possible application in today's organisations. In fact, Aristotle's book itself can be read more as a self-help manual than a philosophical treatise, though there is a danger that particular words in the original Greek do not easily translate into modern English and can be misleading. Fortunately most modern translations have extensive notes to help with this difficulty.

One word which I would recommend noting from *Aristotle's Ethics* is 'phronesis', which can be translated as practical wisdom or even as 'know-how'. This in many ways, when allied to courage, is the key virtue in that having carried out a correct ethical evaluation is of little practical use if you do not know how to put your ideas into practice and do not have the strength of mind, and political skills, to do so! This point is complementary to one made by Hume, which we related to the importance of translating moral judgement into action (see Chapter 5). In summary we might say that motivation, practical knowledge and courage are essential if we wish to translate challenging ethical ideas into organisational reality.

In the hands of the medieval theologians the Aristotelian set of virtues became translated into the four cardinal virtues (temperance, fortitude, justice and prudence) in the context of the religious life. An interesting contrast is provided by Machiavelli, a 15th century political theorist who uses a similar word in Italian (*virtu*) to denote the characteristics of the successful prince. Whilst some 'virtues' might be common to all lists of desirable characteristics, the merciless cunning displayed by Cesare Borgia, Machievelli's inspiration in writing *The Prince*, would not have appealed to the theologian Aquinas, though some management writers have seen parallels with organisational politics, hopefully short of dispatching one's opponents through poisoning, as favoured by Cesare's sister.

Some further concepts from a more recent source might be useful here. MacIntyre (1985) makes a distinction between internal and external goods, the former being developed through practise in the context of a practice. This refers to the development of the virtues over a number of years within a specific social context. To take a non-business example, the development of one's abilities as a tournament chess player (which includes not only ability to play the game but mental toughness and physical stamina) is an example of a practice in this sense of the word. The development of one's abilities as an accountant, say, might be another example.

The point to note here is that we all participate in a number of 'practices' over a lifetime and these all provide differing challenges through which we can develop the virtues, including confidence and self-knowledge. This aggregation of practices is termed a 'narrative quest' with the aim of developing virtues or eudaimonia; a search not only for the good life but also for a better understanding of what the 'good life' actually is!

The business ethics literature which relates to virtue ethics sees organisational life as providing a rich context for such a narrative quest. Management can easily be seen as a practice in the sense given above, as can more specific professional and technical self-development. One point we should, however, make at this point (a distinction drawn out by MacIntyre) is that institutions such as businesses are themselves primarily concerned with external goods (such as money, prestige and power) rather than internal goods. This is inevitable if they are to survive; (most) organisations do not exist to develop you as a manager, except so far as this development in turn facilitates the production of external goods. Therefore the vehicles for the practices which we need as part of our narrative quest are actually 'institutions' which depend on the production of external goods. MacIntyre sees this as a potentially corrupting influence and argues that clarity over the nature of the virtues we are trying to develop and the practices which aid this process is essential.

As mentioned above, Robert Solomon has done much to show the relevance of the ideas of virtue ethics to the organisation (see Statman 1997). He refers to the six dimensions of virtue ethics in a corporate context as follows:

1. *Community*: Aristotle's view of moral development and action was always in the context of membership of a community. We may see an employing organisation as one community we have membership of, and which provides the context for much of our moral behaviour.
2. *Excellence*: the idea of striving to do one's best and aim for outstanding achievement for oneself and one's community is not a recent development despite appearing so in the work of some notable writers of popular business literature! Yet the ideas of business excellence fit particularly well with the virtue ethics approach.
3. *Role identity*: this relates to the idea that to work for an organisation is to accept a full role with its duties and obligations. It will be natural to associate this with the idea of loyalty to an organisation. Naturally the role will differ depending on level in a hierarchy, but all roles carry some moral import in terms of obligation and conformity to rules and standards of ethical behaviour.
4. *Integrity*: the 'wholeness' of our approach to being a moral member of an organisation and the consistency of our actions over time is summarised by integrity. It can also mean courage and stubbornness in the context of a difficult situation, and may even lead to a perception of disloyalty.
5. *Judgement*: this refers to perception, analysis and debate, as well as action. The Aristotelian virtue of 'phronesis' was seen as one of the keys in the application of the other virtues by linking intellectual development with character building. Needing continuous improvement over a lifetime, it is very different from the application of a moral calculus.
6. *Holism*: Solomon asserts that good employees are good people and argues for the integration of business virtues with those we apply in all other facets of our existence.

It is particularly interesting to see how the above are linked. For example, in the context of loyalty, perhaps in opposing some proposed action by the organisation we see as wrong, the notions of integrity, judgement and holism all come into play. Therefore the above may be seen as aspects of an integrated approach rather than as separate individual attributes.

Finally, a very readable view of the virtues can be found in Dorothy Rowe's book *The Real Meaning of Money* (1997), where a short self-test asks us to provide a personal ranking of a list of possible virtues. When carried out within a group this invariably shows that individuals' rankings are different. In my experience it also shows that people mean different things by 'loyalty', 'gratitude' and so forth. Rowe, as a psychologist, then argues that individuals who are extraverts (i.e. for whom relationships are important) tend to choose different virtues from introverts (i.e. who are oriented to achievement and control). The former would choose kindness and generosity while the latter tend to choose truth or ambition. What is also interesting is the effect particular past experiences have on the choice. The point we should take on board here is that our scientific knowledge of how the human mind functions, particularly within social groups, has developed considerably since Aristotle. When considering such deeply personal things as feelings and when using emotionally charged words such as 'courage' and 'ambition' to describe desirable characteristics we should always be careful about how we are using language and the effects this is having on our moral assessments and judgement.

An ethics of care

Feminist ethics is an attempt to redress a perceived imbalance in philosophical and applied ethics as centring on the experiences of men and on a perceived male characterisation of a rational analysis of how we should behave. This reassessment is undertaken in the context of feminist reassessments in other branches of philosophy, as well as other disciplines. It does, of course, have to face up to the obvious counter-argument that what has been characterised as 'male' philosophy is in fact universal and gender-free. Yet even at a superficial level it is easy to see that the language and examples used in many of the classical works of ethics pay little attention to the social and work situations of women. More fundamentally, such writings are often concerned with finding universally applicable principles and rights rather than focussing on human relationships and roles. Where relationships figure strongly, as in Japanese views of business ethics, the emphasis may well be on obligation, 'face' and honour rather than caring for others. Even the original view of virtue ethics is couched in terms of the attributes of the fighter and the politician working in a male-dominated social unit, which perhaps explains its attraction to businessmen!

Therefore we are entitled to at least wonder if something is missing from these classical accounts, and the 'ethics of care' might be seen as another approach or tool to be added to the long list already in existence. Yet a more fundamental challenge, in keeping with a radical feminist critique, would be to the whole enterprise of philosophical ethics and hence to its prescriptions for behaviour in particular contexts, such as business and health care. The latter is beyond the scope of this book but may be approached through, say, Jaggar's article on 'Feminist Ethics' in LaFollette (2000), which does include some discussion on the ethics of care. Jaggar (2000) comments that

> Proponents of care ethics characteristically advocate that ethical priority should be given to the values that they see as central to women's practices of nurturing and especially of mothering: these include the values of emotional sensitivity and responsiveness to the needs of particular others, intimacy and connection, responsibility and trust.

While the above may have always been seen as positive characteristics of personal relationships, the argument is that they should now be viewed as important characteristics of ethical theories and approaches in general. Indeed, modern popular writings on behaviour at work are increasingly likely to emphasise the importance of emotional sensitivity and the need to 'connect' and form strong, genuine relationships. A key phrase in the above quotation is the reference to 'particular others', moving the focus away from universal prescriptions and towards an appreciation of the nature of the actual people with whom we are dealing.

A key writer on care ethics is Gilligan, who argues that

> care is grounded in the assumption that...detachment, whether from self or from others, is morally problematic, since it breeds moral blindness or indifference – a failure to discern or respond to need.

(This quotation is found in Winstanley and Woodall [2000] in the context of the Ethics of Care seen as relevant to HRM practices.)

We may note in the above quotation the reference to the dangers of detachment from 'self' as well as from 'others'. The ethics of care has much to say about how we relate to ourselves and therefore is easily linked to many of the ideas in virtue ethics. Another important point in Winstanley and Woodall is that the practice of care within Personnel and HRM can be based on 'paternalistic and welfarist models' which entail a completely different, and less helpful, view of the discharge of responsibilities of an organisation.

A particularly interesting topic explored by Jaggar (2000) is whether the emphasis on 'human rights' in so much classical ethical theory and practice is consistent with feminist views of ethics. She shows how some conceptions of rights, while meant to be universal, in fact bolster male domination in a number of social settings where inequalities in power and resource distribution already exist. Furthermore the use of language dominated by notions of 'my rights' can often be highly confrontational, producing the exact opposite effect from a caring consideration of the situation faced by others. It can be argued that this has resulted from inadequate conceptions of rights and the social and legal processes associated with them. Thus feminist ethics, emphasising care, can be seen as a challenge to standard characterisations of such notions as 'rights' as well as a path to improving them through an imaginative and different critique.

This brief introduction, as with all the previously discussed theories, can only serve to set the scene for our forays into the foothills of organisational ethics. Further reading of the original texts and references is strongly recommended.

The language of ethics

If you take any business book down from the shelf and thumb through it you might at first be reassured that, unlike some disciplines, it does appear to be written in everyday English (or French, Spanish, Chinese, etc.). True enough there are exceptions to this in areas of finance and the more esoteric branches of the social sciences as applied to organisations, but the impression remains that here is material which is readable; and so it should be given the large and varied audience for such books.

A closer reading might then raise some concerns. The book may mention 'quality' in ways that seem unusual. If we are lucky this term may be defined, though not in a way that we associate with 'quality'. It may tell us that 'quality means conformance to specification', which is reassuringly straightforward. It may or may not be explicit in telling us that 'quality' does not, for its purposes, have the other range of meanings we attach to it in everyday speech. It may or may not bother to give the writer's view on these other connotations of 'quality'. It may not tell us that other writers disagree on this point (see Chapters 12 and 14, which continue the theme of confusion in business language).

Similar issues surround 'excellence', whose meaning will differ depending on when the book was written. One should also be careful of words like 'motivation' that are key words in other disciplines and are the subject of extensive literatures outside management theory. Scientists in areas like physics have long played the trick of taking everyday words like 'mass' and giving them very precise meanings in the context of the theories and models in their subject. Before we know where we are, these specialist meanings have become the 'correct definitions' and we display ignorance by using the words otherwise.

Apart from the embarrassment of appearing ignorant, there is usually little harm in this and considerable advantage in using words with well-defined meanings. An exception can arise in management practice where the correct use of words, often subtly redefined for a given organisational context, can be used as a label to separate those 'in the know' from the rest. Thus a sub-culture of expertise is established, perhaps many, inferring superiority, competence and membership of an elite group. At least this is less dangerous than the brainwashing techniques practised by religious cults and extreme politicians, though some forms of sales training come close!

'Moral language' has a long history and is complicated by issues of translation. Key texts in philosophical ethics are in ancient Greek, German, French and other languages; direct word-for-word translation is often impossible, not least because words are defined in idiosyncratic ways or simply invented. Therefore the whole language of ethics can become impenetrable, quite apart from the fact that the words used may also have common meanings. Words like 'virtue', 'duty' and 'utility' are central to the three different main approaches to applied ethics we use in this book and all have a history of redefinition and debate surrounding their meaning. This is quite separate from their everyday meanings and the religious connotations which may well be present for many users. Even a word like 'pleasure' has an interesting past, as a comparison of writings in ethics with those in consumer behaviour (as a branch of marketing) will show.

This is unfortunate as one of the key points in this book is on a careful use of language and on the need to discuss and clarify 'moral' uses of words (in both senses) in an organisational context. One point made by writers on business ethics is the problem of the moral inarticulacy of managers (or 'moral muteness' in some versions; see Chapter 14), that is though the actions of managers may be moral, the explanations and justifications provided by them avoid moral language in favour of such things as 'it's organisational policy', 'it's in the customer's interests', 'it's more effective' or 'it's the most practical way to do things'. Sometimes management techniques use this to good effect, for example benchmarking not only provides knowledge of alternative processes but allows the justification that 'I'm following best industrial practice'. Another example are the external accreditation bodies such as ISO, IiP and EFQM as well as professional bodies which provide ways of showing actions to conform to 'good, current management practice'. Often to argue from a more basic ethical position that something is 'right' is far more difficult. One suspects that many managers welcome such things as anti-discrimination legislation as providing them with the lever to bring about changes they have always felt were right but lacked the language needed to convincingly express them and the impetus to implement. It can be quite impressive to see senior managers and entrepreneurs who pursue a strategy simply because they believe it is the right thing to do. This is often in the context of a small, expanding company or in a turn-round situation where other employees will accept anything which promises survival.

'Discourse ethics' is the term given to the more formal development of discussion between the stakeholders of an organisation (see Winstanley and Woodall 2000). While many organisational theorists and strategists routinely use the term 'stakeholders' to refer to those who are affected by the decisions of an organisation (i.e. those who 'have a stake' in organisational outcomes as a broadening of the group who have legal rights through being shareholders), this often only means that the impacts on stakeholders will be considered when policies are being devised by managers. Involving stakeholders in policy discussions is more common within public sector management. Discourse ethics sees such as interchange of views as having a base in moral debate, often facilitated by an independent ethicist.

This can be seen in the context of consultative committees, focus groups and a variety of other regular events which are often required in the context of the public sector but more problematic in the private sector. There is a viewpoint that managers are appointed to manage and an excessive apparatus of consultation is a sign of weakness rather than concern. There is also a more Machiavellian stance which uses such 'consultation' as opportunities for an elaborate sales pitch. It is doubtful if staff or external stakeholders are fooled by this, though they may cynically accept such manoeuvrings as inevitable. The positive approach is for senior management to have the confidence to open debates on fundamental (moral) issues and use an independent ethicist to demonstrate this approach is genuine. As we can see from the above, an attention to both moral language and the technical language of the organisation will be essential for such debates to succeed in generating new insights and a consensus, but it can be done.

Guiding principles for a moral community

In this chapter and the previous one we have gradually been developing the idea of the organisation functioning as a moral community. This reflects the Aristotelian notion of the virtues being individual characteristics essential for the effective working of the community, the idea of the community as the focus of moral development, the importance of language and discussion of values within an organisation and the concept of a social contract.

While the idea of the organisation acting as a moral community is very attractive, it would be useful to have in place some guidelines on how this might be put into practice. Bowie (1999) suggests seven guiding principles as shown below. It is interesting to note that Bowie's book specifically relates to a Kantian perspective of business ethics and his notes on these guidelines provide a very useful bridge between a communitarian approach and the theories of Kant.

Therefore, starting from a Kantian perspective, Bowie suggests the following principles as guidelines for rule-making in the moral organisation. It should of course be noted that as these principles relate to the process of making rules, rather than actually give the rules for moral behaviour themselves, considerable autonomy remains with the moral community. This is typical of the Kantian approach, which supports rational, moral decision-making rather than prescribing actual rules for behaviour. The principles themselves are quoted in full from Bowie (1999). A number of technical terms are employed which require reference back to Chapter 7. The full statement of Principle 5 may be found in Bowie's book which includes discussion of some technical points we have omitted here.

Principle 1: The firm should consider the interests of all the affected stakeholders in any decision it makes.

While this principle provides for the scoping of any decision, that is arriving at a view on whose interests should be considered in a specific decision context, it does rely on the coherence of the idea of a 'stakeholder'. It also begs the question of what might be meant by an 'unaffected stakeholder', unless the word 'affected' in the statement of the principle is merely there for emphasis! Perhaps, like Bowie, we really have no alternative but to take the straightforward view that we can arrive at a sensible list of stakeholders in most contexts and the remaining principles are mainly concerned with situations where the interests of the stakeholders conflict. It might be noted that Bowie speaks of 'the firm' and many of his examples are typical of a profit-making context. The notion of an agreed list of stakeholders might be more difficult to apply in a public sector context (e.g. a social services department) or where strong feelings are aroused in particular groups of citizens (e.g. where environmental or animal rights issues are at stake).

Principle 2: The firm should have those affected by the firm's rules and policies participate in the determination of those rules and policies before they are implemented.

Participation is of value in itself, both as a moral attribute of a process and as a practical means to making a process more effective, for example, in the search for new ideas, in communicating ideas to a wide audience and in facilitating implementation through staff development. In a Kantian context it also relates to the 'Formula of Humanity' by respecting that the ends (e.g. aims and objectives) of other people should be fully recognised. If the stakeholder group is large and diffuse there may be difficulties in gaining agreement, though this may say something about the ambitious nature of the goals of the organisation itself. Similarly if participants disagree on fundamental issues then rule-making may not be easy. Perhaps this is inevitable if the idea of a moral community is to be taken seriously.

Principle 3: It should not be the case that for all decisions, the interests of one stakeholder take priority.

This principle runs counter to the idea that one stakeholder (group) has an overriding priority, as might be claimed for shareholders or an entrepreneurial owner of a firm. If it is, in fact, the case that one group effectively runs the show, and its objectives are paramount, then the pretence of a moral community should be seen as rhetoric and spin! It would be better to admit to the reality of the situation so at least we preserve the virtue of honesty. In contrast, it should also not be the case that one stakeholder (group) always loses out!

> Principle 4: When a situation arises where it appears that the humanity of one set of stakeholders must be sacrificed for the humanity of another set of stakeholders, that decision cannot be made on the grounds that there is a greater number of stakeholders in one group than another.

This somewhat emotively worded principle acts to exclude utilitarianism (i.e. maximising utility) as a decision process because the dignity and autonomy of individual persons must be respected.

> Principle 5: No principle can be adopted which is inconsistent..., nor can it violate the humanity in the person of any stakeholder...

Reference back to Chapter 7 will show the necessity for the above principle, which is obvious in a Kantian context.

> Principle 6: Every profit-making firm has an imperfect duty of beneficence.

The idea of beneficence (i.e. doing good to others) is mentioned in Chapter 7 as part of a list of seven imperfect duties due to Ross. An imperfect duty is one where there may be situations where it cannot be performed, for example, due to a clash with another duty. Beneficence is a duty individuals should perform if possible but Bowie strongly argues we should move this across to becoming an imperfect duty for an organisation. On the one hand this may be seen as a reasonable manoeuvre thus encouraging the profit-making firm to donate to charity, help the community and perform similar good deeds. Bowie does note that this idea can be strongly attacked, for example, by the Friedman argument that beneficence amounts to stealing from the shareholders of the firm. Of course, in this instance we would also have a problem with Principle 3 and the notion of a moral community becomes problematic.

> Principle 7: Each business firm must establish procedures designed to insure that relations among stakeholders are governed by rules

of justice. These rules of justice are to be developed in accordance with Principles 1–6 and must receive the endorsement of all stakeholders. They must be principles that can be publicly accepted and thus be objective in a Kantian sense.

The idea of justice and fairness now takes centre stage as a link between the application of the other principles, emphasising openness and objectivity in order to legitimise the application of the resulting rules. It might also be noted that in practice such rule-making is unlikely to happen in isolation from legal requirements and the codes of practice of professional bodies. It would also be prudent to engage in benchmarking with other organisations in order to enrich, though not restrict the autonomy of, discussions within the firm.

It will be obvious from the above that the approach taken here owes a considerable debt to the Kantian framework, that is the various versions of the Categorical Imperative and to strict ideas of duty. It is interesting to speculate if such a framework and technical language are necessary; can not we simply base our rules and processes on common sense? This might, however, entail the unchallenging acceptance of a corporate culture and status quo. We might also wonder how 'common sense' can be defended if its assumptions are critically questioned, as is almost inevitable in ethical debate.

A comparison of ethical approaches

In the last few chapters we have introduced a range of ethical theories. In the remainder of the book we will be applying them in a variety of situations. As an early exploration of such application, consider the following example. We will use three individuals called Don, Ron and Len (reminders of Deontology (Chapters 7 and 8), Results (Chapters 5 and 6) and Learning (Chapters 4 and 9)) as line managers facing issues of timekeeping by members of their teams. In doing this they must have a regard for fairness to staff as well as the effective working of the office.

▶ Don insists on strict timekeeping with no excuses allowed.
▶ Ron makes more flexible decisions based on the information available (the car would not start; the baby-sitter failed to turn up etc.) and the workload in the office.
▶ Len treats each person as different and cares about their attitudes and development.

Don's approach has merits in terms of clarity and fairness. Everyone knows the policy and it is applied in an even-handed manner. This is also an efficient approach, if it works, in terms of the use of managerial time. The problem, as everyone who has been a line manager will recognise, is that some reasons for lateness are so obviously justified (e.g. severe family illness; occasional traffic chaos) that to penalise staff seems unfair. However, how do we separate 'severe family illness' from 'stomach upset'? How do we react to the individual who seems to get caught up in traffic, no doubt vociferously defending their excuse, several times a week?

One problem Ron faces is the adequacy of the information he has available in specific circumstances. Managing an office with very flexible working patterns and a tolerant attitude to lateness ('just work harder and catch up') can be very demanding of managerial time. It can also lead to endless arguments about perceived unfairness. However, there are a number of workplaces where this type of approach is acceptable, often when professional or creative staff are required to be self-managing.

Len has a concern for the development of his staff. He is keen to promote a right approach to work (including timekeeping) in his staff and this approach will be very time-consuming. Yet the needs of the organisation will be met in the long run by the development of its human resource.

Of course, the whole discussion has now moved into the territory of general management and organisational behaviour. Our concern in this book is somewhat narrower in terms of the ethical values inherent in each of the above. We have, in effect, been describing some different 'workplace cultures' and a thorough exploration of this would have to relate to a number of features of the organisation in question. We might consider issues of timekeeping in the context of the emergency services or when time is central to a service on offer (e.g. driving public transport) in a different way to situations where professionals are engaged on project design work which can be carried out at any time within the next few weeks and where staff habitually work extra time when necessary.

A key factor here will be the contract of employment for the individuals concerned and the job descriptions of staff. These define the 'rules of the game' for specific situations and should be drawn up in such a way that appropriate levels of flexibility are built in, along with the management processes, including appraisal, discipline and complaint, that support them. Unfortunately this does not finally solve all moral problems of behaviour in the workplace but it does provide a potentially useful tool for the resolution of problems. Don would, presumably, know these rules and apply them but would still have to cope with exceptions. Ron would either be adopting his more ad hoc approach in the context of supportive rules or may just be ignoring the rules as a bureaucratic nuisance and asserting his 'right to manage'. The latter may simply sound wrong, but can be seen as more defensible if the 'rules' have been carelessly drawn up or are outdated. Some might then argue that Ron should follow procedures for changing the rules but this may all be seen as too expensive and difficult in practice.

Even this basic, elementary exploration of a simple and everyday situation has shown the complexity which inevitably arises when we start to question how things should ethically be done in practice. 'Human activity systems' (to use a phrase from the systems approach favoured by some management theoreticians) are endlessly difficult to characterise and model effectively. Our focus on the use of ethical concepts and language adds an important dimension to such analysis. We bring into the foreground an array of concepts which enrich the use of words such as 'fairness', 'rules' and 'consequences'. Some may find it disappointing that we cannot finally say what 'ought' or 'ought not' to be done (unless we embrace some form of ethical fundamentalism different from the inclusive approach adopted here) but it can be reassuring to know that some problems really are difficult. We are allowed to be baffled, uncertain and ill at ease when faced with ethical dilemmas! What we must not do is ignore them and do nothing about the situations in which they occur.

Summary

Perhaps the most noticeable things about this chapter are the increasing combined use of the theories of normative ethics, the perspective that business ethics has a long-term dimension and the move towards an increased consideration of practical management examples.

The reader will by now have gathered that this book does not finally recommend one ethical theory as being correct at the expense of the others. More concepts will be introduced in later chapters but these will not replace the ones introduced so far. There is also no one, simple, overarching integrated theory which will replace them all. We will continue to take inspiration from the theories considered so far, but also note the problems inherent in their use.

A key perspective we have introduced is the idea of time, of personal and corporate development and a consideration of long-term objectives. This is inherent in virtue ethics and the notion of personal moral development fits well with other approaches to organisational behaviour. Good business systems often have a stability and permanence which reflects sound practical moral judgement and experience. Yet such stability can become complacency and ethical discourse may be essential in challenging a sterile organisational culture.

Reputation, integrity and politics

Purpose and learning outcomes

The purpose of this chapter is to introduce the complementary perspective of power and develop some models for implementing ethics in organisations through the use of the notions of reputation and integrity.

You will be able to

▶ show an appreciation of the importance of the perspectives of power and politics in the practical use of ethical concepts;
▶ explain how a model can be developed to show how reputation and long-term objectives can be included in ethical evaluation;
▶ understand some meanings of the concept of integrity in an organisation and show an appreciation of the problems of implementing an integrity strategy.

Introduction

The first part of this chapter is built around the notion of a reputation. We explore the idea that our motivation to do the right thing may be based on our long-term gain rather than a moral rejection of unfair short-term advantage. It raises the interesting point that what we may see as fair dealing in others may in reality be carefully calculated egoism. Therefore how can we reliably carry out a moral evaluation of a person's acts and motives? Indeed, how can we even be sure for ourselves that actions we do today from what we think is a motivation to do the right thing are not in reality driven by subconscious calculations of our own long-term advantage?

Whatever the deeper, ethical arguments needed to unpick this conundrum, the practical point is that we may never be able to separate apparent short-term morality from personal long-term advantage, for the individual or for the group. In the next section we address this by summarising a model relating political (i.e. power oriented) and ethical views. In this context some new and very important ideas are presented, including the notion of a warrant and the need to preserve reputation in order to be politically effective in the long term.

These ideas are further expanded through consideration of an alternative model of organisational behaviour based on the notion of 'integrity'. These two models are both recent attempts to link ethical ideas with the reality of organisational practice, in particular in contexts of change management which are prone to revealing ethical dilemmas.

This chapter ends with a series of discussion questions relating to Part II as a whole.

Developing a reputation – some initial thoughts

There is an obvious difference, even if we adopt an egoistic view of moral motivation, between working for a short period of time in a business or other organisational context and looking towards a career. In the latter context the idea of a reputation becomes important. Behaviour is judged in terms of a pattern of events and interactions over a period of time. Astute managers will take care not only regarding what they actually do but also of what is said about them. They will seek to influence the consensus view of whether an action was fair, reasonable and justified. This influencing of organisational stories and myths may or may not in itself be ethical, particularly if it involves the apportionment of blame. Managers may be judged by their peers in terms of how fairly they handled the inevitable fall-out from failure and poor decision-making.

Thus if we take a rational economic view of moral behaviour which looks only at personal gain over a long period of time, say a career, the resulting model might comprise a mixture of:

▶ personal gain at various points of time;
▶ the risk of being caught engaged in some dubious or even illegal dealings;
▶ the development of a reputation and habit of straight dealing in order to be in a position to gain in the future.

Incidentally we may note that the first two points look suspiciously like an economic model of criminal behaviour and the third might be translated as simply avoiding a criminal record. The distinction between highly egoistic behaviour and white-collar crime appears to have eluded some people caught up within the collective greed of the financial world!

We can explore this theme further by imagining the following individual, who we will call John. When young and ambitious John needs money to support an impressive lifestyle, he has little to lose and does not have the habit of straight dealing. This might lead to excessive risk taking and unethical behaviour. However, the development of a good reputation will be of great value in the future. So John does not cheat unless there is a good chance of getting away with it or the short-term gain is very large! Future gain (seen here in terms of the development of a solid reputation) is traded against current advantage. For this to make sense the future gain must be highly likely and considerable, or perhaps more speculative and huge!

When older, the reputation of straight dealing has been gained and is profitable (in terms of money and social standing) so is there good reason to continue now when there is less to gain in the future? Perhaps the loss in social standing now becomes important, that is the reputation which was preserved as a meal ticket for the future now has a value in itself as reflected in self-esteem and social regard. Also it should be remembered that there is now more to lose in financial terms. Thus 'straight dealing' moves from being a good bet for the future to become a habit and source of pride and standing.

The above game is rational and egoistic but may have the appearance of altruism and organisational loyalty. How can one tell which form of motivation is actually present? If we move to a Kantian framework, it is clear that actions are not being carried out through a sense of moral duty. In the context of virtue ethics, the calculating individual described above cannot be seen as engaged in a quest for moral self-development. Each of these approaches may consider this individual as morally deficient but how can this behaviour be seen for what it is? The answer, if there is one, will depend on responses to specific challenges and on the reasons the individual gives to explain and justify their actions. In the course of a career it is likely that certain points will arise when an individual must choose between self protection and doing what others will see as the right thing. Similarly one's stated opinions and reasons for action will give others a good idea of one's real motivation.

There is, of course, a quite different response to this challenge of what really constitutes moral motivation. It is to consider long-term egoistic motivation as the norm in an organisation modelled as a political system, that is one where survival and gaining power are the overriding motives for everyone. In the next section we pursue the logic of this approach. You might also wish to relate this discussion to the section on 'Morality or expediency' in Chapter 22.

Ethics and politics

One of the dangers of becoming absorbed in the language and concepts of business ethics is that one can come to view and judge the world by a strict set of standards which are far distant from those which apply in many organisations. If separated from the world of organisational politics one may even come to see organisational behaviour in terms of minor lapses from good conduct with the occasional 'bad apple' pursuing a path which is probably illegal anyway! It is useful, therefore, to look at the alternative literature on organisational politics and the practical 'how to win at business' prescriptions which fill airport bookshelves. It might then come as a surprise to discover that much business behaviour is far from 'ethical' (in the sense described in earlier chapters), though probably not illegal if there is a danger of being caught. A greater surprise will be that many books not only recommend such behaviour but systematically tell the manager how to do it more effectively.

An excellent and balanced approach to organisational politics (subtitled 'Winning the Turf Game'!) is Buchanan and Badham (1999). While developing an explicitly ethical framework, this book also contains a wide survey of the 'how to win the political game' style literature which provides a useful antidote to any complacent view that business is becoming more ethical. Some stunning examples include von Zugbach's 13 'winner's commandments', which include:

▶ Me first.
▶ There are no absolute rules. Other people's ideas of right and wrong do not apply to you.
▶ Say one thing and do another.
▶ Be a team player, but make sure you beat your fellow team members.
▶ Manipulate the facts to suit your interests.
▶ Get your retaliation in first.

Von Zugbach's examples of the behaviour of the 'losing manager', and therefore things to be avoided, include:

▶ Attending meetings when there is nothing in it for you.
▶ Regarding the organisation's rules 'with sanctity rather than contempt'.
▶ Doing things for which others get the credit.
▶ Performing tasks which could have been delegated.
▶ Volunteering.

Now, at one level the above implies a degree of selfishness which may not win many popularity contests, unless well disguised, but it also gives some practical advice (e.g. such as delegating when possible) which is not unreasonable in terms of the suggested action even if the motivation is questionable (i.e. avoiding work rather than developing one's subordinates).

Such lists are also honest about the ambiguities and difficulties of organisational life. For instance, being a 'team player' is recommended by many management writers but the reality of organisational situations involves particular members of the team being promoted or given career enhancing tasks. In making such decisions, the past performance of individuals will be evaluated and it is often not easy to separate this from the performance of other team members. The tensions this gives rise to will be evident to those who have had to contribute to student group-based assignments. Having one's contribution appropriated by another team member as part of their 'performance' can lead to personal reassessment of one's attitude to team working along the lines suggested above! The point is that the writers on practical organisational politics do at least address the issues of power, influence, information asymmetry and risk, even if their recommendations are somewhat one-sided.

One of Buchanan and Badham's positive contributions to this debate is to take on board both the political pressures facing the manager working in a real organisation and the need to provide an ethical framework for action. This recognises the need to employ power tactics but also to maintain organisational stability and the reputation of decision makers. The decision framework they recommend includes the following terms (quotations and definitions are from Buchanan and Badham [1999, pp. 34–38]):

▶ A 'warrant' relates to 'the degree of confidence the change driver has in being able to offer a convincing explanation and justification for their actions in pursuit of particular goals'.

▶ A 'formal warrant' concerns the sanction an organisation formally gives to a change initiative.

▶ A 'tacit personal warrant' relates to the change agent's personal conviction that the intended actions are appropriate and can be defended when necessary (remembering that formal warrants rarely cover all of a change agent's actions).

▶ 'Accounts' are the responses change agents give when challenged about their behaviour and asked to justify their actions. They are the 'public face of the change driver's warrant'.

▶ 'Reputation' is a 'socially defined asset dependent on one's behaviour and on the observations, interpretations and memories of others'. It must be carefully built over time and is fragile; one ill-considered action or damaging allegation can destroy it!

This structure of warrants, accounts and reputations is used in the context of an ethical decision-making process. Ethics enters the discussion in the form of three 'models' which can together be used to judge political behaviour (note that Buchanan and Badham use the term 'constituents' rather than 'stakeholders'):

▶ Utilitarianism (which links to common organisational parameters of efficiency and cost–benefit analysis and includes a wide range of stakeholders)

▶ Theory of rights (which relates to the protection of individual rights and freedoms)

▶ Theory of justice (which is concerned with the fair allocation of resources and the protection of less well represented stakeholders).

The 'ethics test' then follows a procedure summarised below:

1. Gather the facts.
2. Is the proposed act acceptable in the following terms:

    (a) Does it optimise stakeholder satisfaction?
    (b) Does it respect individuals' rights?
    (c) Is it just?

    If so, the act is ethical. If not, go to Step 3.
3. Are there any:

    (a) overwhelming factors which make it reasonable to set aside some of the three ethical criteria?

(b) double effects where an act might have both positive and negative outcomes?

(c) incapacitating factors such that the ethical criteria cannot be applied (e.g. constraints, lack of information)?

If so, the act is ethical. If not, the act is not ethical.

The 'ethics test' is now combined with the 'warrants and reputation framework' and the following questions asked:

1. Is the behaviour ethically acceptable?
2. Did the change driver have a reasonable warrant?
3. Can a plausible account be given of the behaviour described?
4. How has the change driver's reputation changed?

Fairly obviously, one will take a positive view of an action where the behaviour was acceptable, there was a reasonable warrant, a plausible account could be given and the change agent's reputation was left intact or improved. In other cases one's judgement of events will be more guarded and qualified.

A particular strength of Buchanan and Badham's work is that this framework is then tested against a range of case studies to show its appropriateness and feasibility. Though the view of ethics presented in their work is inevitably more limited than the full range of approaches to business ethics (e.g. virtue ethics, a fully developed Kantian framework and discourse ethics are not explicitly present in the framework, though some attention is given to gender issues later in their book) it has the great advantage of addressing organisational politics, that is the feasibility of taking and judging action in real and competitive contexts. Some issues remain, such as the interlinking of decisions, which always presents a problem when the focus is on assessing individual decisions. It is possible, however, that this framework can be adapted to such interlinking (through its attention to human interaction) and therefore be complementary to the more mechanistic cost–benefit models which address financial and informational issues across a range of projects.

Integrity

Whereas the term 'reputation', as developed above, is applied to an individual decision maker, it could also be applied to an organisation. We may often speak of the reputation of a business as a good employer, or even of its brands as providing good value for money. In this section we consider how such a long-term positive view of an organisation may be developed, using the recently developed concept of an integrity strategy.

A simple exposition of the role of an integrity strategy in an organisation is found in Paine (1994), where integrity-based strategies for ethical management are contrasted with compliance-based strategies. The former are seen as operating on corporate cultures and value systems in a positive and constructive manner while compliance is seen in terms of laws and externally applied regulations. It is not argued that the latter should be ignored but that such compliance be internalised into an organisation's own rules, procedures and common working practices. As Paine comments:

> An integrity strategy is characterised by a conception of ethics as a driving force of an enterprise.

While this is an approach we can no doubt endorse from the perspective of organisational ethics, it is by no means easy to see how it can be done in practice. We can explore this further by noting a further quotation from Paine (1994):

> While compliance is rooted in avoiding legal sanctions, organisational integrity is based on the concept of self-governance in accordance with a set of guiding principles. From the perspective of integrity, the task of ethics management is to define and give life to an organisation's guiding values, to create an environment that supports ethically sound behaviour, and to instil a sense of shared accountability among employees.

Thus we can foresee the following tasks as being necessary:

▶ Reaching an agreement on an appropriate set of guiding principles; this will usually involve the external benchmarking of best practice or the use of professional codes of conduct.
▶ Defining the organisation's guiding values and reaching agreement on them; the phrase 'giving life to' is highly evocative of this process, if hard to define.
▶ Creating a supporting environment for ethical behaviour; there is little point in having an agreement on ethical behaviour if the reward system of your organisation, for example, encourages unethical behaviour (e.g. through commission and bonuses for

inappropriate sales activity; by turning a blind eye to unsafe working practices, etc.).

► Instilling a sense of shared accountability; in contrast to a 'blame culture', this will depend on a mixture of accepted procedures for handling risk and other sensitive areas of potential conflict.

Paine (1994) goes further in emphasising the following as 'hallmarks' of an effective integrity strategy:

► clear communication of guiding values and commitments;
► senior management personal and credible commitment and willingness to take action;
► integration of espoused values into decision-making processes;
► systems and structures which reinforce such values;
► employees having the skills and knowledge to make consistent ethically sound decisions on a daily basis;
► the investment of time and resources to facilitate this strategy.

This list is very similar to others produced as essential features for the implementation of any strategy, that is communication, commitment, time, resources, systems and skills development are typically called into play in a wide range of contexts. The very sensible point being made here is that if an organisation wishes to see ethics as more than a Public Relations exercise (e.g. a few paragraphs in its Annual Report) then it must take the implementation of an integrity (ethics) strategy as seriously as it would take the management of any other strategic change.

If one sees an integrity strategy in this way then the serious financial investment involved must be justified to an organisation's stakeholders. Such justification has often been in terms of avoiding corporate liability (e.g. arising through causing harm to customers or employees through unsafe products or working practices) and improved Public Relations. A more sophisticated justification is that an organisation which successfully adopts an integrity strategy improves the effectiveness of its operations, for example, by the increased commitment and motivation, by employees and the use of better processes. The latter might be through the perception of a link between ethical action and quality (see Chapter 14 for an initial exploration of this difficult area).

However, if we take the message of Kantian ethics seriously and apply it to the organisation as if it were a moral individual, we might wish to say that the organisation has a duty to act in a moral way (see Chapter 7). This would be a bold step to take, unless a legal duty for an organisation to act in certain ways was in existence. This may well be the case in a public sector context, for example in health, education or the social services. For a private sector business we might run up against the Friedman argument that the overriding duty is to promote the wealth of the shareholders. It is hardly surprising that most managers who wish to implement an integrity strategy will argue that it combines good morals with long-term profitability! We will return to this point at the end of the section.

While Paine (1994) gives a simple and practical introduction to the integrity concept, there is a noticeable lack of connection with actual theories of ethics. A very useful, integrated theory of organisational ethics is contained in Kaptein and Wempe (2002) and it is their model of corporate integrity which we will briefly summarise in the remainder of this section. Their work provides a more detailed link between the standard theories of ethics, including virtue ethics, and practical policies for organisational action.

It is useful to begin with the notion of individual integrity. Integrity in a person can be positively defined as 'wholeness', 'completeness' or being 'intact'; it includes personal values, judgement, objectives and conduct and is exemplified in an individual who shows consistency between what they say and do over a period of time. Now strictly speaking the above characteristics could hold for someone who behaves in a consistently selfish, unethical and even criminal manner! This is where other characteristics of the notion of integrity might be brought into play, that is integrity also infers 'incorruptibility' and other positive characteristics.

An alternative view is to define integrity as the absence of certain undesirable features, as shown below with useful characterisations:

▶ a person who holds inconsistent values (the opportunist, pragmatist or moral chameleon);
▶ a person's whose values are not consistent with their actions (the hypocrite or self-deceiver);
▶ a person who takes no account of their environment or the roles they play in the world (the rigid dogmatist or bureaucrat).

These ideas are familiar to us from the concept of consistency linked to the notion of sensitivity to the environment (broadly defined, of course). Taken together Kaptein and Wempe (2002) arrive at the following suggested characteristics of individual integrity, which we will quote in full as they are also suggestive of what we might mean by corporate integrity:

1. A person of integrity is first and foremost autonomous and authentic: he or she stands for something, strives for something, and is true to his or her ideals.
2. A person of integrity is capable of integrating his or her values, deeds, and their effects in his or her life in a natural way.
3. A person of integrity is integrated into his or her environment and sensitive to social issues, and willing to account for himself or herself.

Now it should be noted that this characterisation of integrity rests upon the coherence of certain other ideas, such as authenticity and sensitivity. It should also not be taken in isolation from other theories of ethics, in particular because one might argue that the above could characterise some individuals who we might not think of as ethical (i.e. we might use the philosopher's trick of trying to find the most repulsive person who nonetheless fits the above; Hitler is a good starting point). It is also not clear if this idea of integrity is adequate to resolve ethical dilemmas and clashes between other theories in applied ethics. However, if we take this idea of personal integrity in a positive spirit as a notion we can associate with virtue ethics then it has obvious value.

Kaptein and Wempe (2002), however, have a rather more ambitious objective and wish to apply this notion directly to the corporation. This requires a great deal of explanation and analysis in their book and we will briefly introduce some points which are also of more general interest. They introduce what they refer to as the three fundamental dilemmas of the corporation, imaginatively referred to as:

► The dirty hands dilemma: in order to ensure the survival of the corporation, some stakeholder's rights and interests may be honoured in at best a minimalist fashion.
► The many hands dilemma: effective use of teamwork dilutes individual moral responsibility.
► The entangled hands dilemma: effective delegation of responsibilities may lead to irresponsible employee behaviour due to clashes between individual's interests and those of the corporation.

The explicit statement of these dilemmas is useful in reminding us why organisational ethics is different from other branches of applied ethics. Reconciling the competing demands of stakeholders, while maintaining the continuity of the organisation, is a very real problem at the heart of many examples of perceived corporate misbehaviour. The dilution of individual moral responsibility is a recurring theme in this book and will be well known to any experienced manager; when things go wrong, someone else is always to blame to some extent at least!

Kaptein and Wempe (2002) give a Corporate Integrity Model which addresses such issues in the following terms. An overall objective of mutual sustainable advantage is suggested as a desirable consequence for all. The use of the word 'sustainable' (in a general sense, though reminiscent of its use in 'Green Ethics') is noteworthy in suggesting a long-term context for all stakeholders. Conduct is then based on five principles, that is openness, empathy, fairness, solidarity and reliability, which apply in a variety of contexts (clarity, consistency, realisability, supportability, visibility, discussibility and sanctionability). Great care is taken to show how the above three dilemmas are addressed within this model (e.g. see Kaptein and Wempe 2002, Table 6.6).

This work is very useful in providing a systematic treatment of the increasingly popular word 'integrity' as used in an organisational context. Even the above superficial description shows how integrity can be a useful link between other ethical ideas and the model given does show practical policies and organisational practices which go some way towards addressing some difficult issues. However it should also be noted that this work cannot be divorced from the insights provided by philosophical ethics; integrity is not a stand-alone guide to ethical behaviour.

We might also note that one issue which is given considerable attention in Kaptein and Wempe (2002) is whether an organisation can itself be considered a moral entity. This has been a recurring theme for a number of years in business ethics theory. Legally companies have a distinct status but it is by no means accepted that it makes any sense to refer to a company's moral obligations as opposed to the moral obligations of various human agents (e.g. Directors, employees, etc.). This is a very interesting topic for future study if the reader is so inclined!

Summary

This chapter is not particularly long but it is complex and demanding. The models and ideas on reputation, power and integrity presented above refer very directly to organisational contexts and to the work of organisational behaviour and strategy theorists. They show a different approach and perspective from standard ethical theory in that their origin is a consideration of the particular problems of working in organisations rather than broader issues of practical ethics. In that sense they provide a useful bridge into the remaining chapters of the book.

These theories and ideas are of fairly recent origin and are based on organisational research. For this reason they should be of particular use if you are attempting to relate ethical concepts to your own real work situations. These ideas are strongly grounded in public sector practice as well as private sector business ethics. They are, therefore, complementary to the models given in Chapters 18 and 19, which relate strongly to consumer market contexts, and Chapter 20, where business-to-business contexts predominate.

Questions for discussion – Part II

As previously noted in Part I, the 9 discussion questions given below relate to material covered in Chapters 5–10 and may introduce new ideas and perspectives. These questions are meant to challenge rather than review basic learning of the material in these chapters.

Question 1

It can be argued that the implicit use of consequentialist ethics is a management ploy to avoid discussion of intentions, feelings and the other things which actually make us moral and human. It moves any debate on morality into the world of objective facts in which many managers are more comfortable.

Discuss.

Question 2

How can we measure (or even know) if the ethical theories we have been using are successful?

For example, before a decision is made utilitarian ethical evaluation is based on predictions. After the event, evaluation is based on a partial knowledge of the outcomes for a variety of people. We therefore have the problem, typically occurring when evaluating planning systems, of whether we judge the process of decision-making and implementation or the results.

Question 3

What should we actually do with the theories of applied ethics outlined in Chapters 5–10? Should we:

▶ Use them as part of a decision-making process?
▶ Use them as part of a theory in the social sciences (e.g. economics) or business (e.g. marketing)?
▶ Use them as a resource as part of a critical debate of management theory and practice?

Can the same theories be a management technique and be used for fundamental assessment of management practice?

Question 4

Even if we accept that utilitarianism has a number of weakness, do we not all tend to be 'local utilitarians'? (i.e. we feel it is right to produce the best result for those within a narrow range of family, friendship and obligation.)

Question 5

We may easily see organisational duties and obligations as a source of contradiction and dilemma. The most valuable part of deontology is supporting a debate on how to avoid or resolve clashes of duties.

Discuss.

Question 6

A fundamental contradiction relating to individual freedom lies at the heart of management practice. Management seeks to influence and control everything (actions, performance, quality, learning, culture and values) as part of the freedom to manage. Control is seen as a basic feature of successful entrepreneurs, but how far is it legitimate to seek to control everything; that is to get our own way in all matters?

Similarly we might think that our personal values are at the core of our identity. They are something we try to develop in ourselves, to preserve and to use when we evaluate others, including our managers. Thus as individuals we fight against conformity, but as managers we promote conformity. Surely this is hypocritical – we want to be free but to control the freedom of others.

Discuss.

Question 7

Most roles in society encourage an integration of the self with the performance of the role. Managers play out a role where the self is dominated by the organisation's culture and objectives. Is this morally healthy?

Question 8

A major issue in business ethics is group agency, that is can an organisation (rather than a person) be viewed as a moral entity. Is to talk of an organisation as a moral entity a paradigm shift or an elementary mistake?

Below are some possible reasons why an organisation cannot be viewed as a 'person':

▶ Its survival is not essential.
▶ Its freedom or liberty is not a fundamental issue.
▶ Its happiness is not an intelligible concept.

Do you think these arguments can be overcome and is it reasonable to speak of an organisation as being moral or otherwise?

Question 9

It can be argued that only if an individual is in a position of power or influence can the consequences of their actions be identified. You can only be moral or immoral if you have power. Perhaps most of us (in ordinary social and organisational life) prefer to avoid power, influence and moral responsibility. A further issue is whether an organisation (or part of it; or a professional role) can be said to exhibit ethical behaviour in a consequentialist sense. The augmented power of an organisation might make the identification of consequences easier in many contexts.

We may also argue that a consequentialist view of moral behaviour is only bearable (for the person who really wishes to be virtuous) if the full, possible consequences of our actions are unknown. Fortunately in a social context it is often difficult to identify the consequences of our actions from within the endless web of interaction. Maybe we can only talk of possible influences. Does all this lead to a deontological viewpoint of personal ethics in an organisational context, that is the best we can do is follow the rules?

Discuss.

Part III   Topics and cases in business ethics

Introduction

In Part III we move on from a consideration of theory and business background to the examination of a series of topics in business ethics. Each topic is of general applicability, that is it does not relate solely to one functional area (such as personnel or marketing) nor to one type of organisation. However, topics may be introduced in a specific context in order to make them clear and relevant. An example in Chapter 14 is where the general notion of 'moral muteness' is associated with ideas of quality management; it might equally well have been introduced in other contexts but the association with quality ideas is useful and memorable. In Part IV we will move towards a more explicitly functional view of business ethics.

In writing these chapters there was a great temptation to link them explicitly with the theoretical material in Parts I and II in order to simplify what is becoming a complex structure of theory and application. For example, the material on unfair discrimination and diversity in Chapter 13 can readily be seen in the light of the ideas on human rights in Chapter 7. However, on reflection, we can also see discrimination in consequentialist terms, perhaps as consistent with the narrow and short-term perspective of an individual who is engaged in unfair discrimination but in contrast to the long-term benefit of an organisation and its stakeholders. To pursue this further, we may see an individual who habitually discriminates in unfair or ill thought-out ways as someone who needs to become more self-reflective and to develop the virtues of judgement and even-handed discrimination. We may continue this line of argument, but the point is obvious. A simplistic linking of theory and practice will not exploit the resources of ethical theory and may well lead to a narrow and inadequate view of a problem context.

A further feature of Part III is the use of range of case exercises. These are summarised below, following a brief guide to chapter contents.

Readers are strongly encouraged to attempt to relate this material to their own organisational context through reflection, discussion and the writing of case studies reflecting their own experiences.

Chapter contents

Chapter 11 is distinctive in that it is based around two specific tasks. The first is the analysis of ethical case studies, which is a new feature in Part III and requires some explanation and advice. It is strongly recommended that this section is read before embarking on case analysis and also referred to in the future. Many of the points made are relevant to case analysis in general. This is followed by a listing of a number of the ethical principles included in this book in a 'question' format in order to help the reader in the often difficult and confusing task of relating theories to case contexts.

The second part of Chapter 11 is a guide to research ethics. This is of obvious relevance if live project work (e.g. surveys or in-company investigations) is to be carried out in any branch of management, that is it does not relate to 'researching ethics' but to being professional and ethical in all forms of primary research in organisations. It should, however, also be studied even if no such project is immediately planned as it contains a number of ideas relating to such things as confidentiality and the control of information.

In Chapter 12 we move on to the topic of language and context, exploring first of all the vexed subject of truthfulness and otherwise in an organisational context. This is also the point where we include some alternative uses of language to show their possible effects on ethical evaluation. We also show how the evaluation of an act may be affected by context.

Chapter 13 is devoted to the single and highly important topic of unfair discrimination and the related idea that the promotion of diversity might be an organisational objective. The case study in this chapter includes a substantial analysis in order to encourage the reader to think broadly about such issues. Chapter 14, as mentioned above, discusses moral muteness before moving on to another particularly fraught area of ethical concern in organisations, the management of whistleblowing.

Chapter 15 uses the idea of 'other cultures' to broaden out the debate once again, now taking into account some different styles of management (e.g. Japanese management, which has been much researched following the success of Japanese manufacturing companies in the latter part of last century). This leads to a more general model of cultural diversity and inevitably to question the extent to which 'Western ethics' really is the one rational approach to value formation in business.

The quality concepts in Chapter 14 and the background to Japanese management in Chapter 15 are often considered as part of the subject of Operations Management. In many ways Chapter 16 also relates to operational concerns, though now with a focus on risk management. It includes consideration of one major disaster and looks at the important theoretical and practical issue of the extent to which senior managers may be held responsible when disasters occur.

Case studies in Part III

In Parts III and IV we include a number of case studies and exercises, which should be seen as an essential part of the text rather than an optional attachment. The cases in Part III are described below with some comments on how they might be used in a teaching context.

Chapter 11

The two simple cases, given at the end of a section on research methods, may be used by individuals or groups. As well as exploring problems in carrying out empirical research, both also relate to possible issues facing students in completing course assessments.

Research case exercise 1

A student uses a market research questionnaire as part of a course assessment. This is completed mainly by family members and friends see the results in order to help with the presentation. What are the potential ethical problems in this situation?

Research case exercise 2

This case explores the ethical issues inherent in a student using a structured research interview in a commercial workplace context in order to explore worker attitudes to management.

Chapter 12

The two cases included here are intended as a major vehicle for exploring the issues raised previously in the chapter. They may be read simply as interesting narratives, subjected to extensive analysis or used as the basis for group discussion. In the latter case, group members with organisational experience might be encouraged to describe real situations they are familiar with. As with all cases, an effort should be made to generalise from these specific contexts and to reflect on the difficulties inherent in managing (or avoiding) such situations.

An exercise in alternative case descriptions

This case explores the use of language and the nature of 'objective' descriptions of situations in which emotion and politics play a major part. It relates to the closure of a department in a large organisation. Three alternative descriptions of the situation are given:

1. a management report on the closure giving an 'objective and factual' account from a management perspective;
2. an alternative report focussing on the roles played by various participants in the crisis;
3. an 'informal conversation' giving a different and more overtly political view of the roles played.

These reports are not consistent in their view of events but show some ways in which the actions of staff may be discussed and reported. The task is to reflect on how the student, in a management role, might attempt to make sense of such a situation, how to manage the flow of information (and misinformation), how they might seek to avoid such problems or to manage them as events unfold. Ethical issues underlie the events portrayed but their resolution may well depend on which version of events is accepted as valid.

A case showing different contexts

While the previous case explored the validity of descriptions of events, in this case we do something slightly different.

A basic description of a situation is given, relating to the absence from work of a key member of a project team. As this individual's line manager you need to respond to this potential crisis. However, first of all you need more information. You are given five separate (and different) sets of possible background information relating to the character, reputation and previous performance of this individual. A common-sense view might lead one to take a different approach when the current crisis is seen against each of the five different backgrounds.

You are asked what action you would take and the extent to which this is influenced by the 'background statements', whose validity might also be called into question. You are then also asked some more general questions about the extent to which such background statements should be taken into account and also how far one should go in pursuing such details, for example if they involve medical or other confidential personal information.

Chapter 13

Discrimination: A case with analysis

The situation at the centre of this case is one where an accusation has been made that a manager has unfairly discriminated against some individuals when making an appointment. In a long narrative, the actions taken by a range of individuals are noted. Three tasks are set for the reader.

The presentation of this case is different from most others in this book in that an extensive analysis is presented to show the reader some of the ways in which ethical analysis may be conducted. In response to the first task set, a number of quotations are taken from the case and their validity as evidence is challenged. Then the ethical perspectives shown earlier in this book are used as a way of structuring the information given. The other questions are left for the reader to work on in a similar manner.

Though other forms of analysis may be carried out on this case, the above is consistent with the view that the language used in describing actions and the selection of 'facts' to be presented are not ethically neutral. It also reinforces a key message of the book that common sense should be combined with the considerable resources of ethical theory when analysing cases as well as taking action in the real world.

Chapter 14

The early part of this chapter deals with issues of quality management and moral muteness. Though case exercises are not formally separated out in the discussion, there are a number of anecdotes which may be used as the basis for individual reflection or group discussion.

Whistleblower cases

The latter part of the chapter relates to whistleblowing. Following two sections which discuss this difficult area, a series of four short cases are given. Each is based on accounts reported in the media and are followed by comments in brackets. The set of cases is followed by some general comments.

These cases may simply be viewed as an extension of the previous text or as the basis for discussion. Perhaps a more useful approach, noting the frequency with which reports of whistleblowing are seen in the media, is to look for similar cases. It is also useful for students to consider whether or not their own organisations have effective policies which address whistleblowing.

Chapter 15

Once again the general text in this chapter contains anecdotes and cases which may be used as the basis for group activities. The exercises noted below may be seen as an extension of the text or may be used imaginatively as a starting point and a support for activities aimed at uncovering the real, personal problem inherent in working in different cultural contexts.

Gifts, hospitality and bribery (case exercises)

The final section of this chapter is an extended set of scenarios based on the above theme. This is followed by a discussion of the issues raised. A range of different activities might be based on this material. In particular students may wish to consider similar instances which arise in their own employment situations. Some texts which cover international marketing give examples and advice, often related to operating in different countries and cultural contexts. There is also a considerable challenge in relating the theories covered in Part II to this chapter as a whole.

Chapter 16

The discussion on risk management includes some examples. In particular the section 'Health and safety in context' has a couple of brief examples of dilemmas in operational risk management. It is not difficult to extend these by reference to published sources or experience of working practices. The ethical implications of issues in this area are considerable and will require much time and preparation if they are intended to be addressed in a teaching context.

Clapham Junction Railway Accident

This case study is based on the formal accident report of this tragic incident. The main emphasis is on the management of maintenance activity and how the blame for such accidents may on the one hand be attached to a specific event or may alternatively be seen as the result of ineffective management systems at all levels.

Unfortunately there have been a number of rail accidents in the UK in recent years. These are always investigated in great depth and the published reports, and media articles, give considerable scope for the ethical analysis of safety systems. These, in total, form a valuable resource for project work, as do similar reports from other countries and other areas of transportation, such as Air travel.

Other public disasters, for example the Hillsborough football ground tragedy, are similarly well reported and often generate arguments (and compensation claims) which continue for many years. It is useful to analyse not only the direct causes of each incident but also the ways in which management handled information during and after the incident as well as the extended issues of compensation, blame and systems improvement.

11 A guide to ethical case analysis and organisational research

Purpose and learning outcomes

The purpose of this chapter is to provide support and guidance in the ethical analysis of case studies and to introduce some of the ethical issues present in the design and implementation of management research.

You will be able to

► use a structured approach to case study analysis;
► comment on the ethical acceptability of a proposed research design.

Introduction

In many ways this chapter is similar to Chapter 1 in that it presents guidance on how to carry out certain tasks, though some new concepts are introduced. The early sections on case analysis and the summary of principles should therefore be used as a resource and referred back to when using the case studies which are a key feature in the remainder of this book. I would, however, suggest that you thoroughly familiarise yourself with this work before moving on to the next chapters.

The first section gives some advice on case study analysis. Cases are a key feature in almost all management courses and without doubt one of the most useful ways of bringing theory to life. This is especially true in the context of ethics where the general principles we have introduced so far are only the start of any attempts to untangle the ethical dilemmas we meet every day.

One of the most difficult aspects of applying ethical theory is that there is so much of it and it is difficult to see which principles to use in a given case study or real-life context. To help with this process of theory use, our advice on case analysis is followed by a summary of the concepts used in this book. This summary is intended to support case analysis and case writing and is presented in the form of a series of questions to be used when carrying out ethical evaluation of a case or a real situation. The resulting list of questions looks quite formidable but its use becomes easier with practice.

Most institutions and professional bodies which commission or carry out academic research now have in place a code of practice to protect the various stakeholders in such a process. The final section in this chapter introduces some of the basic ethical principles relevant to academic research design. Though much of this material relates to protecting the rights of respondents, it should be noted that one leading text on business research design, Easterby-Smith *et al.* (2002), emphasises the political nature of business research. Similar principles carry over into the design of Market Research, which is not explicitly dealt with in this text, though Chapter 18 deals with a selection of topics in marketing ethics.

Working with business ethics case studies

There is inevitably a great deal of complexity and ambiguity in case studies dealing with issues in business and managerial ethics, particularly when these are drawn from real-life situations rather than written as simple exercises to illustrate theories. Interesting cases centre on dilemmas where it is not clear how decision makers should proceed or what ethical evaluation is appropriate. Business ethics thrives on situations of real-life difficulty; indeed situations which show clear criminality are often of less interest to the business ethics analyst than those where apparently immoral action can somehow be defended.

Whereas philosophers exploring the basic principles of ethical action may choose to use very simple situations where a dilemma is crystal clear yet hard to resolve, one of the themes of this book is that dilemmas may specifically arise in business ethics where there is confusion regarding the facts and the decision makers are operating with a lack of knowledge regarding key pieces of information, for example, relating to the future or to competitor action. Reflecting such problem areas may require a more complex description of a real or hypothetical situation, in order to capture the rich interplay of variables. If such a difficult situation is to be considered it is often then also worthwhile to reflect a real dilemma or an example typical of those an employee may meet in practice. By doing this, we may combine reflection on theories and principles with a developing understanding of ethical behaviour in an organisational context.

The result of this is that published cases in business ethics can be complex and difficult to follow. Similarly if one uses other forms of publication, such as reports of public inquiries and stories reported in the press, as a source of ethical cases then one has to be careful in structuring the information in order to facilitate ethical analysis. Furthermore if one wishes to engage in case writing, using original organisational materials and collecting evidence from those involved, structuring materials for clarity as well as eliminating unintentional bias in reporting can be a forbidding challenge.

For these reasons, it is essential that a systematic case analysis methodology is used. This should be of value in the analysis of published (i.e. secondary) cases and reports and should aid case writing, though we must emphasise that the latter requires further skills normally taught under the heading of research methods. The following set of questions is suggested for preliminary examination of any business ethics situation. The list of questions is intentionally long and many may not be relevant in a specific instance. With practice, you will also, of course, find many other questions to ask!

Context of the case situation

▶ What is the organisational, managerial and business context described in the case?
▶ Does the case have specific business (e.g. competitive) or public sector (e.g. political) issues in the background?
▶ What is (are) the source(s) of the information in the case?
▶ How reliable is the reported 'factual background'?
▶ Are there obvious sources of bias in the reporting (intentional, as when a protagonist is explicitly arguing a given point of view, or unintentional)?
▶ Does the report involve statements of opinion or judgement which may be hard to objectively verify?
▶ Who are the stakeholders?

▶ Who are the directly involved participants and decision makers?
▶ What is their background (including professional, managerial and technical attributes)?
▶ What are the relevant organisational, social and cultural issues?
▶ How reliable is the particular information relating to the actions and motivation of the key participants?

You will note the need for a high degree of care and considerable scepticism in the evaluation of the facts. You might also consider the assertion often made in the social sciences that all apparently objective facts are underpinned by values and assumptions which may not be explicitly stated. You might then attempt to uncover the hidden values in reported statements and in assumptions made by the case writer. This may involve things which are not said as much as things which are said!

Dilemmas

▶ What moral dilemmas are revealed in the case study?
▶ Who are the decision makers facing a dilemma?
▶ Are there conflicts of interest?
▶ What information is available relevant to the moral dilemmas?
▶ What information was available to each stakeholder at different points of time described in the case?
▶ What arguments are presented in the case in support of each stated moral stance?

Theories and argument

▶ What theories are potentially relevant to the case?
The following may be used as a short checklist or reference made to the theory profiling contained later in this chapter.

Consequence-based theories:

1. Egoism (whether self or relating to a small group)
2. Utilitarianism (how broad a range of 'stakeholders'?)

Rights-based theories:

1. Rights, duties, obligations (to whom and why?)
2. Liberty and freedom of action (e.g. a 'right to manage')
3. Legal frameworks

Agent-based theories:

1. Virtue ethics
2. The organisation as a community of purpose
3. Ethics of care.

▶ For any theory under consideration, what is the ethical acceptability of the moral stance of each of the key participants?
▶ Do the theories considered provide a consistent evaluation of each moral stance?

Recommendations

▶ How might the main actors have done things differently (change short-term behaviour or change procedures and systems)?
▶ What changes in policy or behaviour would you suggest in the light of the above analysis?
▶ How might such changes in policy or behaviour be implemented?

Note that it is important you support your recommendations in terms of the theories used in the analysis.

Ethical principles and issues – a guide for case analysis

In this section we show a list of ethical principles and potential issues which may be of value when analysing a case study or real decision situation where there are ethical concerns (i.e. all decision situations!). This list brings together some of the various prescriptions given in other parts of this book. It is extensive but by no means exhaustive. It is unlikely that reference can be made to all the items below in any given context. It should be used, and added to, as a source of ideas rather than as a formal model of ethical decision-making.

For simplicity the list is given as a series of questions. They are given in the order of their first occurrence in this book. The source of the principle is given so that the relevant chapter may be referred to. This should be done on the first occasion a particular question is used in order to avoid misunderstandings. Some of the questions are reasonably straightforward. Others will require some thought and practise in their usage.

The list may be used in a variety of ways. It may be used as a series of prompts when beginning the analysis of a given case study, particularly if you have difficulty in articulating ethical issues, that is you may instinctively feel that a given action presented in a case study is somehow wrong but you find it difficult to say exactly why. It may be used as a checklist to help avoiding a biased analysis. For example, a case may be presented in a way which emphasises consequences and it might therefore be useful to be reminded of rights, responsibilities and moral development as potential issues.

Another use of this, or similar, lists is when writing up the analysis of a case. It is important that you clearly state the reasons (based on facts or theories) for your judgements, conclusions and recommendations in case analysis and this should involve reference to background principles and include references as appropriate.

The list looks forbidding but do not be discouraged. You will soon see patterns and similarities in the questions and find favourite questions which can be used a number of times. Their most important value is to get you started in analysing a situation.

Internal or external focus
Are we concerned with internal (organisational or managerial) ethics or external (business or public sector) ethics? – Chapter 1

Focus
Are we primarily concerned with intentions, actions or consequences? Do we note deficiencies in ethical awareness, poor judgement or inappropriate behaviour? – Chapter 2

Ethics and the law
Are observed or intended actions illegal, immoral or both? – Chapter 2

Stakeholder scope
Is a comprehensive group of stakeholders included in ethical analysis? – Chapter 3

Simple egoism
Is the primary focus on maximising the self-interest of the decision maker? – Chapter 5

Altruism
Does concern for the well-being of others come above concern for oneself? – Chapter 5

Group egoism
Do group concerns come ahead of other factors? – Chapter 5

Cultural relativism
Are the moral norms in use based on social approval within society or a relevant group? – Chapter 5

Ideal observer
Would a fully informed and impartial observer choose this action? – Chapter 5

Belief consistency
Is the action based on beliefs and principles which are consistent? – Chapters 5 and 10 (integrity)

Belief and action consistency
Is the action consistent with our beliefs? – Chapters 5 and 10 (integrity)

Action consistency
Is the action consistent with similar actions in comparable situations? – Chapters 5 and 10 (integrity)

Utilitarianism (act)
Does the chosen action maximise utility over the population? – Chapter 6

Utilitarianism (rule)
Does the chosen action follow a suitable rule which tends to maximise utility in similar cases over the population? – Chapter 6

Freedom
Does the action affect the basic personal liberties of any individual, including the ability to protect themselves from harm, to be physically free and secure, to be free from danger, to participate in political action, to own property, have the means to survive and be treated with equal dignity to others? – Chapter 6 (Mill on utilitarianism)

Information base
Is the range of information used to inform ethical judgement sufficiently broad, rich and free from bias? – Chapter 6 (limitations of consequentialism)

Predictability
Can the results of our actions be adequately predicted? Can we adequately link cause and effect? – Chapter 6 (limitations of consequentialism)

Chaos
Is the action being taken in a situation where small changes in relevant factors might lead to dramatically different results? – Chapter 6 (limitations of consequentialism)

Complexity
Is the action being taken in a potentially unstable situation (e.g. dramatic organisational or environmental change)? – Chapter 6 (limitations of consequentialism)

Competition
Might the action be seen as part of a competitive 'game' and hence lead to counterintuitive consequences? – Chapter 6 (limitations of consequentialism)

Human rights
Does the chosen action preserve the generally accepted human rights of all individuals affected? – Chapter 7

Golden rule
Would I be willing to be treated in the same way as I am treating others by this action? – Chapter 7 (Kantian ethics)

The Categorical Imperative or Formula of Universal Law
Is the action consistent with the norm: 'Act only in accordance with the maxim through which you can at the same time will that it be a universal law.' – Chapter 7 (Kantian ethics)

The Formula of Humanity or Formula of the End in Itself
Is the action consistent with the norm: 'Act so that you use humanity, whether in your own person or in the person of any other, always at the same time as an end, never merely as a means.' – Chapter 7 (Kantian ethics)

Autonomy and the Kingdom of Ends
Is the action consistent with the norm: 'We should so act that we may think of ourselves as legislating universal laws through our maxims.' – Chapter 7 (Kantian ethics)

Fidelity
Is the action consistent with any promises made? – Chapter 7 (Ross)

Reparation
Does the action compensate for previous harm done? – Chapter 7 (Ross)

Gratitude
Does the action show some return to others who have previously benefited us? – Chapter 7 (Ross)

Justice
Does the action redress unfair distribution of utility? – Chapter 7
(Ross)

Beneficience
Does the action do good to others? – Chapter 7 (Ross)

Self-improvement
Does the action lead to increases in our knowledge or virtue? –
Chapter 7 (Ross)

Nonmaleficence
Does the action harm others? – Chapter 7 (Ross)

Discrimination
Does the action unfairly discriminate against any group or individuals? –
Chapters 7 and 13

Justice
Does the action treat all involved fairly? – Chapters 7 and 8

Contract
Is the action consistent with all agreed norms of behaviour applicable
for this group in comparable situations (including actual agreements
and contracts)? – Chapters 7 and 8

Moral development
Does the action contribute to the moral development of the agents
involved? – Chapter 9 (also Chapter 4)

Moral debate
Have the underlying moral issues been surfaced within a debate
involving all relevant parties? – Chapter 9

Moral articulacy (moral muteness)
Has moral language been used in the process of debate leading up to
the decision? – Chapters 9, 12 and 14

Moral clarity (moral muteness)
Has the analysis and decision been expressed in clear moral language? –
Chapters 9, 12 and 14

Care for others
Do observed actions and attitudes show the values of emotional sensitivity and responsiveness to the needs of particular others; intimacy and connection, responsibility and trust? – Chapter 9

Warrant
Does a formal or tacit warrant exist to support the decision maker? – Chapter 10 (Buchanan and Badham)

Account
Can the decision makers articulate a clear, moral account of their actions? – Chapter 10 (Buchanan and Badham)

Reputation
Does the action preserve the reputation of all individuals, groups or organisations involved? – Chapter 10 (Buchanan and Badham)

Integrity strategy
Does the strategy of the organisation demonstrate integrity, that is, is it characterised by a conception of ethics as a driving force? – Chapter 10 (Paine)

Personal integrity
Do agents demonstrate the characteristics of authenticity, integration of values and deeds, integration into their environment, sensitivity to social issues and willingness to account for themselves? – Chapter 10 (Kaptein and Wempe)

The dirty hands dilemma
In order to ensure the survival of the corporation, are some stakeholder rights and interests honoured in a minimalist fashion? – Chapter 10 (Kaptein and Wempe)

The many hands dilemma
Does the effective use of teamwork dilute individual moral responsibility? – Chapter 10 (Kaptein and Wempe)

The entangled hands dilemma
Does the effective delegation of responsibilities lead to irresponsible employee behaviour due to clashes between individual's interests and those of the corporation? – Chapter 10 (Kaptein and Wempe)

Privacy
Does the action intrude on anyone's privacy? – Chapter 11 (Research ethics)

Informed consent
Is the action based on the obtaining of informed consent by all individuals involved? – Chapter 11 (Research ethics)

Deception in data gathering
Is data or information gathered by means that are open and transparent to all involved? – Chapter 11 (Research ethics)

Deception in information use
Does the action entail the manipulation of information and its presentation with the intention of misleading others? – Chapter 11 (Research ethics)

Confidentiality
Are the rights of all individuals and organisations respected in terms of data protection and use? – Chapter 11 (Research ethics)

Vulnerable groups
Does the action exploit vulnerable individuals or groups? – Chapter 11 (Research ethics)

Unfair discrimination
How effective are organisational policies and practices in discouraging unfair discrimination? – Chapter 13

Whistleblowing
Do effective mechanisms exist for surfacing legitimate employee concerns? – Chapter 14

Risk assessment
Do effective policies and practices exist for risk assessment and management? – Chapter 16

Top level responsibility
Are senior managers aware of risks and willing to take full responsibility? – Chapter 16

Performance assessment
Does the way in which individual performance is measured encourage unethical behaviour? – Chapter 17

Societal constraints
Have all social and legal constraints been observed? – Chapter 18 (Robin and Reidenbach)

Market system
Is the decision in line with the ethos of market behaviour in encouraging risk-taking, hard work and creativity? – Chapter 18 (Robin and Reidenbach)

Human limitations
Does the action recognise and respect the constraints of human capabilities and limitations? – Chapter 18 (Robin and Reidenbach)

Adiaphorization
Does the action assume or make others less ethically worthy of consideration, for example through not being members of a select group or through distancing or objectification? – Chapter 19

Research ethics

All universities and colleges which expect students to carry out empirical research (i.e. gather data from real situations or experiments) have policies, principles and procedures to ensure that such work is carried out in an ethical manner. There are a number of ways in which such research can go badly wrong and it is our intention here to explore some of these rather than provide comprehensive advice on how to carry out research in management, which is itself the subject of a number of texts.

You are strongly encouraged to find out the rules and procedures for ethical approval of research which apply in any University in which you are working. This is an essential part of any training in academic research (e.g. as part of a PhD programme) but the ideas are still valid in other forms of commercial and organisational research and consultancy. These are based on fundamental concepts such as transparency, fairness, obtaining consent and data protection and therefore have wide potential value.

We might first of all ask what is the point of designing potentially time-consuming procedures? The objectives of a process of ethical approval and implementation can be summarised as follows:

► to protect the rights of external stakeholders (e.g. the privacy of respondents; non-disclosure of sensitive company information);
► to inform and guide learning by the researcher through a clear process of ethical approval and implementation (i.e. to support the researcher in what can be very difficult work);

- to give the supervisor confidence that agreed research methods are within ethical guidelines and are being implemented (i.e. to ensure that research has actually been done as agreed);
- to protect the reputation of the Institution or body sponsoring the research.

Now this may all sound very straightforward, but a number of quite difficult issues arise when we actually try to do research, particularly in those controversial areas where research is particularly valuable. Some problems and issues which might arise are briefly described below, in no particular order of priority.

On occasions, we may need to research vulnerable populations of respondents, such as children, patients in hospital, the elderly and so forth. It should be noted that any research which relates to the Health Service will inevitably require an extensive approval process based on very detailed descriptions of intended work. This level of planning and approval is reasonable and should not be seen as a nuisance or unfair constraint.

One particular area of difficulty is the use of deception in gathering primary data and evidence. This relates to situations where we may feel that identification that research is being carried out on a given, perhaps emotive, topic will be counterproductive. Respondents may not come forward or permission to carry out such work in an organisation may not be easy to obtain. An exception might be where the deception is later revealed and the participants have the right to destroy the evidence that has been collected. This is a problematic area, but covert observation is a method used in the social sciences, preferably by experienced and well supported researchers. Unless you have been trained in this type of work, fully understand the ethical issues involved and unless clear rules are in place and appropriate permission granted it should be avoided.

A very basic point is that we should avoid exposing participants or researchers to increased levels of physical harm or likelihood of damage to reputation. Some criminological research, for example, can pose considerable dangers for the researcher.

We have an obvious issue with the collection and use of highly sensitive company information, that is information too sensitive to be handled by normal security processes such as passwords on files (see below). Many businesses will not agree to be involved in research because of the potential leaks of commercial data. Others will not wish dubious practices to come to light, though it is hard to assess whether this is the case due to lack of research! This is an interesting point; there are limits on what we can research because organisations have the power to ensure that some things about them should not be known. However, see the section on whistleblowing in Chapter 14.

We must avoid the collection and use of sensitive personal information unless full permission has been given by the individuals concerned. A related issue is the importance when designing questionnaires and interview prompts to avoid forms of 'open-endedness' which might lead to sensitive information being received which is beyond the scope of the research objectives (e.g. allegations of malpractice). Do not give blanket assurances of confidentiality! However much our natural sense of curiosity may lead us to uncover all manner of interesting information, remember that material beyond the agreed and communicated scope of the investigation is not our legitimate concern. Be prepared to say 'Don't tell me that . . .' and if necessary to terminate the interview!

Following on from this point, there is a form of organisational research where employees of participating organisations are encouraged to give data or opinions which might be problematic if revealed to other employees or management of the organisation, particularly if specific individuals or groups are identified. The use of large samples may be a way forward, provided it is effective in ensuring anonymity in sensitive cases. The exception is where all parties concerned have fully consented to the process of data gathering, analysis and dissemination.

We must always obtain informed consent from participants; that is consent based on a knowledge of what the research is about and how the findings are to be used, usually in the form of a short summary given to intended respondents before they give consent through signing an appropriate form. An exception might be where implied consent is achieved in completely non-sensitive contexts such as street or telephone surveys.

Sensitive data and any derived material (e.g. notes for analysis) must be stored in a locked place (paper) or in computer files with passwords. It must not be shared with others without agreement of the participants. Care should be taken when material is being used in an office, for example if a computer screen can be overlooked. It is good practice to preserve the anonymity of all sensitive data by using a code to identify individuals, groups or organisations as appropriate. The key to the code should, of course, be kept in a secure place!

If at all possible, any final report of academic work should be presented in such a way that it can be 'published'; that is made generally available in a University library and to other researchers. If its availability is restricted (e.g. for commercial reasons) then it must be agreed in advance how this is to be handled. It can be frustrating for a researcher if data is gathered for one purpose and then its use is requested for another purpose outside the scope of the original permission obtained from participants. However, data should not be handed on and recycled in this way unless new permission can be obtained.

The notes above are presented as practical advice, but it is fairly straightforward to link these with duties relating to disclosure and data protection. The framework operating here is contractarian in the sense that, through the consent obtaining process, we reach an agreement with respondents and organisations about the rights and duties of all parties involved. This agreement then forms the basis of the relationship within the context of professional practice (as defined by various codes of practice such as those for psychologists, sociologists, etc.), normal expectations of academic research practice and the law. While major funding bodies have extensive procedures for managing research, smaller projects and those outside recognised professional and academic structures may be a problem. It can be a great temptation to use the label 'research' to hide selling activity, journalistic intrusion or sheer nosiness! It should also be remembered that even small-scale research, such as surveys and primary data gathering for class use and assessment, must be carried out in a planned and ethical manner.

Research ethics cases

Case exercise 1

Anne is a second year Business Studies student at her local University. As part of a Marketing module she is required to undertake a piece of market research. She has chosen to investigate the buying of designer-labelled fashion clothing by people in their early teens. To do this she has created a questionnaire to be used in a street survey. This consists of a series of short questions which gather some basic information about the respondents (e.g. gender, age and postcode) and then some information on what adverts they have seen, what clothes stores they use and what labels they would buy.

Unfortunately she has had little helpful response when using this information in the street and therefore has decided to use it with members of her extended family. A total of 23 intelligible responses have been received and she has now written this up as a report. To check she was going about this in the right way, she shared this information with a group of friends who made a number of helpful suggestions on presentation. The report has now been submitted as coursework.

Do you think there were any ethical issues with the actions Anne took in completing this assessed work? In what practical ways might this work have been carried out to avoid ethical problems?

Case exercise 2

Brenda is carrying out empirical work as part of a postgraduate thesis on attitudes to stress in the workplace. She is currently a full-time student though has considerable work experience, including at Company X which has agreed to be part of a survey.

She has informally agreed objectives for the survey with her research supervisor and has designed a structured interview to be used with a sample of employees of the company, which is involved in the telephone selling of a range of products. The interviews will explore employee perceptions of the attitude of management to the support of the direct sales employees. This will be followed by interviews with selected managers.

As part of a compulsory research methods module, Brenda was introduced to key concepts in management research ethics and the University's procedures for agreeing empirical work. What questions would you ask Brenda about how she intends to proceed with her empirical work.

Summary

The case analysis advice given above includes a number of comments which are standard for all case analysis, in particular the emphasis on detecting the presence of ethical dilemmas. These often provide a useful focus in a complex and confusing case-based situation and hopefully match dilemmas which occur in real life. The list of useful ethical questions should be seen as a 'starting pack' to be annotated and added to with practice.

The research ethics notes are based on a series of briefing sessions for staff and students at Staffordshire University Business School and my considerable thanks are due to co-developers and presenters. All higher education institutions which carry out research, as well as bodies which commission academic research, will give similar advice for management research, though with possibly different emphasis for research in other social sciences. There is no reason why similar advice and strict standards should not apply to commercially sponsored research, including market research.

Below are a small number of references relating to the final section on research ethics. These are somewhat more advanced than the guidelines presented above and might best be used in conjunction with a course of research methods.

Easterby-Smith, M., Thorpe, R. and Lowe, A. (2002), *Management Research: An Introduction*, Sage, London.
Hollis, M. (1994), *The Philosophy of the Social Sciences*, CUP, Cambridge.
Resnick, D.B. (1998), *The Ethics of Science: An Introduction*, Routledge, London.

12 Language and context

Purpose and learning outcomes

The purpose of this chapter is to explore the nature of 'truth-telling' in organisational situations and to reflect, through the use of cases, on several aspects of the effect of language and context.
  You will be able to

▶ demonstrate an understanding of the complexity of 'truth-telling' in an organisational situation;
▶ carry out a basic analysis of some simple case situations where differences of context are important.

Introduction

We now move into a series of chapters where there is less emphasis on the introduction of new theory but an increase in the application of ideas to business and organisational contexts. The first section in this chapter does this through a discussion of the idea of telling the truth in a variety of situations. The next two sections present case contexts where the use of language and interpretation of information are important. These sections are possibly best used as the basis of group discussion or in a class situation where tutor comment is available. However, there is no right answer to be found and individual reflection on the lessons which might be learnt will be of value.

Truth and lies

In John Grisham's book *The Rainmaker*, the characters are discussing the ethics of their work, which in this instance is the more down-to-earth end of legal practice, soliciting work through 'ambulance chasing'! They arrive at the 'Big Three: Fight for your client, don't steal, try not to lie' (Grisham 1995, p. 137). Of course, lawyers spend a fair amount of time during their training on ethics in legal practice and on Jurisprudence, the philosophy of law. The point explored in Grisham's novel is how this works out in practice, in the competitive world of legal practitioners chasing work to survive.

The 'Big Three', though obviously a tongue in cheek summary, present an interesting contrast. The first one 'Fight for your client' is a good starting point in that it is a statement of an overriding objective rather than a constraint. It can become very easy to take a constrained and rule-bound view of ethics where the objective becomes to keep a clean sheet rather than actually score any goals, to use a football metaphor. In a highly competitive context, someone who only keeps the paperwork tidy and does not break any rules is missing the point; this type of behaviour is at best a necessary but not sufficient condition for success. Indeed the point made above is that it may not even be necessary, remembering that many of Grisham's novels are about whether rules may be broken in particular circumstances. In this case, if you do not play hard and rough then you will lose! The serious point is if you have as an objective the role of championing a client or a project in a difficult situation, then how far can you ethically go in doing this?

The second of the Big Three is an absolute 'don't steal'. One suspects that a number of other 'don'ts' would be included here if Grisham was writing a textbook rather than a novel, but 'don't steal' can stand in their place. The third point is particularly interesting; 'try not to lie'. Why is lying different from stealing? In the first place, stealing is illegal (by definition) whereas lying is not unless particular conditions exist, for example not telling the truth in a contract or other formal, signed document or making untrue public comments about somebody. However, I do not believe Grisham is making some statement here about the niceties of the law; like many writers he is exploring the grey area between absolute truth-telling and downright, malicious lying. The 'white lie', being 'economical with the truth', 'need to know', the tactics of exaggeration and misleading opponents are the stock in trade of communication and power plays in business and politics as well as social life.

Of course, we may argue that not giving someone a piece of information they might otherwise expect (e.g. an early indication that there is a problem with a delivery deadline) is not actually a lie; but it is not the straightforward and open truth, and it is the ethics of such manoeuvres we are exploring here, rather than the obvious wrongs of libel and contract breaking. (*Note*: Is it ever ethical to break the law in the ways just mentioned? This is an interesting, but separate topic.)

Let us approach this from a different angle. Why should we tell the truth? I suggest you jot down a few ideas on this and then compare these with the one given below.

Absolute rule

We tell the truth because it is an absolute rule that we must. This may be based on religious beliefs or in conformance with some ideal such as the Golden Rule (behave towards other people as you expect them to behave towards you) or the Kantian categorical imperative (see Chapter 7). Problems, as always with absolute rules, arise with potential exceptions. Would you still tell the truth if it was cruel and hurtful, for example telling an employee under intense personal stress that they are hopelessly incompetent. Would you tell the truth if it was counter-productive in some other way, for example would you tell a customer that their goods are in the post, or admit that you had forgotten to send them and genuinely intend to post them immediately? The question is not how you would respond to the two examples given above but whether or not you would even consider that exceptions could exist.

Fear of the consequences of lying and deception

We may fear the personal consequences of being caught in a lie or we may fear the consequences for our workgroup or organisation. Personal consequences can be embarrassment or damage to our reputation. In most organisations it is 'common knowledge' that there are some people who are straightforward and others who are devious and whose word should not be trusted unless there is documentary evidence. Of course, we have to judge whether the stories told about people are themselves truthful, a complex game typical of the operation of a working culture. Organisational consequences can similarly be highly destructive, as when a company's advertising claims are discovered to be misleading.

Virtue

We always tell the truth because that is the sort of people we are. This is not related to beliefs or some complex calculation of duties or consequences but is a matter of pride and self-esteem. At first sight this appears to run into the same problem with exceptions that plagues absolute rules. However, if we see such behaviour as well-intentioned in the context of personal moral development (i.e. a personal moral 'kaizen') then we will see potential problems such as 'painful truth' as a challenge we must learn to cope with through learning new skills and increasing our sensitivity and empathy towards others. If we can clearly show that where we have 'bent the truth' this was for good reasons then our reputation may even be enhanced, though probably not if the 'good reasons' benefited mainly ourselves! A habit of truth-telling may or may not be a less stressful and more profitable approach to organisational life depending on organisational circumstances.

Organisational culture

We tell the truth because that is how we do things here, that is this is our working culture. It can also be an elaborate and devious game. Perhaps this can be seen as part of the 'social contract' of an organisation.

Fairness and openness

We have a duty to be fair and open to other people, a broad agenda of which truth-telling is an important part. Other people have a right to know facts and perceptions which affect them, even if this is painful and even counter-productive in the short term, as shown in the examples given above. In particular we must not evade our responsibilities to be open because this might be difficult for us.

The above list of possible reasons why we might encourage truth-telling obviously link to the main categories of ethical theory we introduced earlier. It might be useful here to consider some of the more acute problem areas which particularly relate to business ethics and to situations where our way of doing things may clash with other employees or with company policy. Let us do this through some brief examples, as shown below.

Product sales

We are employed to sell a product, either face to face or over the phone, and we have been trained to follow a detailed script. Not surprisingly this involves emphasising the merits of our product and glossing over its less attractive features. When dealing with a particular customer we may see that their needs will best be met by a rival product, but do we simply continue to 'play the game' and follow our script; after all, that is what we are paid to do and the customer expects us to behave like this? This situation becomes more difficult if the client contact is prolonged and the client begins to see the salesperson as acting professionally and offering their own, real advice. If the salesperson is likely to have continuing contact with the client after the sale, then there is greater personal incentive to be honest in terms of advice given.

So, if you are designing a sales campaign and you want your sales staff to follow a dubious script and not start telling the customers the truth, you have to set up the sales pitch and the training with this in mind. Are you going to be truthful with the sales staff that this is what you are doing? Or do you assume that if they have any sense they will know anyway? We are now into a devious game which may backfire badly.

Another example, which is slightly more subtle, is the following. Many consumer goods are sold in conjunction with a finance package and a service agreement. The finance package may involve interest rates above those easily obtained from banks. They can also be used to sell high-priced luxury goods to people who will have difficulties in making the repayments. The service agreements are often very profitable to companies as they may exaggerate the risks of theft and breakdown. The retail company will expect its employees to try to sell these lucrative financial products in conjunction with the goods, even though they have little financial training and will have no further customer contact. Is this being 'fair and open' with the customer?

Maintaining confidentiality

You are part of a management team which is involved in a complex and difficult programme of organisational change. A wide range of time-consuming consultations are in progress with individual staff on changes to their roles and responsibilities. However, other staff are becoming rightly concerned about these changes and an unpleasant atmosphere of secrecy and mistrust is developing, even though some general announcements of impending change have been made. Increasingly staff have been asking you if their jobs will be affected; often this is the case but you have been told not to say this. Your boss, who is leading this change programme, is insistent that individual talks with key managers must be concluded before other staff are briefed. This is justified as a necessary protection for these key managers, some of whom may be leaving the organisation. Is this a situation where 'open management' cannot be practised as it would be unfair to individuals in a sensitive personal position?

A more dramatic situation occurs when you know, for example, that a factory is to be closed down but you have to maintain secrecy for commercial reasons, yet must continue to work with this group of employees on a daily basis. What do you do when rumours start to fly and you are directly asked if the future of the factory is safe? To admit there is a problem or even to refuse to answer might lead to employee action or to commercial disadvantage. The answer, of course, is that you should not have been put in this position, either by your management or by the employees who asked the question. Alternatively you should have thought it through in advance and come up with some suitably evasive reply. At the very least, we should all admit that such situations are not easy to handle.

In summary, the simplest rule is 'always tell the truth'. This may be because you believe some absolute rule applies or because this is the type of person you are. In some ways this is an easy rule to adopt (e.g. you don't have to remember what lies you told to whom!) but it may lead you to not being told important facts in case you pass them on. It may lead you to being brutally honest in unfortunate circumstances and you will not avoid some dilemmas caused by loyalty to colleagues and the organisation.

Another straightforward rule is simply to be truthful or otherwise depending on the situation and what you are trying to achieve, that is truth-telling is not important in itself. This may be consistent with a short-term consequentialist ethic, but is hardly likely to match other ethical norms. It is unlikely you will have a good reputation, but that may not worry you!

The most difficult path to follow is to agree that telling the truth is very important but to see this as part of a rounded approach to being ethical and effective at a personal level and being part of an organisation which values integrity. Thus truth-telling becomes the 'default setting' unless there are very good reasons (i.e. a 'warrant' you could eventually defend, see Chapter 10) for doing otherwise. Such reasons should not consist mainly of your personal advantage!

An exercise in alternative case descriptions

The task

This extended case is designed to show different perspectives of a difficult employment situation and illustrate ways in which language is used to argue a point from such perspectives. The case is structured as three reports. No attempt is made to reconcile the differences between the reports and you might like to consider if such reconciliation is possible. How could you arrive at an objective view of these events? You might also like to draw on your own experience and identify similar situations. What are the implications of the points made here for the conduct of your own work roles?

The background

The Business Services Unit (BSU) was a small section within a major organisation and provided training and development in the area of business systems, as well as some low-level, short-term management development programmes.

A management report on the closure of the BSU

The BSU had run with moderate success for seven years, initially funded by the parent organisation and then operating on a break-even basis as a service to the local community. Around 60 per cent of its revenue came from client organisations which were small to medium-sized businesses. Further funding came from public sector training grants (25% maximum), the balance being made up by notional revenue from the parent organisation in return for internal services. The latter part of the business was not obtained on a competitive basis and was a source of some concern to departmental heads who would have preferred to have had a free choice in the selection of service providers.

In 1999, the BSU was taken under the umbrella of the Consultancy Services Department with John Merritt becoming line manager of the senior staff in the BSU, following the departure of Jane Wilson (who had been the BSU section leader up to this point). In 2002 John followed normal practice in the organisation by carrying out a management audit of the work of the BSU, along with constructing financial projections for the remainder of the current year and the next. The latter showed that the BSU were likely to miss their external revenue target by around £1.6m in the current year, with only minor external grant income to set against this and little or no internal consultancy work planned. The best estimate, taking into account all planned work, was a loss of £1.2m in the current year. The poor state of the management information system in the Unit made it impossible to estimate the scale of loss in future years, as client liaison appeared to be on an ad hoc basis.

After consultation with staff and employee representatives, a plan was put forward by John to the senior management of the corporation to rectify this unacceptable situation. This plan involved some of the remaining viable work of BSU being taken into the Consultancy Services Department along with four of the remaining 17 staff in the Unit. The other members of staff were offered a generous severance scheme with opportunities to apply for other posts in the organisation as well as support for re-training and re-location. As a result there were no compulsory redundancies.

Though a number of staff expressed concern regarding this development, it was also felt that John had acted promptly and decisively in reducing potential financial loss and also in reducing the damaging uncertainty which would have had a detrimental effect on the morale of staff in the Unit as well as in the Department as a whole.

Another report on the closure of the BSU

The BSU was set up in the mid-1990s following pressure from the local community that the organisation, as a major employer and centre of business expertise in the town, should contribute towards the regeneration of the local economy. The new unit was initially supported with considerable public funding and under the leadership of Jane Wilson a nucleus of experienced and talented professional staff was formed. This group proved adept in communicating with local firms and soon built a reputation for high-quality training and consultancy work.

The BSU was operated as an autonomous unit with its own management controls and budgets. All finance was agreed in a quarterly meeting with the group accountant and Jane had a monthly meeting with the Marketing Director of the organisation. The BSU was encouraged to offer internal training and consultancy services by Personnel and the resulting events invariably gained high satisfaction scores by participants, as did the external training programmes.

In 1999 the Consultancy Services Department was formed, through an amalgamation of three departments in the organisation, and had an initial staff of around 90 employees, though this had dropped to around 55 by 2002. This Department took over the internal training role and it was planned that BSU would now concentrate on external work. However, there was still considerable internal demand for their services as the various budget holders in the organisation showed some preference for the provider who had given good service in the past. This led to some tension between BSU and Consultancy Services.

Jane left the Unit shortly after and was succeeded by her deputy, Frank, with the Head of Consultancy Services nominally in charge. Unfortunately this change was at the same time as a reduction in demand for the services of the BSU by local firms, due to a worsening economic situation, a number of company closures in the area and the success of the local College in developing new training initiatives based on grant revenue. Frank did, however, manage to maintain the morale of the BSU team and the Unit continued to deliver a large number of training events, often with all the staff of the Unit working to a maximum on direct client contact. As a result, less attention was paid to maintaining the planning system.

The decision to close the Unit came as a complete surprise to all staff except Frank, who was given a few days to agree the figures prior to John Merritt's plan being put to senior management of the organisation. Due to the heavy workload on staff, Frank had decided to work with John in the full expectation that the accounting data would demonstrate an acceptable position. His view, strongly stated to John and to the Marketing Director, was that the revenue projections simply did not take into account work which would be undertaken when contract details had been completed. It was common for the smaller organisations the BSU dealt with to be slow in negotiating programmes of work but then require immediate delivery! Frank resigned and found employment with Jane's new company, as did several other BSU employees. Other employees were found work within the organisation, thus eliminating the need for compulsory redundancies.

An informal conversation on the closure of the BSU

The problems all began with Jane not being offered the head of the new Consultancy Department. She would have brought the BSU straight into it and created a really useful outfit. With her entrepreneurial flair the whole thing would have buzzed and everyone would have been happy. But the job went to a paper-shuffler who messed up the new Department and then got himself back in favour by targeting the BSU as another part of his mania for cost-cutting.

The staff in the BSU did not know what hit them. They were just so snowed under by work (not helped by staff off ill and the usual lack of resources and planning) that there had not been the usual staff get-togethers and everyone was off-site for much of the time.

It is all down to politics really. After the early days when the organisation gave us a pat on the back for its public spiritedness it just did not want to know. The fact that the Unit was a success was just a nuisance. They would have preferred us to have been useless so they could have closed us down a lot earlier. We just did not fit the organisational structure and the politics just became horrendous.

Discussion

Having now seen the three reports, look back at the task set at the beginning of the section. If you were in a senior management role in this situation, what action would you take, if any? Are there lessons to be learnt in how to avoid such situations?

A case showing different contexts

The purpose of this final section is to demonstrate the effect of context on the meanings we attach to statements of 'fact' and therefore to show how we need to be aware of a range of factors in making ethical judgements. Though dependent on one basic situation, five alternative contexts are put forwards and you are asked to consider how you would act in each. This is followed by a short discussion raising some points you might have borne in mind, though you may well have raised other, equally important, points for consideration. You should obviously be very aware not only of the information you have at hand in each context but also of the information you might wish to obtain, remembering that gathering information may itself present ethical problems.

The basic situation on Wednesday morning

It was noticed that Alan had been off work in the latter part of last week and had not returned by Tuesday of this week (i.e. yesterday). This was very serious as a key project required his attention and needed some parts writing by him before this Friday at the latest. In particular his attendance had been required at a meeting on Monday, for which permission to not attend should have been requested in advance or an email explaining such absence sent at the earliest possible time. A brief message from his wife had been left with reception last Friday saying he had a stomach upset but nothing has been heard from him so far this week. This behaviour is contrary to the rules of the company which require formal notification of such absence.

The task

As Alan's line manager you now have to take some appropriate action in response to this breach of discipline. However you need to take into account some background information. Below are five examples of alternative background information you might have available. For each of these in turn, how would you address the issue of Alan's absence in the short term (i.e. what would you do now) and in the long term?

Some alternative examples of possible background information:

1. Alan has a history of genuinely poor health but he tries very hard to attend work when at all possible.
2. Alan has a history of poor attendance at work for which he has been warned on several occasions. He appears to attempt to enhance his allowance of holiday time through days off sick, particularly when the local football team is doing well.
3. Alan is an absolutely solid worker who rarely if ever takes time off. His colleagues are sure he took some of the project documents home at the weekend.
4. Alan has a tendency to play the system and take time off for a variety of reasons but this is tolerated as he is the first to put in extra work in an emergency. He will probably come in on Thursday and work solidly until the project is finished (though he might claim overtime!).
5. Alan is one of the most highly skilled and qualified members of the team with a very strong reputation for good work. For this reason his tendency to turn up when he likes is tolerated as it would be near impossible to replace him in the short term.

Discussion and points for further consideration

It is likely that you decided on differing lines of action dependent on differing pieces of background information. However, the breach of discipline was the same in each case. Should the context matter, in the sense that 'rules are rules' and a level playing field should exist for all staff? Should rules in general always be applied in the same way (showing impartiality) or should their application be sensitive to context (recognising the inadequacy of general prescriptions and the need to be sensitive to contexts)?

As Alan's line manager, to what extent do you feel you should be free to manage this situation based on your own perception of the needs of the organisation and the characters of the individuals concerned? How far does your own autonomy and 'right to manage' extend?

If you feel you should have a high degree of autonomy in managing such a situation, do you have the information to make good decisions? In the above case, some of the information is confidential (Alan's medical history and state of health) or impressionistic. (Is Alan really lazy and taking advantage of the organisation? Is he really so valuable to the organisation?) Is there not a danger that we base our decisions on poor or incomplete information and possibly prejudiced interpretations of the information we have to hand?

Summary

Many current theories of ethics revolve round the importance of debate, discussion and agreement within a moral community. As the medium of debate is language we must be very clear what 'moral words' mean and attempt to communicate facts and our arguments in ways which are non-ambiguous. In the later sections of this chapter we show some of the problems of doing this, mainly through descriptions of reality being selective and depending on assumptions of context. Such problems underlie many of the discussions and cases in this book as a whole.

Discrimination and diversity

Purpose and learning outcomes

The purpose of this chapter is to introduce some of the basic issues in
handling unfair discrimination and promoting diversity.
 You will be able to

▶ demonstrate an understanding of the background issues in the
  management of unfair discrimination and of diversity;
▶ show a developing ability in ethical case analysis.

Introduction

This chapter is devoted to one main topic, handled through a discussion
of the key issues in the first section followed by an extended case
study. The initial discussion of discrimination and diversity introduces
a number of important issues, not least the idea that discrimination in
itself is not necessarily unethical. We all make discriminating judgements when we select an applicant for a post, prioritise one project
ahead of another and so forth. Hopefully such decisions are made on
the basis of criteria which are open and fairly applied. Ethical issues
arise when we make such judgement and decisions in a way which is
unfair. Obviously much of the debate must centre on what we mean
by 'fair' and 'unfair'. A further set of issues arise when we contrast
diversity (roughly characterised as an open and inclusive approach)
with unfair discrimination. Not surprisingly, the promotion of diversity
raises its own thorny problems.

 We follow the discussion with an extended case exercise. In this
instance we not only present the background to a case, including a set
of questions for discussion, but also give examples of the sort of
discussion and conclusions one might aim for. There is no suggestion
that these are the 'right answers'. The intention is to show how the
principles of ethics may be used in case analysis and to stimulate
creativity in case analysis.

Discrimination and diversity

In this section we will explore some of the concepts and language underlying this difficult area of management. It will be useful to start by making some basic points about key words which recur in the debate on equal opportunities in the workplace. The first word we will deal with is 'equal' when applied to humans rather than in the precision of mathematics. It is natural to assert we are 'all equal' but what does this mean?

Self evidently we are not equal in terms of physical characteristics, gender, race and age. We can demonstrate different abilities when faced with tasks requiring a physical or intellectual response. We belong to different social groups and have differing beliefs, including religious beliefs, which may exercise a strong constraint on how we behave. Thus we can see why Maclagan (1998) gives his very useful chapter, 'Equality and the Management of Differences' analysing these issues such prominence.

The above individual differences are due to a range of genetic factors as well as upbringing and a series of decisions we have made over the years relating to lifestyle, work, membership of social groups and the development of beliefs and attitudes which structure our social world. They reflect our experiences and responses to opportunities, challenges and threats. They will affect our relative success in gaining the sort of employment we would like and our ability to perform the work tasks our organisation requires and to make an original contribution in the workplace.

We began by talking about equality but very soon went on to differences. So in what ways are we equal? Fundamental is the notion that we are all human beings and are 'equally' together in this world. We are communally affected by the economic and political context, though the word 'inequalities' springs to mind when considering the distribution of society's rewards and ills. In the modern world we assume that adults have equal human rights and children and others who are less capable of making decisions and managing for themselves are entitled to protection. Earlier societies, and some today, would view the idea that humans have equal rights to be nonsense, children to be an economic resource and the unfit to be disposable. Hence our assertions about equality are to some extent a political statement and an ideal. How this applies to an organisational context is of concern to business ethics.

A complicating factor in this debate is the extent to which we also use the word 'differences' to apply to groups rather than individuals. We speak of gender differences, racial characteristics, problems of disability, gay rights and ageism on the assumption that we can make meaningful statements about the common differences of groups of people. At one level it is very useful to cluster issues which are common to groups in order to engage in political debate and form policy agendas. This is often done by people who are championing the rights of all members of such a group. Unfortunately it can also focus opposition on an individual through the use of stereotyping; 'as you are a man you will be poor at multi-tasking' or 'you are over 55 so you won't be able to cope with the pressure of work here'!

It would be nonsense to see an organisation as a watertight world in itself rather than as part of a social environment within which discrimination against particular groups may be widespread. Attitudes from the 'outside' will leak into the organisation and may reinforce a culture which condones unfair discrimination. An interesting debate is the extent to which businesses and public sector organisations have a role in countering this through strong cultures and practices which act against bias. An example from the past would be an organisation with strong policies regarding wheelchair access for either staff or customers. While a hospital needs good access to be able to function, a sporting venue which encourages and makes possible access and good services for everyone is sending a strong message relating to its core values, even if this is also good business sense. Such an example is only from the past as the law is changing to enforce such good practice, as in the case of the Special Educational Needs and Disability Act (SENDA) which is highly prescriptive in the context of the educational sector.

However, the greatest problem in a work context comes from the fact that most work tasks do require particular skills and attributes of the individual who is to perform them. Therefore management has a duty to match individuals and tasks. If job roles are seen as aggregations of tasks and responsibilities, then recruitment and selection are difficult but essential functions within an organisation. It is also important to note that management's responsibility to ensure fairness as well as effectiveness does not end at job appointments. The design of an organisational structure and the management of organisational change can be the key to allowing flexible working patterns or to setting a rigid hierarchy and career structure in place. The latter may favour a male-dominated, conservative meritocracy while the former may allow participation by a wider range of individuals. Management are also responsible for setting levels of pay and remuneration, for appraising staff performance and facilitating staff development. They are also responsible for ensuring policies and practices are in existence to protect staff from harassment and bullying and to ensure a safe workplace. Failure to implement such policies in an effective way can discriminate against individuals and groups just as much as biased selection procedures.

Maclagan (1998) uses a helpful model to explore two further aspects of this situation, the possibility of unconscious bias and the possibility that bias is built into an organisation's policies and procedures. Taken together these give four possibilities which we briefly mention below, using Maclagan's numbering to facilitate reference to the original text:

1. Individual (or group) conscious or deliberate bias against specific individuals or groups because of gender, sexual orientation, race and so forth is the most obvious case of unfair discrimination. Though the bias originates from individuals, the management of the organisation has a responsibility to eliminate it.

2. Deliberate bias may result from an organisation's rules and policies. Particular occupations such as the Armed Forces or the Police may have, or have had, views on the suitability of some work roles for women, the disabled or people over a certain age. Some Christian churches have strong views on the eligibility of openly gay men or women for religious office; at least this issue has now been surfaced and is a matter of open debate. Most organisations ban some activities (e.g. smoking, alcoholic drinks) on their premises. The debate on whether such action is fair (assuming for the moment it is legal) depends on whether such policies are relevant to the work of the organisation and whether an individual can surmount the obstacle put in place. The latter often relates to accepting training and development or the acquisition of further useful experience, typical responses to the unsuccessful job applicant. Difficulties arise when the obstacle relates to age or gender, for example, and effectively bars an individual from some type of work.

3. Individuals (and groups) can act in an unintentionally biased way through habit or ignorance, often by the unquestioning acceptance of past practices and the status quo. In some ways this is no excuse, as professionalism dictates we should continually question our

motives and attitudes. Perhaps a more practical point would be our response when some examples of our unconscious bias are pointed out to us. An immediate acceptance that this is an issue, allied to changes of behaviour, are positive signs! However, damage may already have been done to others, and once again the organisation has a responsibility to raise awareness of issues of unfair discrimination through training and the example set by senior staff.

4. An organisation may display 'unconscious' bias through a culture of high-pressure working, a casual acceptance of discriminatory language, a culture of harassment or an unthinking approach to issues of disability, to give a few examples. As in 3 above, if we assume that such problems will be rectified if the issues are surfaced (or at least be debated as in 2 above), the key is the raising of awareness through, for example, staff actively participating in the work of professional bodies, attendance at external training events, the use of management audits and participation in benchmarking activities with exemplary organisations.

The solutions to problems of unfair discrimination may therefore involve changes to rules or procedures, or even to terminating the employment of recalcitrant staff! They may involve awareness training, the surfacing of old prejudices and working with other organisations. There may be technical solutions involving automation, for example, where manufacturing tasks were previously physically very demanding. This is particularly true where obstacles in carrying out tasks, for example, relating to sight or hearing impairment, may be countered through the use of computer-based equipment.

A more drastic approach is the use of affirmative action, sometimes called positive discrimination, to counter problems of unfair discrimination. Typically a quota system is introduced whereby some number of individuals from disadvantaged groups must be appointed to certain jobs, or jobs may be specially created for individuals who would otherwise not find suitable work. Such systems are more prevalent in the USA and reference to the papers in Larmer (1996) or to other US-based texts is appropriate here. The ethical debate surrounding such deliberate, systematic and legally enforced discrimination is considerable.

Affirmative action is perhaps the strongest and most controversial way of countering unfair discrimination. A more subtle approach is taken in the debate on 'diversity' as shown by Liff and Dickens (in Chapter 5 'Ethics and equality: Reconciling false dilemmas' of Winstanley and

Woodall [2000]). The basic argument here is that in recent years (in the UK in particular) the ethical debate has moved on from arguments about duties, rights and social justice to a more utilitarian stance in which promoting equality is seen as being good for business.

Now at one level, it has always been the case that organisations have considered the groups we have been referring to as potentially disadvantaged to be stakeholders (as employees, customers or members of society) and therefore legitimate parts of the utilitarian calculus. The problem with such a view is that these concerns are not taken as absolute rights but as interests which must be balanced against the utility of other agents. Hence an organisation might not think it cost-effective, on balance, to incur the large capital costs of making wheelchair access to their premises possible and the law may have to step in to protect the rights of wheelchair users, as with the SENDA legislation mentioned above.

This is countered by an argument which is similar to the 'Green Business' approach to management and the natural environment. The argument centres on the idea that diversity in a population is highly valuable, that is that differences are not a nuisance to be ironed out, compensated for or simply borne as a cost but a source of value and originality which is of benefit to an organisation. If we openly acknowledge 'difference' as a normal part of any society (as we did at the beginning of this section, you may remember) then we should value and use such diversity.

A key to this may be how we view an organisation. If we adopt a 'machine metaphor' and try to see an organisation as a well-oiled mechanism then it is likely that 'difference' represents a threat. Engineers tend to favour standard components, an unfair generalisation, of course, and not intended as discriminatory! A 'biological metaphor' might be more appropriate and the idea of preserving genetic diversity can be extended to diversity of individuals, ideas, cultures and approaches. This is a theme extensively developed in texts on organisation theory and on systems behaviour.

Thus we are led to a view in which diversity is to be celebrated as a positive source of value to an organisation in the short term and perhaps an essential ingredient in ensuring long-term survival. It may, however, be prudent not to abandon the practical advice given earlier on countering unfair discrimination until the value of diversity is more widely accepted. A less positive view is to see 'diversity training' as little more than a Public Relations exercise; it is useful for an organisation to say it has run such events if challenged on its policies to counter discrimination.

A further negative point we must recognise is that organisational procedures, intended to counter unfair discrimination, can be used to 'cover the backs' of individuals who have no intention of eliminating bias against groups they do not favour. In this case the observance of the letter, if not the spirit, of anti-discriminatory processes (e.g. in job selection and appraisal) can be used as a politically correct defence mechanism. Shortlisting and interviewing members of particular groups may not lead to their being appointed, as women fighting against 'glass ceiling' restrictions on promotion have found out. The issue here relates more to the moral development of senior managers, moral muteness (see Chapter 14) and the real recognition of value and human rights.

A final point is that 'unfair discrimination' usually relates to issues of gender, sexual orientation, race, age, disability, religion, belief or culture. Each of these present unique as well as common problems, have been taken up by different pressure groups, are the subject of specific legislation and affect different organisations in different ways. There are many agendas here as well as a bewildering array of opportunities and challenges which cannot be hidden by using such bland words as 'difference' and 'diversity'. In reality, though we can debate them as a totality, individual case by case management will present us with a wide range of practical and ethical problems to which our general debate will have hopefully been some guide.

Note that all the references given above contain a far greater wealth of detail, argument and case analysis than we have been able to present in this short summary. This is a major and continuing area of concern. In the UK, new legislation (from December 2003) is aimed at countering discrimination and victimisation in training and work on the grounds of sexual orientation and belief. This follows on from previous legislation on race relations and so forth.

Discrimination: A case with analysis

The task

This is a fairly long case, though only a tiny fraction of the evidence has been presented that would be available to a formal investigation. The case centres on the comments made by David in response to accusations that he has been unprofessional in making an appointment. An important further issue is the role played by Mary and the personnel function in this situation. Some questions to consider while reading and analysing this case are the following:

1. Has David actually done anything wrong, and if so what?
2. How adequate are the company's procedures in this context?
3. Mary's response to this situation appears to be based on political objectives rather than ethical concerns. Is this a fair comment?

At the end of the case we include a discussion relating to the first of these questions. The other two questions are for you to consider in similar fashion, as far as the evidence permits.

Case report

The position of Procurement Department Manager had become vacant at the Swindon factory of IZT International. In reality this has traditionally been a supervision job looking after a team of around 15 buyers and progress chasers for a large assembly plant and distribution centre, but the pay was reasonable and this post was probably the limit of the ambition of many staff in the office. The previous manager had retired and it was generally expected that Jim Smith would get the job, a point contested by Alan Jones who, like Jim, has worked in the office for a number of years. Jim had been acting department manager for the previous month.

The selection process was managed by David Wilson, the Regional Procurement Manager, in consultation with Personnel and the Swindon plant management. A simple format was used whereby the post was advertised throughout the company, shortlisting for interview was carried out by David and the plant general manager, and formal interviews held a couple of weeks later. Jim, Alan and the holder of a similar post in Leeds were interviewed and Jim was appointed.

There was some adverse comment made in the office; 'the usual farce' and 'why didn't they just promote him straightaway if that's what they wanted' were typical remarks but David had no doubt that the right appointment had been made and it was 'business as usual'. The situation became more serious when Judy Lockwood, who also worked in the office, put in her resignation and had a long interview with Personnel on the 'jobs for the boys' culture at this plant. The Personnel function had recently been centralised by IZT which meant that Judy's comments came to the attention of the Group Personnel Director, Mary Leeson. In the past Judy would have received lots of sympathy but little else. However, IZT were becoming alarmed by the staff management processes in some of their recently acquired units.

Mary discussed Judy's concerns in an abrasive interview with David Wilson. David's response was that the procurement function was critical to the Swindon plant, the office had been well run in the past and had largely met its financial targets for reducing procurement costs while maintaining quality and delivery times. It needed to be run by someone with experience and good local knowledge. It was normal to try to make an internal appointment from the Group and the job had been advertised. The shortlist included the only three people to meet the criteria for appointment. On the day, Jim had performed the best in the interviews; Alan had dried up and the guy from Leeds had rambled on about stuff which was irrelevant to the Swindon plant. David had become increasingly irritated at having to explain his actions in this way; 'You've given me the job of managing this outfit so why not get off my back and let me get on with it. Sack me if we make a loss but don't expect me to do my job with my hands tied behind my back.'

After her discussion with David, Mary wondered if there was any situation in which he would not have promoted Jim or Alan. Judy had not long worked for the company and had pointed out that many of the procedures in the office were sloppy and uncritical. Suppliers were rarely changed, unlike her previous employers where a really sharp approach to supply contracts was adopted. However, Judy had no problem in getting another job and had no intention in putting up with the hassle of going through the grievance procedures.

Things became far more serious when Des Wainwright approached Group Personnel with the intention of putting in a grievance claim, citing amongst other things racial discrimination. Des had worked in the Swindon office for five years, though he had felt he had been increasingly marginalised in the past two years. Des was 38, born in the UK of Afro-Caribbean parents. He was well qualified, exceptionally smart and punctilious and very good at dealing with overseas suppliers, though he felt he was being sidelined into working on fairly minor supply contracts. This had been a source of continual argument with the previous department manager, on and between the infrequent occasions when the appraisal system was formally used.

David Wilson strongly defended his decision not to include Des on the shortlist for the Department Manager's post. 'The main part of that job is getting the team to work well together and I don't believe Des had any chance of doing that. Also he hasn't got the breadth of experience in dealing with our big suppliers. That's where the real savings are made, not on those piddling overseas bits and pieces. I know his application looked good; that's typical of him. Nobody would seriously think he could run that office. What do you want me to do? Make him "Manager of Overseas Contracts" with a few extra quid a year?'

Mary walked out of the meeting where David made these comments and requested a meeting for later in the day with the Chief Executive of IZT. She would request, and get, a formal internal investigation which would cover the company's back in terms of any threat by Des and Judy, or anyone else who might now summon up the courage to complain or to go to an employment tribunal. A reorganisation of the procurement function was long overdue and should sort out dinosaurs like David, as well as countering the complacency in the Swindon plant.

Discussion and points for consideration

Let us consider in detail the first of the questions asked at the start of this section.

Has David actually done anything wrong, and if so what?

If we take David's own version of events we have the following quotations with some introductory comments:

'...the procurement function was critical to the Swindon plant...'
Presumably all the functions at the plant are important and there is no evidence that procurement is critical at this time, for example there is no mention of dramatic changes in suppliers or delicate negotiations in progress. 'Criticality' can easily be used as a defence of the status quo.

'...the office had been well run in the past and had largely met its financial targets for reducing procurement costs while maintaining quality and delivery times.'
What is the evidence that the office had been well run and what does 'largely met' mean in this context? Furthermore, is the intention behind this argument to show that Jim was a good manager during his recent temporary promotion; if so, how was this demonstrated?

Alternatively, if the argument is that there is a good team in the office, what are the implications of this for the new appointment?

'It needed to be run by someone with experience and good local knowledge.'
Obviously 'experience' is necessary but exactly what experience is needed, and why is local knowledge important? The argument here is far too vague!

'It was normal to try to make an internal appointment from the Group and the job had been advertised.'
If correct advertising procedures had been followed, this is not David's fault; but had they?

'The shortlist included the only three people to meet the criteria for appointment.'
Shortlisting for interview is a very important activity and should be given the same amount of time and care as the interviews themselves. This is one point at which misconceptions about the post under consideration may be surfaced. It is interesting that no mention is made of such basic documents as a job description and a specification of the necessary and desirable characteristics of the applicant.

'On the day, Jim had performed the best in the interviews; Alan had dried up and the guy from Leeds had rambled on about stuff which was irrelevant to the Swindon plant.'
All a matter of opinion! Who did the interviewing and how was the interview structured?

'You've given me the job of managing this outfit so why not get off my back and let me get on with it. Sack me if we make a loss but don't expect me to do my job with my hands tied behind my back.'
A cry that is still sometimes heard but is nonsense! Managers work in the context of organisational rules and procedures as well as external legal constraints. If the company did make a loss, do we imagine that David would go quietly?

We may note several points from this:

▶ the need to challenge every statement that at first sight appears to be common sense, in particular to challenge the logic of casual statements of cause and effect;
▶ the need to ask for evidence;
▶ the avoidance of overt discussion of motive and intent, though there is a considerable subtext here suggesting that David was taking a minimalist approach to this task and that he resented being challenged.

From this it appears that David has been politically inept in his handling of this situation (see Chapter 10) and that the recruitment and selection procedures are either inadequate or have been poorly implemented in this case. The result of the latter is that Des and Judy may be able to make a case for discrimination, that is they did not, as employees, have a fair opportunity to compete for promotion in this case and may not have been well managed in the past. Notice that no mention has been made here of race or gender in reported conversations.

In addition to all this, we have not made explicit reference to business ethics! In what way, if any, have the characters mentioned here said or done things which could be labelled as 'unethical' within any of the frameworks we have mentioned so far? We can make some preliminary comments:

▶ If we adopt a 'virtue ethics' framework, the protagonists appear to be 'mute' in terms of using moral language and do not seem to consider the issues raised here as important for their personal development or in their functional roles as managers.
▶ If we use a Kantian perspective, making appointment decisions in this way might be seen as illogical in the sense that always following the status quo removes the need for an appointment decision-making process; appointing Jim was hardly a decision! This is not a particularly compelling use of the categorical imperative but the alternative formulation (see Chapter 7) is more useful. David does indeed appear to be using his staff as means to an end with no apparent concern for their objectives and development.
▶ If we use a 'justice' framework, it does appear that Jim is going to 'get the job', but is this actually unfair if he is the best person to do it? Yet one could also argue that Jim is always going to be the best person if 'the job' is in effect defined in such a complacent way. Discrimination may occur prior to the selection decision through setting up the 'job' as something favouring one particular person or through grooming a person over a long period of time.
▶ A consequentialist perspective might appear to be the one used by David if his insistence that his actions were taken to maintain the company's financial success are accepted. However, it is doubtful if this is true even in the narrow sense and if we take a broader and more long-term view of consequences for a range of stakeholders then it is very doubtful if David is behaving ethically. Mary's view is more consistent with this position, which may be reflecting IZT's concerns.

Thus it appears that David's actions are dubious in terms of all the ethical frameworks mentioned above. The same might also be true of other players in this drama, though we have not presented the evidence for that in this short narrative.

Summary

If you began this chapter with the idea that focussing on a single management topic would lead to simple solutions then you may be surprised by the complexity of the result. This is not a peculiarity of this topic; almost any topic in management ethics could be the source of heated and endless debate. This does not mean that progress and resolution of some difficulties can never be achieved. It does, however, suggest that ethical issues should be approached with some degree of caution and care.

We do not include such detailed analysis of cases throughout this book, not least because it might well act as a disincentive for the reader to work hard at analysing them in the first place! In writing this analysis I was continually aware of other points that could have been made and other lines of discussion which could have been followed. This is typical of ethical case analysis, even more so if the analysis is being carried out by seasoned managers who continually see comparisons with their own past experience.

14 Moral muteness and whistleblowing

Purpose and learning outcomes

The purpose of this chapter is to review some ethical issues facing organisations as a whole, with particular emphasis on moral muteness and whistleblowing. The first relates to situations where employees feel unable or unwilling to express moral concerns directly. The second is the opposite extreme where they do so publicly.

You will be able to

▶ show some ways in which moral muteness is present in organisations;
▶ apply the concepts of business ethics to issues in whistleblowing.

Introduction

In this chapter we continue the theme of language and communication but in a rather different fashion. Our first main concern is with the idea of moral muteness, that is with situations where employees find it difficult to articulate moral concerns. This may arise for a number of reasons, for example due to the lack of an agreed ethical language and set of concepts or from the perception that 'moral talk' is not acceptable within a given organisational culture. Now an intriguing possibility is that other management terminology and systems act as a substitute for openly moral language. One candidate is the idea of 'quality' which, despite a confusing history, can be a rallying point for those who wish to argue against perceived unethical behaviour. Thus a 'quality inspector' may see customers being given a bad deal by shoddy products and carry out a crusade against lax production management, using written quality standards and the external validation of quality systems as a necessary defence if threatened with dismissal.

Therefore at the beginning of this chapter we open up some ideas of quality management which are then linked to the idea of moral muteness. Though the use of alternatives to explicit 'moral talk' may be seen as positive in that moral issues surface in a practical way, the point being made here is that real moral discussion is being avoided. This may, of course, be generalised into all manner of other organisational situations. This form of action may be contrasted with the external action of whistleblowing dealt with in the later part of the chapter.

The next sections relate to whistleblowing, that is where an employee of an organisation decides to publicly expose some practice which they feel is unethical. This topic is discussed in almost all texts on business ethics, not only reflecting its practical importance but also the nature of an acute dilemma. It can be, and often is, argued that such whistleblowers are acting unethically and with disloyalty as their actions may damage the interests of their colleagues as well as their employer. The sensitive nature of this issue is reflected in the excellent practical advice which has been generated to manage such situations and which is briefly presented here.

The chapter ends with four short cases, typical of the instances of whistleblowing which occur in the press. It will be noted that this chapter includes an increasing number of references to current issues in the media. It is expected that you will by this stage feel confident to explore books, media and the Internet, as well as your own observation of management practice, for relevant examples of ethical and dubious practice.

Quality and ethics

For a number of years the management of 'quality' has been a key ingredient of courses in Operations Management and more recently within general management. Originally seen as a very technical issue within manufacturing operations, Quality Control (QC) was a topic dominated by statistics and graphs. Yet the word 'quality' has always had a broader meaning which can be used to illustrate some subtleties of how language may be used in an everyday working context.

Quality control has traditionally been an area of conflict where often quite junior (though highly experienced) staff have taken on roles with titles such as 'quality inspector' and a responsibility to maintain quality levels. Financial targets relating to output volumes are a key motivator for both managers and workers. Counteracting this are the levels of customer complaints and cost of waste which drive quality inspectors into a 'policing' role, that is an antagonistic stance which could be difficult to maintain if the opposite point of view ('we must get this batch out today or we'll lose the customer') has been articulated by a senior manager. In the past, quality inspectors tended to win the argument mainly in the context of military contracts or subcontracting to large companies where the industrial customers also had strong quality inspection processes for in-bound goods. The sheer wastefulness of this whole scenario was one of the reasons for the development of external quality certification bodies such as the British Standards organisation, now evident in the proliferation of ISO standards and a range of other bodies such as Investors in People.

The other main factor which led to change in the 1980s and beyond was competition from Japanese companies who turned an obsession with the elimination of waste into a powerful management tool. Increasingly managers in the UK would give examples of 'ridiculous' quality targets set by their Japanese customers, but easily met by Japanese suppliers! The Western consultants, academics and business managers who investigated this Japanese 'quality phenomenon' discovered an excellence in engineering allied to an organisation-wide appreciation of the need for business processes which incorporated 'quality thinking' and a real zeal to make goods which met the customers needs. This provided the impetus for such developments as 'Total Quality Management' (TQM) in the West.

Quality language and moral muteness

It should be evident from the above that 'quality' can provide an arena of conflict within an organisation as well as with its suppliers and customers. The above comments most obviously relate to a manufacturing context where one might think that the formal specification of customer requirements and measurement techniques within engineering would be sufficient to resolve issues. From the narrow perspective of Quality Control this might be the case but organisational human behaviour as well as the competitive context of industry provide a context in which problems are not so easily resolved.

In Service Operations there are additional difficulties. Service quality can be hard to define and if the customers are present they will naturally have views which may be articulated at the time. A personal service, such as a haircut, is delivered in real time to a customer who may have strong views on their needs. Of course this can be an advantage in that a dialogue can develop to everyone's benefit. More contentious areas include healthcare where a frightened patient and their relatives are trying to cope with a situation where they do not understand a treatment being offered which has been explained in technical language and is likely to radically affect all their lives. The 'quality concerns' extend, here, not only to the treatment but to the whole experience of the healthcare situation.

One of the major breakthroughs in the literature and the practice of Quality Management is the understanding that language is important. The word 'quality' has multiple meanings. It can mean something superior, something which meets your needs, or which is in line with a promise (e.g. in an advertisement). It can have a technical meaning in terms of products or processes which 'conform' to a stated standard or specification or can be implicit in a context of human contact, say between a patient and a medical professional. It can be an unapproachable ideal in a mission statement, a brilliant and innovative action or a routinely met goal. It should also be said that most 'quality gurus' would agree with some of the above characterisations of 'quality' and disagree with others, though unfortunately not all gurus will favour the same ones!

It is interesting to note the use of the word 'guru' in this context. Whether this is a misunderstanding of the 'Asian' origin of the impetus towards quality (gurus tend to be associated with the Indian sub-continent rather than East Asia) or a perception that 'quality crusades' have a quasi-religious feel is not clear. Perhaps the uncertainty surrounding the meaning of the word 'quality' has been compensated by the fervour of the consultants selling programmes of change management based around 'quality' ideas. What is clear was the passion communicated by the adherents of the quality movement and disciples of the gurus in the latter part of the 20th century with 'quality' concepts now being accepted as common currency in most organisations. Whether the language is matched with action is something we might all consider on an ongoing basis, and in the context of other case studies in this book.

However, a point made by some authors (in particular see Pratley 1995) is the lack of a link between Quality language and the concepts and models of business ethics. Even if Quality is a technical and practical issue, then such a link will still be relevant, as with issues of productivity, effectiveness and so forth. This reflects the human behaviour and organisational factors seen above. If we see Quality as somehow having overtones beyond the merely practical then a more sustained philosophical analysis is appropriate, as some feel is the case with environmentalism and business.

An idea explored by a number of writers in the area of business ethics is 'moral muteness' in relation to the apparent unwillingness or inability of managers to articulate their actions, decisions and policies in moral language. At a general level, Pratley (1995) quotes three possible explanations for moral muteness as:

1. *A threat to harmony* – moral talk can be intrusive, accusatory and confrontational; it can bolster an image of personal moral superiority.
2. *A threat to efficiency* – moral talk is simplistic, inflexible and inexact; it leads to pointless, never-ending debate.
3. *A threat to the image of power and effectiveness* – moral talk weakens the managers' image of competence and knowledge through the use of a language in which they are not the obvious experts.

Hence by avoiding 'moral talk' in favour of the technically complex and subtle vocabulary of TQM, management control over the agenda and debate can be asserted. Once again following Pratley (1995) we may show the results of moral muteness in TQM as follows:

▶ *Moral amnesia* – achievements in quality management are presented as a technical activity when they, in fact, are often examples of progress in responding to moral demands.
▶ *Narrow conception of moral debate* – often moral language is only used in the context of blatant wrongdoing rather than the analysis of all activities; the latter are presented as technical and practical concerns.
▶ *Moral stress on the individual* – issues in quality management often deeply affect the practitioners who see injustice and bad practice and feel frustrated in how to respond constructively; the language of TQM does allow the expression of such frustrations even if their moral source is only implicit.
▶ *Neglect of moral abuse* – as we saw in the cases above, poor quality management is also bad management; also note that TQM

207

programmes are examples of the management of change, which may also raise moral issues of the treatment of employees affected by change – the 'moral' status of a change to 'improve quality' may be questionable.

▶ *Decreased authority of moral standards* – if the successes of TQM are always presented in non-moral terms, then moral muteness is reinforced and moral debate in the future becomes more difficult.

The above are obviously linked in a number of ways but the overall effect is to show that an area of managerial work with obvious moral implications may seek to hide this to the detriment of future debate.

A final point can be made here to reinforce the problems presented by moral muteness. It should not be thought that quality control staff are the only group who use an alternative 'moral language'. Another area of Operations Management is production planning and control, an area which has attracted a similar group of experienced but junior staff (in the sense of organisational hierarchy) who are, nonetheless, crucial to the success of their companies; a group whose contribution is now recognised through the development of computer-based planning and control systems and the realisation that fast-response systems are feasible in a Supply Chain context. Though the technical content of their work was quite different from the quality inspectors, the imperative of keeping delivery promises leads to what is in effect a moral debate couched in terms of order promising, lead times, excessive stock holding and delivery performance. Underlying this is a very real sense that customers are not always getting a very good deal. While these issues have been strongly addressed in highly technical language, often embedded in computer-based systems, overtly moral language is rarely evident.

Whistleblowing

'Whistleblowing' is the everyday term given to the situation where an employee of an organisation goes beyond normal procedures in reporting instances of alleged wrongdoing by other employees. Though we will explore the broader scope of the use of the term, it is often narrowly applied to the highly emotive situation where an employee makes a public disclosure of wrongdoing in their organisation and suffers severe consequences, such as dismissal, as a result. Thus whistle-blowing raises issues of loyalty to one's employer and colleagues as against the public duty of disclosing something which is wrong. There is an obvious ethical dilemma here, which is why this topic appears in most texts on business ethics.

In practice, as the cases below show only too well, actual instances of whistleblowing are diverse in nature. Whistleblowing, or its threat, may also be viewed in a less than positive light as an attempt to extract some advantage from an organisation. For instance, an employee facing disciplinary charges relating, say, to cheating on expense claims in a public sector organisation might attempt a defence on the lines that 'everyone does it' and threaten to expose this in a local newspaper. Long-term grievances against specific managers may also play a part in a decision to 'go public'.

On some occasions the disclosure might not be public but to another part of the organisation. An employee in a local branch of a retail business may decide to go over the head of her local boss and draw the attention of Head Office staff to dubious local practices. Whether we would call this an instance of whistleblowing or of organisational politics matters less than the key point that normal reporting procedures have been short-circuited.

Typical organisational responses in the past have often been to retaliate strongly against the whistleblower even if the disclosed information is correct. That well-known saying 'don't shoot the messenger' has often been ignored, particularly if the disclosure was public. This is particularly worrying if the disclosure relates to harm suffered by members of the general public (as in some Health Service-related cases) and the whistleblower has made real efforts to raise their concerns within the organisation before going public. In such cases, the disclosure may have been against particularly powerful members of the organisation who have been adept at protecting themselves against audit and internal investigation or have successfully threatened potential supporters of the whistleblower. If this happens, whistleblowing may be seen as a heroic act rather than the betrayal it will no doubt be painted as by those whose actions are now exposed to scrutiny.

With this in mind, professional bodies and the media have become champions of whistleblowing through encouraging it as a public and professional duty. A particular issue arises in the case of the accounting profession where auditors obviously have a professional and legal duty to endorse, or otherwise, reports on the financial health of an organisation. For this reason an unfavourable financial audit is not really an instance of whistleblowing. However, internal accountants also have professional duties and codes of practice relating to the surfacing of problems. An example from the media is the 'Whistleblowers' column in the *Times Higher Education Supplement* which encourages disclosure of problem areas in Colleges and Universities.

The responsible, and politically astute, organisation will now take a proactive stance in managing the potential for whistleblowing. You will note from the opening paragraph, above, a reference to 'normal procedures'. An organisation which has thought carefully how it should respond to the possibility of damaging external disclosure will pay careful attention to lines of communication within the organisation. If a middle manager is doing something which is wrong (e.g. favouring some members of their team by promotion or bonuses for reasons other than their legitimate work performance) and is adept at covering their tracks, then senior management will obviously wish to find out about this for practical as well as ethical reasons. One way to do this is to ensure that confidential comments can be made to senior management by any concerned employee. Thus procedures are put in place, and widely publicised, to support staff who wish to air such concerns. In conjunction with grievance procedures and protection against organisational bullying, an organisation can be seen to have taken considerable steps to avoid the risk of public disclosure and can also be seen in a more favourable light if public disclosure nevertheless happens.

Of course, things are not quite as easy as this in practice! If one takes the example in the paragraph above, a complaint against the middle manager may well come from a member of their team who has not been as favoured as others. This can lead to retaliatory accusations of 'sour grapes', social pressure against them by other team members and a raking up of any evidence of unsatisfactory performance by the employee who has 'broken ranks' and 'been telling tales'. In fact, one of the biggest problems faced by the would-be whistleblower is the gathering of evidence to support their accusation. In the above 'favouritism' case it is more than likely that the accused manager can produce appraisal and performance data to support their actions to some extent at least. The accuser may simply not have access to such data.

Interestingly the position may well be very different if an official disciplinary investigation is undertaken. A more senior investigator will have access to a wide range of performance data as well as memos and emails over a period of time. It may now be difficult for the accused to justify their actions and explain every informal comment made in a private meeting or aside made in an unguarded email! The well-meaning but disorganised and casual manager will be at a disadvantage compared with the careful, calculating politician. Hence such investigations may not uncover malpractice but will be expensive, disruptive and capable of generating a climate of fear and caution in managers who feel likely to be threatened. This, in turn, can be used by a disaffected employee to ensure disproportionate attention is paid to their grievances.

A further and rather obvious point must be made. All the above organisational procedures will have little effect if the whistleblower perceives the problem to relate to top management and the fundamentals of company policy and practice. An employee in, say, a major engineering company which is systematically cheating in claiming costs for government work may well be doing a great public service in whistleblowing but is likely to end up unemployed or moved into meaningless work.

Practical advice for whistleblowers and management

We can now try to draw this material together into a brief classification of situations in which 'whistleblowing' (broadly interpreted) might occur through asking a number of questions:

Is the 'harm' which is being reported against the individual doing the reporting? Some possibilities are:

► Harm solely to the whistleblower (e.g. a grievance such as discrimination)
► Harm to a group of employees which may include the whistleblower (e.g. favouritism)
► Harm to the organisation (e.g. fraudulent expense claims or theft)
► Harm to other stakeholders (e.g. through selling unsafe products).

It should be noted that harm to one group (e.g. customers) may then rebound onto others (e.g. the organisation through product liability claims). Most whistleblowers can argue that their actions are in the long-term beneficial to the organisation, though perhaps not to current management! Whistleblowers may be seen to be more plausible if less likely to directly gain from their actions.

Is the 'harm' sufficiently serious to justify the disclosure?
Serious potential harm to the general public is a context where whistleblowing, however unwelcome to the organisation, is obviously justified. A minor personal indignity is not likely to command respect if publicly disclosed, however much it may be wrapped up as a matter of principle.

Does the whistleblower currently work for the organization?
It is often easier to accuse a previous employer and so avoid some of the social pressure of such an act. If you can argue that your reason for leaving was unconnected with the complaint then you may appear more objective. However, evidence may be hard to find, particularly if possession of documents can be seen as theft. A typical organisational response, after a protracted investigation, may be to admit past problems but give assurances that all is now well.

Is disclosure external and if so was an internal report made initially?
Solving a problem without external disclosure, or at least attempting to do so, is usually seen as desirable unless the nature of the problem makes this impossible.

Is the disclosure anonymous?
If so, it is likely to carry less weight unless backed up with strong evidence or can be seen as part of a pattern of complaint. Of course accusations of such things as sexual misconduct bring with them a whole range of issues of anonymity.

Michael Davis (in Larmer 1996) makes a good point in referring to the 'tragedy of whistleblowing'. In the short term, whistleblowing is bad for everyone. It is stressful and costly for the accuser, the accused and everyone else involved. Investigations throw a spotlight on all manner of organisational activities, may highlight inconsequential failings and damage the confidence of all concerned. Trust is broken and networks of loyalty and mutual help are negatively affected and reconciliation is often so hard that the whistleblower is ostracised and marginalised in the organisation.

The solution is for organisations to avoid whistleblowing through good procedures, lines of communication, education and the encouragement of reporting 'bad news' through appropriate channels. Davis also makes the interesting point that employees can also avoid becoming whistleblowers through the following excellent pieces of advice (adapted here with some contextualisation):

▶ Choose the right job! Though there may be some naturally investigative and crusading individuals who choose morally challenging areas of work, most people find it preferably to work in jobs where they feel at ease with the industrial sector, organisational culture and norms of behaviour.
▶ Be political! Network widely, both formally and informally, and seek to influence events and opinions through developing alliances with other key players. The motivation to 'blow the whistle' can arise from a feeling of isolation, frustration and lack of influence.
▶ Use moral language! A point we mention frequently in this book is the importance of language and conversation in setting a climate of ethical expectation. By widely and openly discussing problem areas, attention can be focussed which hopefully affects actions in a positive, moral fashion.
▶ Be aware of any relevant professional codes of practice and make it known that you take them seriously and will act on them if necessary. The use of an external reference point, for example code of practice, benchmark information ('this is what the best firms do'), quality standards and so forth, adds considerable credence to a moral stance.
▶ Develop the skills of presenting bad news! Telling people things they do not want to hear is a considerable skill and one may speculate that some whistleblowing, at least, could have been avoided through the use of sensitive communication at an early stage.

It should be noted that our discussion has moved on from the 'rights and wrongs' of whistleblowing and any calculus of cost and benefit to a consideration of the skills and character of the whistleblower. While this form of internalisation will not address all the issues in this complex area it is a considerable advance which, taken with improved organisational procedures and culture (i.e. the organisational equivalents of competence and character), may reduce this mutually destructive form of engagement.

Below are some final questions you may wish to address:

▶ What is loyalty?
▶ Who or what should we be loyal to?

▶ When is disloyalty wrong and why?
▶ Can disloyalty be morally acceptable?
▶ Is it loyal to act in the best interests of others even when they do not agree your action is in their best interests?
▶ Is whistleblowing always a betrayal of trust?

Whistleblower cases

In an article in *The Guardian* on 14 October 2003, Clare Dyer draws attention to the legal protection afforded by the Public Interest Disclosure Act and to the charity Public Concern at Work which supports whistleblowers. She mentions a number of cases, the bare facts of some of which we summarise below. I have included a few brief notes (in brackets) after each case in order to stimulate discussion. I would strongly suggest you follow up such references as examples of ethics in practice.

Case 1

A branch manager in a retail outlet was forced to resign after revealing that the regional manager had sexually assaulted two women employees. The regional manager was allowed to leave. The whistleblower was later disciplined on 'bogus grounds' and subsequently felt he had to resign. However, he eventually took his case to an employment tribunal and won a substantial award in compensation. The regional manager was prosecuted for indecent assault and jailed.

Though one can only speculate on the complex reality underlying such a case, it seems barely credible that:

▶ the sexual offences were not treated more seriously by the company;
▶ the whistleblower was in a vulnerable position as a result of his actions;
▶ retaliatory action was taken by the company.

Many less recent cases do, however, seem to have this characteristic of a crude, almost tribal, attitude being taken to any perceived disloyalty to colleagues and the organisation, even when harm has been done to other colleagues. The sexual nature of the offence may be significant here, remembering the ambivalent attitudes to sexual harassment at work evident in many organisations.

Case 2

Some years ago, an anaesthetist who gave information which led to the uncovering of incompetence in the performance of children's heart surgery at a major hospital eventually had to leave the country in order to restart his career. More recently another anaesthetist was able to report another surgeon (now accused of manslaughter through gross negligence) using accepted National Health Service (NHS) whistleblowing procedures.

Hence we can see that things can improve! It really would be scandalous if they did not and malpractice in healthcare could be covered up with ease.

Case 3

A junior manager exposed bribe taking by a senior manager but soon left as he felt he now had no chance of a career with the organisation. After encouragement from the company chairman he returned and now occupies the senior manager's post. The dishonest manager was convicted of fraud and received a substantial jail sentence.

The company could have made their positive view of the whistleblower's actions known at an earlier stage and encouraged an appraisal of his future prospects.

Case 4

An accountant raised concerns about whether a stock exchange prospectus would mislead investors and about other matters with a company chairman, who threw a digital diary at him and threatened to destroy his career. The accountant won a substantial award under the disclosure act.

One's view of the professionalism and common sense of top managers is hardly enhanced by accounts of such behaviour, quite apart from their revealed ethical preferences.

General comments

The overall impression given by this set of cases, and a number of other anecdotes in the original article, is that things are improving to a great extent either in a company's treatment of whistleblowers or in the compensation they may receive in case of retaliation. A similar situation appears to be developing in the USA where *Time Magazine* referred to 2003 as the 'Year of the Whistleblower', no doubt influenced by the uncovering of such scandals as Enron.

Whether this positive development applies also to European business and the bureaucracy of the European Union may be judged from an article in the *Sunday Telegraph* (28 September 2003) referring to the problems besetting on auditor charged with uncovering fraud in the European Union's Committee of Regions. The extent of expenses fraud as part of a 'what can I get away with' culture is vast, but the auditor who has opened this to the light of day has made a large number of enemies and has been treated with spectacular rudeness by his colleagues.

One might speculate whether the attitude to whistleblowers is culturally determined. One finds it difficult to believe that such activity would be regarded as heroic within organisational and national cultures which value group working and mutual personal obligation. Yet the point remains that much public and shareholder money is diverted into the wrong hands in ways that can only be uncovered by whistleblowing, thorough audit and investigation. Public disclosure of such wrongdoing is a vital safeguard in those instances where internal controls are ineffective.

Summary

Moral muteness is one of those pervasive issues that can be seen to occur in many different organisational contexts. The link with quality management was chosen in the early part of this chapter as 'quality language' may be seen as a substitute and robust way to talk about ethical concerns. However, this does not provide a comprehensive solution as 'quality' may itself be seen as a technical construct and some unease in its connotations may be behind the use of alternative words such as 'excellence'. In conclusion we might say that there is no substitute for an informed use of the 'ethical words' (rights, duties and such like) which business ethics has been using for a number of years. Getting people to actually use this rich resource in an organisational context might be more difficult.

The complexity of the issues underlying whistleblowing, the major topic in the latter part of the chapter, should not be underestimated. Action by a past or current employee against their employer may be motivated from disaffection and malice as much as any felt need to disclose to the general public some information of concern. It can also result from an honest misjudgement of facts and issues. It may also relate to malpractice in a small part of an organisation which was unknown to the senior management. For these reasons it is in everyone's interest that robust internal processes exist which have a good chance of effectively handling accusations before public disclose becomes inevitable.

It is interesting to note that similar arguments also apply to allegations of bullying, discrimination and corruption within organisations. Internal investigation and disciplinary processes within organisations are certain to be controversial and difficult to manage. Hence they might well be avoided by all concerned in the hope that problems will go away. This in itself is hardly an ethical approach to management. Accompanying formal processes will be the management of an organisation's values and working culture. This is a difficult area which can easily sound paternalistic and interfering but cases show that the effort is worthwhile.

15 Perspectives from other cultures

Purpose and learning outcomes

The purpose of this chapter is to show how the basic ideas of business ethics developed in a mainly Western context may be complemented by perspectives from some other cultures.
  You will be able to

▶ understand the different perspectives of ethical management as described in studies of management styles in different countries;
▶ apply ethical concepts to some problems of management where different cultural perspectives are relevant.

Introduction

One of the dangers we must attempt to avoid in any analysis of human behaviour is the assumption that there is one correct way to do things, whether this royal road to success or ethical behaviour is based on our theories, our culture or our organisation. The 'our' in the previous sentence may refer to an academic tradition, a national culture or an organisational setting which is confident in its analysis and prescriptions. It goes without saying that the Western academic tradition, favouring scientific rationalism and logical analysis, is a dominating intellectual structure as are the theories supporting the market economy, the political institutions and the industrial and commercial organisations in the west. Though these can be critically assessed from within the Western tradition, there is a danger that such challenges may lack freshness and originality.

  One way we can improve our ability to critically challenge assumptions is to see how things are done elsewhere. Of course this can lead to the alternative danger of over-estimating the advantages of other cultures and under-estimating their problems. However, on balance this approach can be seen to yield considerable benefits in combating complacency.

The recent interest in Japanese management in the west was triggered by the opposite of complacency! The industrial success of Japan in the late 20th century startled the USA and Europe into a reassessment of widely accepted working practices and produced changes of value to many organisations. In the first section of this chapter we reflect on the contribution of Japanese working practices. It should be noted that a more extensive study of Japanese culture is necessary to deepen any understanding of Japanese management. We also do not deal with the difficult issues involved in the adaptation of Japanese working culture into factories in other parts of the world.

The next section broadens out the debate by briefly considering a model which attempts to reflect international cultural diversity. The resulting variables are of some interest when compared with the ethical concepts introduced earlier in this book.

We follow these theoretical sections with a discussion of gifts, hospitality and bribery. Most practical handbooks on how a company representative should behave abroad include advice and anecdotes on how to deal with bribery and corruption. Here we include a simple analysis of some of the relevant issues, partly referring to behaviour abroad.

Japanese management

In this section we will do something quite different from our earlier work, and very different from the material included in many ethics texts. We will briefly look at the management practices which have evolved in a non-Western cultural setting. It is very important to note right from the start that this is an exercise in descriptive rather than normative or prescriptive ethics. For this reason it would not be accepted as ethical debate by many writers. However, it does give us the opportunity to look at management practice from a fresh perspective. Some ideas relating to Japanese management practices have already been mentioned in Chapter 14 and will be relevant to Chapter 20 when we deal with Operations Management.

In the 1980s, there was a great deal of interest in Japanese management practice for the simple reason that the USA and Europe began to appreciate the very positive achievements of Japanese companies in penetrating worldwide markets. The Japanese were seen as a threat! The sense of danger to Western companies was increased when business managers went to Japan and noted that management practices in that country, and in Japanese owned firms in other countries, differed in a number of important ways from Western practice. Such practices as 'Just-in-time', Kaizen and Japanese approaches to quality control were initially dismissed as simply wrong by Western theorists. But managers are pragmatic; if ideas work, as these techniques seemed to do, then you really should take them seriously and learn from them. This was done in the 1990s, with some ideas being adapted to Western corporate culture (thus 'Total Quality Management' was born), some being ignored as more appropriate to Japanese industrial structure, history and culture, and some castigated as authoritarian.

The new range of techniques in, say, Operations Management, product design and HRM (initially relating mainly to manufacturing) have therefore become standard in the context of firms which operate within a worldwide context or interact with global supply chains. However, academic theorists and consultants have not been slow to realise that if Japan can evolve different, and valuable, management ideas then so can other countries. This has given rise to a strand of research and publication in the area of cultural diversity in business. What is unusual and profitable in the way in which European companies do business? More recently much attention has focussed on Chinese management practices. In particular, if we wish to go beyond the 'tricks of the trade' described in popular management practitioner texts, we must ask in what fundamental ways are such practices different from the ideas developed throughout the 20th century by mainly USA- and Europe-based managers and theorists? Much recent work has combined insights from the social sciences (sociology; anthropology, etc.) with organisation theory in a positive way, which includes reflection on the ethical underpinnings of management.

We can illustrate this with a particular example from Hampden-Turner and Trompenaars (1993). A more recent book expounding this material is Trompenaars and Hampden-Turner (1997) (which uses an extended data set and a sophisticated statistical analysis, as described in its appendix). However, the specific example we are using is from the earlier book and makes a particular point we will refer to several times. The authors (in both books) give a number of small case studies which pose dilemmas. These cases have been used by them for a number of years with a range of students from a variety of countries, thus enabling the authors to report the diversity of responses. In this example we are exploring the difference between universal and situational rules and the example is quoted in full below:

> While you are talking and sharing a bottle of beer with a friend who was officially on duty as a safety controller in the company you both work for, an accident occurs, injuring a shift worker. An investigation is launched by the national safety commission and you are asked for your evidence. There are no other witnesses. What right has your friend to expect you to protect him? (Hampden-Turner and Trompenaars 1993)

The authors report that while 94 per cent of respondents from the USA said he had 'no right' to expect protection, only 66 per cent from Japan and 53 per cent from France gave this response (the UK figure was 82%). The inference is that managers from the USA are more likely to follow 'universal' rules than be affected by differences which are situationally dependent. This nicely parallels the debate found in ethics between universal and culturally relative moral norms and reflects the difficulty that proponents of unbreakable rules have with exceptional cases. We must repeat once again that this is a description of diversity rather than a prescription; there is no logical argument given here that one or other approach is 'right', even if such a proposition is meaningful.

The interest in this specific case is in a reported classroom event which the authors use to illustrate just how complex decision-making can be in even a simple case. Evidently a number of Japanese students were very unhappy with this scenario and insisted on giving a group response, as quoted below:

> Promise your friend your support in the version of events which he wishes to present, but plead with him, as a friend, to tell the truth. In this way, you can remain friends and the workplace will be made safer. (Hampden-Turner and Trompenaars 1993)

Several points can be seen from this interesting reaction:

▶ The need to give a group rather than an individual response.
▶ The chosen response is individually crafted to the case, rather than a stock response which would have applied to any of a range of similar situations.
▶ The response attempts to maintain a relationship with the 'friend'.

▶ The key point is made that the 'friend' has an obligation not to place you in the difficult situation of having to lie to help him. Such an obligation might well have different force in different cultures.

▶ There is an underlying suggestion that you may both be breaking rules by 'sharing a beer' (are you on duty as well?); will this affect your response?

▶ The 'friend' appears to be male; is there a gender issue here also, which may well affect culturally conditioned responses?

▶ How would we characterise this case and its responses from the point of view of a 'feminist ethic' (see Chapter 9) where relationships and mutual care take centre stage?

The point I am emphasising here is the complexity which can be seen even in a very simple case. A description of a real situation of this type would no doubt involve other relationships, the history of safety management in the organisation and the working culture of the organisation. A 'universalist' might, however, say that none of this matters; 'a rule is a rule' and there is nothing here to make us deviate from telling the truth (see also Chapter 12 on 'truth and lies'). This can lead to a simple way of dealing with such situations. However, if we are to accept a far more sophisticated view of personal relationships and obligations, which is archetypically Japanese, then we must accept the implications of this.

Looking at the above case study once again, when you sit down for the beer, does it enter your mind what you will do if an emergency arises? In particular, should your friend have already taken account of this and either not had a beer with you in this situation or have immediately owned up in order to save you the embarrassment of lying or pleading with him. As your friend did not do this (i.e. by Japanese standards behaved crassly) is your obligation to him dissolved?

Taking a slightly different line, if you follow the rules and tell the authorities your friend was neglecting his duties how will he, and your other colleagues, react in the future. If, for example, your good behaviour is rewarded by promotion to safety controller, how will they react? Will they assume your behaviour had this as an underlying motive, and can you be really sure yourself that it didn't? Such a debate opens the proverbial can of worms! Moral rules which take into account a wide range of situational factors are difficult to operate but I suspect they are far closer to the way in which many experienced individuals react in everyday moral decision-making.

Let us return now to a characterisation of Japanese management, the above example having primed us regarding the complexity of a culture where relationships and personal obligations are of key importance. Whilst many companies will say that people are the most important asset, descriptions of Japanese management practice show the implications of this. Family relationships are the building block and appear to be the model for a range of other social and work relationships which are life-long. The individual is a member of a range of inter-connected social networks which confer long-term advantages and obligations.

One implication of this is a sharp division between 'insiders and outsiders'. It has often been noted in the international business literature that while the Western manager favours time-effective negotiations based on the completion of a binding contract between companies, his eastern counterpart will only come to an agreement when a relationship of some trust and understanding has been built and the resulting agreement is between individual people. The 'outsider' has to become an 'insider', to some extent at least. This can take time and considerable social effort but the resulting relationship can positively affect business dealings for many years. This makes best sense in the context of traditional lifetime employment within one Japanese corporation or a Chinese family firm but can be a problem with an American corporation with fast turnover of staff. In the latter case, business dealings are with whoever at a given time is 'Marketing Manager (East Asia)' and not with the original contact.

Underlying this, therefore, is a notion of 'moral distance' which is highly problematic in the context of much Western philosophical ethics (see Chapter 19). The utilitarian ideal of the greatest happiness of the greatest number is converted to a calculus where obligations within the group count and those outside do not. The individual now has a boundary of concern defined by such social groupings. The language of deontology (i.e. universal rights and duties) is difficult to apply except as a formal structure which is ignored if the demands of actual relationships get in the way. One point we must make here is that this may be a better description of how much of Western society actually works than we may be willing to admit. The Japanese, with a different history, religion and culture, may simply be more open about it!

To return to management concerns, the Japanese promotion of group working and the ability to develop and to manage conflict and co-operation within an intersecting network of personal relationships naturally fit together. There are a number of sources of good description showing how this works in practice (e.g. Whitehill 1992). While promotion traditionally depends on seniority in a hierarchy rather than performance (which may sometimes be unfair but does reduce in-fighting), work is carried out by teams which interact in a more egalitarian manner. Job descriptions (like contracts) are not seen as central to the reality of working relationships. Leadership tends to be intuitive with an emphasis on the manager working as a coach in the development of subordinates. Design and problem solving activity is carefully considered in order to maintain working harmony – the 'quick fix' is not looked on favourably!

Some unusual features have been observed, for example an emphasis on courtesy (except in timekeeping; it is more important to end one meeting on the right note than rush to the next), care (even reluctance) to contribute in a formal meeting (speak only if you have something to say, thus respecting others in the meeting) and not saying 'no' (i.e. use your skills to work round a difficult issue). At a more technical level, the consensus form of decision-making has often been noted where wide consultation and a search for real agreement precedes any formal signing of an agreement or adoption of a plan.

The work ethic and motivation of Japanese managers in the 1970s and onwards has become legendary. It is interesting to speculate how this has evolved in the new century and how this now compares with Britain and the USA. The changing economic circumstances of Japan and the growing strength of other Asian economies must have an effect at the national level as well as in terms of organisational structure and the perception of the work–leisure balance by current Japanese managers. The description of the traditional Japanese organisation will inevitably be dated, with organisations around the world adopting each others' best practice.

An interesting issue is the effect of the development of mobile communication as well as computer systems. The skills of face-to-face communication have inevitably to be adapted as email and personal phones change the nature of communication itself as well as the structure of networks. The Japanese have long been regarded as expert in non-verbal personal communication, including the use of silence. These skills have of course been seen as desirable in the west and techniques such as Neuro-Linguistic Programming (NLP) have been developed to improve them (see Chapter 17).

Finally, it has been noted that a strength of Japanese management, as characterised by the studies reflecting practice in the 1970s onwards, has been the way in which a number of features (life-long employment; relationship building; consensus decision-making) fit together and are mutually reinforcing. As the environment changes, some of these features may no longer be viable and it is interesting to speculate on the effect this may have on the structure as a whole. When Western companies have taken parts of the mix (e.g. quality circles) and attempted to introduce them in a different context the results have been mixed to say the least. Sometimes the inherent good sense of an individual technique has won through, with some adaptation, but on other occasions it simply draws attention to the shortcomings of the host company.

The value of this discussion for any consideration of business ethics is first of all to break out of any 'royal road to success' complacency which can surround a traditional hierarchical, rule-following view of organisational structure. Implicit within this complacency is a language which mixes moral and practical prescription in a rhetoric of the 'right way to manage'. This can now be challenged. Perhaps the most obvious attacks are on the nature of stakeholders (i.e. the extent of the networks of concern to an organisational decision maker) and on the way we relate to each other in an organisational context. It should be noted, however, that this critique hardly touches the fundamental nature of the business enterprise in a competitive market economy. There is an important strand of economic literature on the different industrial structure of Japan and how this affects managerial actions. However, the West and Japan agree on the need to compete, as does the emerging Chinese business system. If we require a critique of the business environment as a whole we must look elsewhere.

A model of cultural diversity

Having noted in our description of Japanese management that some analyses of cultural diversity have been made, we now turn our attention to a more formal model based on Gatley *et al.* (1996). Their 'Cultural Profiling and Analysis System' (CPAS) is an attempt to model the diversity in culture and attitude between individuals in organisations in different countries. In this sense it has a similar scope to Trompenaars and Hampden-Turner (1997) and both books may be viewed as basic introductions to this type of work. Our concern is to link the definitions of the cultural variables with concepts in ethics rather than reflect on the national scores the authors have measured. These variables are based on a wide range of concepts drawn from organisation theory and the social sciences and are summarised below (based on Table 8.3 in Gatley *et al.* [1996]).

In each of the following a cultural variant is introduced with a short description and some note of the expected extremes of behaviour. This is followed by a brief comment on the moral implications of this cultural variant having a significant effect on behaviour.

Time

This may be seen as a sequence of events or as a circular process. The former is associated with short-term thinking and the latter with long-term thinking. Within consequentialism, a long-term view is often preferable to fully appreciate the implications of actions (e.g. relating to environmental concerns or client relationships).

Emotion

The expression of emotion in the workplace is being explored here, the range of behaviour being between feelings expressed and feelings not expressed. This distinction is important within Humean ethics, ethical discourse and in an ethics of care, though other approaches (e.g. Kantian) may see this as irrelevant.

Hierarchy

Organisational structure is referred to here with a flat, 'bottom-up' structure compared with a vertical, 'top-down' structure. Bottom-up structures are thought to encourage participation and a flow of information.

Relationships

The separateness of organisational and private lives is a key variable with their total separateness being contrasted with the situation in some cultures where work extends into private affairs. Situations where public and private responsibilities overlap can lead to self-interested decision-making.

Status

It is interesting to ask how is status allocated, the opposites being through achievement as contrasted with such things as age or social standing. Issues of fairness may arise if achievement is ignored, inadequately measured or seen as less important than such things as social standing.

Profit
Are the goals of business exclusively profit or social contribution, some mixture being represented by a middle point on a scale between extremes. We might link this to the range of stakeholders to be considered.

Systems
The systems orientation is usually seen as a contrast between a task orientation and a people orientation, though one might ask if these are mutually exclusive. A human orientation should be present (e.g. to preserve dignity and participation) even if task effectiveness is necessary.

Ambiguity
We might ask how situations of ambiguity are managed, the suggested range having an empirical and experimental approach at one extreme and an analytical approach at the other. A combination of approaches seems desirable to ensure ethical decision-making.

Rules
We have often commented on the contrast between universal and situationally sensitive rules. This is a very important area of ethical concern and fundamental disagreement.

Control
The style with which people assert control is modelled as ranging between assertive and confident on one hand and reflective on the other. Assertive and (rather than 'or') reflective seems to be desirable.

Gender
There is a considerable popular literature contrasting masculine independence (see as dominant and ruthless) with feminine interdependence (seen as sensitive and supportive). A supportive culture recognising inter-dependence seems ethically appropriate in many situations, though the need to take decisive and unpopular action will always occur in many business contexts.

Group
Moral responsibility may be seen to apply to individuals (as in highly individualistic styles of leadership) or to groups. The latter relates to the problem of moral agency; moral norms usually apply to individuals, but is this appropriate in an organisational context?

A quick glance at the above would place the USA at the first of the mentioned 'extremes of behaviour' and Japan at the second. This is borne out by the data collected, with the exception of the 'gender' column where Japan scores very strongly as 'dominant and ruthless'. This demonstrates a tendency to cluster orientations for these countries, but others (e.g. Italy and France) score with a mixture of orientations.

The point we are making here is that descriptions of cultural diversity show systematic variations, linked to country of origin, in organisational behaviour. These variations have implications in terms of how managers view organisational life and the fundamental values inherent within organisational contexts. This is all in addition to the organisational cultural diversity which seems to arise as a result of the history of a company and the people who play a key role in its development. These variations can also be linked to some factors in business ethics, which may be fundamental (e.g. whether rules as seen as universal or situational) or practical (e.g. support the application of the principles of ethical business in real world contexts).

Gifts, hospitality and bribery (case exercises)

Scenarios

In the late 1970s, Ian was a regional sales executive for a large firm selling materials to companies. Every Christmas he had the task of going round the purchasing departments of all his major clients and delivering large turkeys and other seasonal fare. This was done quite openly by Ian, by his competitors and by the reps of other major suppliers to this industry. There were a small number of companies which had strict policies discouraging such activity, though all companies would be sent Christmas cards, calendars and similar routine, low value items. This type of activity was seen as traditional and expected behaviour and few would admit that it affected the buying patterns of the recipient companies' staff, though it did help to maintain ongoing relationships. Privately, Ian would admit to being irritated by the whole business, which would take most of December to organise and carry out and resulted in the waste of excessive goods received by most buyers. It also led to petty jealousies within and between recipient firms.

Frank also worked as a sales executive but his work was quite different, involving selling large items of sophisticated equipment made by an overseas supplier. It was normal to take senior staff from the prospective purchasing company to see similar machinery working in other firms and at the manufacturer's plant, trips which could involve overseas travel, with accommodation and meals paid for by Frank's company using high standard hotels. Frank's company also paid for trips to exhibitions and conferences which inevitably involved some relaxation activities for all concerned. Occasionally such activity would be challenged as unnecessary so Frank was careful to ensure that schedules were reasonably tight and the trips were seen as businesslike in terms of information gathering. The major problems that did arise were often when public sector clients were involved and such trips were challenged as a waste of public money. The high cost of this activity was, of course, eventually borne by the clients as part of the price paid for the equipment. Though Frank was adamant that clients did gather a great deal of essential, practical information from some of these visits, it often seemed to be the case that excessive numbers of client staff needed to make, and repeat, the trips! Perhaps the client's manufacturing director did have to take his technical staff on one visit, and then have to repeat the trip with his finance director and the managing director, but the whole process seemed excessive.

Ted worked in a similar situation to Frank, but in a context where several companies directly competed for the sale, which was usually decided through a tendering procedure. He had no qualms about the number of visits, the luxury of the accommodation and the scale of entertainment. He did, however, expect some helpful information would come his way to help with bid preparation. This might be through the usual social interaction during visits or extra information received at later crucial points in negotiations. He would never directly pay for such information but favoured building long-term relationships with companies and staff.

As Frank's company expanded their activities he found himself involved in overseas sales. At first he was confident that his way of working and large circle of contacts would continue to guarantee success. However he soon found that in some countries the norms of behaviour differed, sometimes being unreceptive to the proffered levels of hospitality and sometimes expecting more! The greatest variation was in public and government agencies where 'fees' were expected by agents and a variety of other well placed individuals. When challenged it was simply stated that these people were providing a service and expected remuneration.

Discussion

It is all too easy to characterise bribery as a secretive payment made to an individual in a situation of power and influence in order to gain some unfair advantage. This might be to ensure a decision is made in favour of the person making the payment or for the receipt of some crucial information. A variation on this theme is coercion, where the recipient insists on the payment using a threat to disadvantage the payer. It is quite clear that such activity is the perversion of a process intended to provide fair competition or resource allocation.

The above scenarios attempt to show that life is not so straightforward. Ethical dilemmas can still exist. In the first scenario, Ian may be seen as taking part in no more than a harmless social ritual. Yet this activity is wasteful of time and money and causes friction both within purchasing departments and between them and other parts of a firm. Most firms would now have procedures which tightly control the receipt of even token gifts. An effective supply relationship can be built without an expenditure which does not benefit other stakeholders. We could therefore simply use advantages and disadvantages for other stakeholders as a means of analysing this type of problem.

The second scenario shows Frank engaged in activity which can almost certainly be justified as providing essential information for major equipment purchase. Hence we could argue that other stakeholders will benefit from such information gathering. It is not sensible, therefore, to simply ban such trips but it can also be seen that they can lead to problems. The issue is where to draw the line; after a tough day visiting factories abroad, how much hospitality and entertainment does the tired executive really need and who should pay for it?

Perhaps the public sector cases where officials and elected individuals are criticised may give us some way of approaching this issue. Assuming that no direct charge of corruption is being made, the reputations of the individuals involved will be affected, perhaps damaged to the extent of making their roles untenable. Public office requires that the trust of the general public is maintained. Therefore the individuals involved would be wise to ensure they had good, publicly expressed reasons for trips abroad. We can see that the framework shown in Chapter 10 involving 'warrants and reputations' is relevant and useful.

Ted's approach is closer to the 'anything goes, provided it's legal' ethos which is the public's view of how much business is conducted. Provided Ted does not actually offer bribes for information, then his view is that anything which happens to come his way in terms of useful information is well and good. The need to be ethically responsible is turned round onto the recipients of his largesse. The pressure is social rather than financial in a crudely direct manner! Is it unethical to tempt other to behave unethically? Issues of reputation and of moral development might be brought into play here, particularly if we view the firm and its suppliers as a moral community. There is an obvious, and accepted, need for such a 'community' to find effective ways to regulate its affairs.

Frank's overseas work raises a standard problem in international business ethics, that is the extent to which local norms of behaviour should be adhered to or ignored in favour of the norms of the developed economies. The latter are usually termed 'universal norms', though this might be thought an example of ethical cultural imperialism! This issue may be explored through the use of the integrative social contract theory given in Chapter 8, though no easy practical solutions should be expected.

Summary

The literature on international cultural diversity and management practice is of considerable interest in its own right. Relating this to business ethics provides further challenges which reflect the moral dilemmas likely to face the business practitioner operating across national boundaries. While it might be easiest to assume that Western business practice (like the English language) is internationally recognised, this not only ignores what Western business might learn from other working cultures but exhibits an alarming complacency in the face of growing competition from increasingly powerful economies around the world.

This chapter has included a mixture of description and situational analysis. The description of the working practices of other cultures is based on published research which has been growing in volume for a short time. The status of the explanatory models used by the authors quoted above is not fully established but clusters of similar behaviours can be identified and related to ethical concerns, particularly in relation to the nature of duties and obligations within quite narrowly defined social groups. This can be related to the discussion on moral distance (see Chapter 19) and is of continuing ethical concern.

The final topic included in the latter part of the chapter explores some important issues in ethical management. Bribery is a standard issue dealt with in most texts on business ethics, the aspect we have concentrated on being the difference between the legitimate giving of gifts and actual bribes. These last two topics are of general interest though international comparisons add considerable flavour to the discussion.

Managing risk

Purpose and learning objectives

The purpose of this chapter is to apply ethical principles to the analysis of organisational risk and the responsibility of senior managers when disasters occur.

You will be able to

▶ demonstrate an understanding of the language and concepts of risk management when applied within an organisational context;
▶ be aware of the practical need to apply risk management in areas of potential danger;
▶ understand some of the complexities of carrying out risk analysis and apportioning blame when disasters occur.

Introduction

The discussion on risk management in this chapter has some links with other chapters as well as some new ideas which are important from both an ethical and a practical perspective. Issues in health and safety management are mentioned here and again in Chapter 20. This work is followed by a summary of a classic case study concerning the rail accident at Clapham Junction.

We then move on to the linked issue of the responsibility of senior managers when a disaster occurs which involves their organisation. This interesting topic gives us the opportunity to explore the relationship between ethical responsibility, time, risk and information in a specific context, thus allowing us an opportunity to draw together some of the main themes in this chapter, and indeed in this book.

This chapter ends with a set of discussion questions relevant to Part III as a whole.

Risk management

As risk and uncertainty are concepts which figure more strongly in this book than most on business ethics, we shall now take some time to explain the basics and draw out some elementary ethical points. We are also concerned here with the subject of risk management, an organisational process which has become far more widespread in recent years and would usually be regarded ethically correct and even necessary.

A simple definition of risk might be 'a possible future event which may harm us'. It will be worth our while to expand this using some accepted terminology:

> An identified risk is an event or situation which we have predicted may occur in the future and which, if it does occur, will be disadvantageous to some stakeholders of the organisation.

The first point to note in all this is the linking of the word 'risk' with harm or disadvantage, that is risk is seen in negative terms. This fits well with the idea of risk assessment as part of a Health and Safety audit, for example. Here we would be happy, though unlikely, to eliminate all risks. We would do well to remember that in a commercial context we seldom make profits without accepting some degree of risk. The hackneyed phrase 'speculate to accumulate' sums this up quite well! Strategic planning sees risk and uncertainty in markets as desirable in that these may be situations which can be exploited. We note in our discussion of 'Precipice Bonds' (see Chapter 19) that the higher rates of interest available should have been seen as indicators that greater risk was present in some way.

Our next point concerns the idea of an 'identified risk' which we have predicted may occur. It is useful to draw a distinction between risk and uncertainty, seen in some economic literature though not universally accepted. We can sum this up by another commonly used characterisation: 'If you don't know which of a number of outcomes will occur, but you can assess the odds, that's risk. If you don't know the odds, that's uncertainty.' It was more elegantly expressed by the economist Frank Knight in the 1920s:

> Uncertainty must be taken in a sense radically distinct from the familiar notion of Risk, from which it has never been properly separated... It will appear that a measurable uncertainty, or 'risk'

proper... is so far different from an unmeasurable one that it is not in effect an uncertainty at all.

Similarly Keynes wrote the following, referring in the 1930s to the chance of another war with Germany:

about these matters there is no scientific basis on which to form any calculable probability whatsoever. We simply do not know!

Note: These quotes, and many others, may be found in Bernstein [1996] which is a good general and non-technical introduction to the idea of risk.

I am labouring this point because it seems essential to grasp the difference, from a practical and an ethical point of view, between decision-making situations where we can assess risk and those where we have to recognise that uncertainty is present. We can often assign responsibilities for the management of risk whereas the presence of uncertainty is organisationally more dangerous, even if it is inevitable. Thus when we are discussing the management of a risk, we assume we have the following advantages:

► knowledge of the structure of the problem or decision;
► an understanding of the range of outcomes;
► some ability to assess the likelihood of each outcome.

Our understanding of the risk situation may be imperfect, or may even be wrong, but we have the basis for management and therefore such situations are preferable to uncertain ones where even this structure is lacking. Bernstein (1996) expresses the implications of this very well:

The essence of risk management lies in maximising the areas where we have some control over the outcome while minimizing the areas where we have absolutely no control over the outcome and the linkage between cause and effect is hidden from us.

Bernstein's last point should be carefully noted. Risk management is often more than accepting that a risk exists; it entails doing something about it! However, if we take action to mitigate a risk (see below) we must be able to assess the effect that this action is likely to have.

Before moving on to some details of how risk management works, it is necessary to point to a difference of opinion between scientists working in this area. Those working in the area of the physical or natural sciences and the technologies which accompany them will traditionally assume that risk assessments can be made in an objective manner. This is usually expressed through mathematical models involving probabilities which have been based on observed data of one kind or another. Such 'objective probabilities' also underpin the forms of risk management which have grown out of attempts to control technological risks, for example, relating to the performance and quality of everyday household goods. Such work can be technically highly sophisticated; the province of experts.

However, much has been written in the social and behavioural sciences (e.g. by sociologists and psychologists) on the subject of risk perceptions and dread. Risk perceptions are seen as being personal and based on judgement of a range of factors while 'dread' (i.e. real fear of particular consequences, often extreme harm or death) is seen as strongly affecting attempts at arriving at objective probability assessments. A phrase seen in the literature is that risk is 'socially constructed'. Some management situations, for example health care, must obviously take heed of the ways in which populations characterise and assess risk.

In fact there has been a technical literature on 'subjective probability' for many years and it is unfair to caricature technologists as being unaware of this contrast between objective and subjective risk assessment. From an ethical perspective it is obvious that situations where it is assumed that risks can be objectively assessed lend themselves to a utilitarian calculus, that is we can still base our decisions on results but things are now more complicated in that probability assessments enter the picture. Economic models of decision-making tend to have these characteristics. Where risk assessment depends on the perceptions of individuals it seems more useful to engage in some kinds of discussion and sharing of perspectives in order to understand the ethical context.

The risk management procedures currently used in organisations are mixtures of the two approaches. Much operational risk assessment, particularly when considerable data history is available (e.g. quality control of manufactured goods; setting insurance premiums for commonly occurring risks as in car insurance), is biased towards objective probability assessment. By way of contrast, long-term planning and strategic management often has to recognise major sources of uncertainty and more consensus-based approaches (e.g. scenario writing and role playing) are preferable. In all situations, we then have to recognise the human and organisational element implicit in setting responsibility and taking action.

If we look at typical sources of business risk we will find the following:

► The environment (political, economic, social and technical)
► Competitor action
► Supplier problems
► Failure of designed products, processes and projects
► Customers
► Inadequate systems and procedures
► Employees.

It is difficult not to notice that this list is similar to a list of stakeholders! Indeed many risks come from problems in an organisation's relationship with its stakeholders or with failure in things the organisation has designed (products, services and processes). This strengthens the view that working with stakeholders may be appropriate both ethically as well as reducing risk. The environment may well be a source of uncertainty as well as risk (see the section on 'Chaos and complexity' in Chapter 6).

The basic risk mitigation tactics consist of variations on the following themes:

► avoid the risk, often by taking on an alternative risk;
► transfer the risk to another party (e.g. by insurance) or share with a partner;
► reduce the risk; this will involve either reducing the likelihood of harm or mitigating the effects of any harm which may occur;
► managing the risk, for example by increased vigilance, better staff training;
► accept the risk and provide a contingency fund.

The ethical implications of each of the above will depend on the situation. For example it may be reasonable to accept the risk of a project delay due to bad weather in some situations rather than in others, depending on the implications for each stakeholder. It is unlikely that accepting the risk of injury to staff without trying to find a better solution is ever an ethical approach.

It is particularly important to note that the effect of the various management tactics will differ between stakeholders; indeed changing the impact on stakeholders is often the whole point. Your insurance company is better able to accept the risk of your house burning down so you pay them an insurance premium to do just that. A company which suffers from overdue deliveries may work in partnership with the supplier to shift the financial loss due to lateness of supply on to the supplier. This is not simply dumping the problem on the supplier as the supplier will now be motivated to do something about it; the 'win–win' situation to be aimed at in such a relationship.

We have referred to the approaches above as 'tactics'. These can be contrasted with more long-term and radical 'strategies' which aim at managing the context of risk taking. Some examples of these might be to move into more profitable markets or even to improve the organisation's capability to manage risk. The latter, an example of a learning organisation, is particularly worthy of note as a possibly ethical way forwards in situations where ignoring risks can harm stakeholders.

Another way of viewing risk management is not through the specific tactics but through the infrastructural characteristics which are intended for risk management. These may be briefly listed as follows, it being assumed that some combination is likely to be effective in practice:

▶ *Rules and procedures*: large, technological organisations will often have extensive rules and processes for managing all kinds of risk. These may be highly detailed, actions being recorded and responsibilities defined by role in an exhaustive manner.
▶ *Organisational structures*: concepts of risk ownership and personal responsibility may figure strongly as ways of ensuring that people are fully aware of their individual responsibility. Professional responsibility may be a part of this.
▶ *Organisational culture*: the everyday habits of organisations and the routine use of simple procedures can be valuable in many ways, for example in avoiding accidents through good working practices.

We mentioned earlier the contrast between technological and social science views of the perception of risk. A more comprehensive working through of this theme is found in Hood and Jones (1996), on which the notes below are based. This contrasts seven pairs of contrasting attitudes to risk management. The views found in the first of each pair, or in the second, do not necessarily fit together or are likely to be consistently seen together in existing organisations. However there may be a tendency for some such association of ideas to be seen in practice. We are presenting this here more as an aide-mémoire of some interesting features of risk management rather than as a comprehensive organisational theory.

- *Prevention*: risks can be anticipated and managed proactively using known cause and effect relationships.
- *Resilience*: anticipation of key risks is not effective in complex systems (and may be counterproductive) so resilient systems must be developed.

With a prevention strategy, risk is seen as a technical problem with widely disseminated responsibility for working to established risk management procedures. The development of a resilient organisation is a strategic management responsibility and may well have considerable financial implications.

- *No blame*: a 'no-fault' approach promotes information flows, effective crisis management and organisational learning.
- *Strong risk ownership*: targeted blame give a strong incentive to risk owners.

While this shows a practical contrast between differing blame cultures, there is an obvious ethical dimension to the acceptance of responsibility and obligation beyond the motivation of targeted blame.

- *Quantification*: measuring risk factors leads to rational decision-making and avoids political manoeuvres.
- *Judgement*: most risk factors can not be quantified.

Care must be taken when making assumptions about the perception of risks by stakeholders, particularly when a paternalistic or non-engaged culture exists and clients are not fully informed.

- *Organisational science*: knowledge and organisational learning can improve organisational design.
- *Art*: there is no secure knowledge for improving organisational risk management.

The latter cannot be taken to mean that responsibilities can be ignored if risk and uncertainty is present. The former should not be allowed to lead to overconfidence.

- *Risk management is good management*: other goals are complementary.
- *Risk management is an expense*: safety, in particular, is a trade-off against other goals.

Though safety is an obvious ethical priority, it is not clear whether or not it is always in fact an additional expense. One of the roles of external agencies, such as the Health and Safety Executive (HSE) in the UK, is to ensure that failures of attention to safety issues (in products, facilities and in working practices) is always expensive, if necessary through the legal process awarding punitive damages.

▶ *Closed management*: risk assessment is a matter for the experts.
▶ *Open management*: broad discussion avoids errors and improves information availability.

Our previous discussion on the promotion of moral dialogue in organisations would obviously favour the second alternative. However such broad discussion needs to be informed by appropriate research, particularly in health contexts where the dread of some negative outcomes may have a massive effect on stakeholder opinion.

▶ *Structure*: a top-down approach based on hierarchy and procedures.
▶ *Culture*: top management should develop an effective risk culture in the organisation.

Both have their place!

Health and Safety in context

Having engaged in a considerable discussion on the principles underlying risk management it might be useful to look at some issues in Health and Safety management. On the face of it, the carrying out of risk assessment in the context of Health and Safety at work must be a good thing to do. However, we can easily come up with a number of examples to argue that this view is too simplistic, including the following:

1. A travel operator notes a slight risk of a fault in its transport and withdraws a service, stranding a large number of passengers. The obvious alternative form of transport, the car, has far higher accident rates.
2. A manager's assertion that the time spent filling in Health and Safety documentation is diverting him paying full attention to the operational safety of his company.

These point to the complexities of cause and effect in social systems and the inevitable tensions between risk taking by individuals in an organisation and by the organisation as a whole. Risk assessment obviously tends to focus on specific, targeted types of risk and is a powerful tool in establishing actions and responsibilities relating to identified risks.

Where the action is to 'not do something', then sufficient attention has to be given to the alternatives. In the travel example above, what alternative forms of transport were provided? If these alternatives (or a 'do nothing' approach) also carry risks then these are also relevant, but attention to them may not be part of the job description of the individual directly involved.

There is more to this than an obsession with Health and Safety. If risk assessments are carried out at an operational level they may well lead to prohibitions which are not accompanied by less risky alternatives, finding the latter being someone else's job! Strategic risk assessment should look at the broader picture and make explicit trade-offs involving risk. However, if you are the manager who will end up explaining your action in court, surrounded by 'experts' armed with hindsight, then you might feel that a very conservative approach to risk is the right way forwards.

However, this discussion is put into perspective by the scale of loss and injury caused when major disasters occur. It is sobering to note that such events may be directly caused by a small mistake, though it is our responsibility to look at broader patterns of cause and effect and the responsibility of management in such situations. The next section gives, without comment, a summary of one such major disaster. You are invited to draw your own conclusions.

Clapham Junction Railway Accident

The narrative below is based on the official Report into the accident (Hidden 1989). The Report relating to this accident is particularly useful in its analysis of management responsibilities and provides a useful bridge to the next section in this chapter. In view of the number of railway accidents which have occurred subsequently, the lessons contained in the Hidden Report may need revisiting. The details below provide a brief summary of the narrative and analysis contained in the Report. These are extremely clear and easily related to the earlier text in this chapter. They are followed by a brief discussion. No specific case analysis tasks are set, though points for discussion are obvious from the case text. Some possibilities for more general tasks are noted.

At around 8.00 in the morning of Monday, 12 December 1988, three trains were moving towards a cutting close to Clapham Junction Railway Station. There would have been nothing unusual about this situation if the signalling equipment had been working correctly. The passenger train from Poole had passed signals in its favour at some speed, but on clearing a left-hand curve (where visibility had been obstructed by the bank of the cutting) the driver saw the Basingstoke passenger train stationary in its path on the same line. Despite full braking the Poole train collided with the rear of the Basingstoke train, the collision forcing it out into the path of a third, fortunately empty, passenger train travelling in the opposite direction. All near the front of the Poole train, 35 people, died in this accident and 69 people were seriously injured.

The actions taken by the train drivers were correct in terms of the information they had available at the time. The accident happened because the signalling system had not worked correctly. During alterations to the system a few days earlier, a wire was not removed when it should have been and this prevented a signal turning to red. We therefore turn our attention to how this had been allowed to happen.

The wire in question was not removed by H, a senior technician who was working in the relay room on Sunday, 27 November. In addition to this, H made a number of errors that day which were part of his normal working practice and similar to those made by other workers. The specific error which caused the accident should have been noted in an independent wire count which did not take place. H worked large amounts of overtime around this time, earnings being doubled by working the weekend after a full week. This is likely to have affected his vigilance. He fully accepted responsibility for the mistake but the investigation uncovered a culture of excessive working, lack of supervision and inadequate training in correct working practices.

H was considered to be a good worker, capable of planning and carrying out work by himself. However he appears to have learnt his skills through experience and watching others rather than through training in sound and robust working methods. Though documentation existed which set the standards for working practices, H (in common with other workers) found this material difficult to understand and never grasped either the detail or its significance.

B had responsibility for supervising H but he did not even enter the relay room on that day, being heavily involved in other work (much of it manual rather than supervisory). He therefore did not carry out an independent wire count, expecting H to do it himself as was customary practice. He was not aware that such wire counts were required for this project and did not know of them being carried out in such a context.

British Rail (as it was at that time) put safety as the key objective in running the rail system. Earlier in the year a policy of TQM had been adopted, though the 'quality plan' for this department had not yet been put into action. The accident investigation noted two incompatible aspects of the statements of workers and management:

► a completely sincere emphasis on the overwhelming importance of safety;
► a widespread failure to communicate and implement the working practices which would improve safety.

While the direct cause of the accident was work carried out in the relay room, errors and omissions permeated the organisation. In the report 16 errors are listed along with 28 recommendations.

it is the task of management to be aware of the working practices to which its workforce works and to ensure that those standards are of the highest. It is the task of management to ensure that its instructions to its workforce on how work is to be done are clear and that they are in fact obeyed. It is the duty of management to see that its workforce is properly trained and that such training is renewed from time to time. It is the duty of management to ensure that the efforts of the workforce are properly monitored and supervised so that the quality of the work may be maintained at the proper levels. (Investigation Report, Section 17.9)

Discussion

The official report is particularly useful in drawing out the responsibilities of managers at various levels in the hierarchy. You may wish to read the original report to fully appreciate the detailed arguments. You should also consider this incident in the context of the discussion in the next section on the moral responsibility of senior managers.

Unfortunately there have been a number of serious rail accidents in the UK both before and after Clapham. A very useful project is to compare and contrast these events in terms of the evolving risk management approaches they demonstrate. It is interesting to note that while rail employees and participating organisations will always emphasise the over-riding importance of avoiding accidents, serious events of this type do seem to recur.

Disasters: The moral responsibility of senior managers

The main theme of this section is the moral responsibility of senior managers when their organisations have caused a major disaster to occur. A subsidiary theme is the interplay of time, risk and information within an organisation and their effect on channels of communication in a management hierarchy.

In recent years there have been a number of disasters where large corporations have been involved. These include such things as Bhopal and the Challenger Shuttle case. Much has been written about whether or not the senior management of such organisations, in particular the Chief Executives, should take the blame. In this section we will air some arguments surrounding this issue which have broader application as well as providing an example of ethical analysis. Our main reference is a paper by Bishop, with a response by Larmer, in the collection of papers Larmer (1996). These two papers, like this section, are concerned with the nature of moral responsibility in such contexts rather than the highly technical issues of legal liability.

In simple terms, the issue we are exploring here is whether or not the senior executives of large corporations should be held morally responsible for disasters which occur as a result of some action or omission by their employees or a sub-contractor acting for them. The focus is on large businesses because one of the key concerns is the flow of information in such an organisation, as we will see below.

In order to construct a compelling general argument, rather than analyse a specific case, it is useful to consider some boundary instances where an attribution of moral responsibility is clear. At one extreme we might consider what is usually known as an 'act of God', the usual shorthand for an event which is thought to be beyond anyone's control. Both of the above writers consider this to be a clear case where executives cannot be held morally accountable. This is quite simply because it is usually considered as a fundamental axiom that if we are to be held morally responsible for something then we must have been able to do something about it. This would mean that we have both the necessary information and the wherewithal, that is the authority, power, resources or whatever was needed to intervene.

This seems clear and straightforward but we might pause and check exactly what this means in an organisational context. Let us assume that damage was caused by an earthquake to a building our organisation had constructed in a way that was inadequate to withstand such catastrophic events. The actual occurrence of that particular earth-quake might have been unpreventable, or even unpredictable, but if the building was situated in Japan, a country prone to such events, we were surely remiss in allowing it to be built in this way. Even if it had been built before we assumed our responsibilities as a senior manager it might be argued that we should have had an adequate risk management system to show that this was a possibility. If the building was in England and had been constructed in such a way that all appropriate building regulations had been complied with, then it is difficult to see what it would mean to say we were morally responsible. In some business cultures (e.g. traditionally in Japan), it might be normal for the Chief Executive or the President of a corporation to resign in such a situation. This does not, however, signify an acceptance of personal moral responsibility in the sense outlined above. It is, rather, a corporate way of saying 'we are very sorry this has happened'; a way of empathising with the victims rather than an admission of guilt or legal responsibility. The individual who has resigned would be found an appropriate position and remuneration.

Therefore for a senior executive not to be held morally responsible in any way we should really consider both the recent event and the organisation's degree of preparedness and risk management. If manage-ment can really say it had done everything that was necessary in advance and at the time to the highest possible standards, then any attribution of moral responsibility would seem perverse and a dilution of the idea of 'moral responsibility'. Nothing is to be gained by defining moral responsibility in such a way that all managers are culpable when-ever anything goes wrong, quite apart from whether they could have had any effect on the cause of such an event.

The other extreme case is where a senior executive not only knows that a grave risk exists but fails to do anything about it even though they could have, that is prevented the occurrence or given a warning. This may happen as a result of a commercial gamble to avoid the costs of prevention or the loss of revenue due to the withdrawal of a service. Issues of personal gain or managerial incompetence may also be present in such a case. Once again, though this situation may be thought incontrovertible, businesses do take risks and things may go wrong. If a comprehensive risk analysis and mitigation exercise has been undertaken and the organisation fully communicates the risks involved to all stakeholders in a context where the benefits are generally held to be considerable, then the decision to go ahead might, in hindsight, have been wrong but are the senior managers morally responsible? If, as I mentioned above, personal gain has clouded the issue or management is simply not competent for the tasks in hand, then we will be more certain in our moral condemnation. Note that this form of risky action may be justified on a utilitarian basis (i.e. through risk analysis and cost–benefit comparisons) or by arguing that the managers had taken all reasonable steps to prevent a problem occurring within an industrial context that was admittedly risky.

Thus extreme cases can be constructed, though attention to time and risk is necessary. This is not explored in the above way by Bishop or Larmer who do, however, concentrate on a particularly tricky situation which exists somewhere between the two extremes. This is the situation where the senior executive was not personally in possession of the information that a disaster might soon occur even though this information was held somewhere within the organisation. It is a recurring theme in the extensive case analyses of disasters that 'somebody knew' the key facts but they did not communicate them.

First of all we might ask why such important information might get stuck at a level where inadequate attention or action resulted. One possibility is habit. A recent disaster (involving the 'Herald of Free Enterprise', see Allinson [1993]) involving the sinking of a car ferry was due to the ship moving off when its bow doors were still open. Evidently this had occurred regularly in the past but not to the same extent. Similar causes may exist where poor working practices result in disasters, as in the Clapham Junction accident (see in pp. 241–244). Another possibility is the ineffective use of communications channels, for example where a dire warning is presented within a complex technical report sent to senior managers who simply do not appreciate the significance of the information it contains. Another possibility is that the relevant information is outside normal information flows, for example, with a sub-contractor. It is also possible that the relevant information is held piecemeal within the organisation but nobody has sufficient overview of all the facts to feel they need to sound a warning.

Human factors can also be to blame. Individuals may feel they have already 'told their boss' and hence the problem is no longer theirs. If the culture of an organisation is to 'shoot the messenger' then nobody will be keen to bring potentially bad news to senior management. Even the opposite can occur, where an employee who is always telling management about potential risks is eventually ignored, reminiscent of the fable of the boy who shouted 'wolf'.

Of course, there can also be good, practical reasons for making sure that bad news and warnings are transmitted upwards, such as showing one is diligent in one's job or making sure your back is protected! The key point is that the effective management of information flows is not a new concern of organisations. It has always been an issue and the need to manage information was well known even before the advent of IT-based systems which have greatly increased the potential for problem visibility. Hence it may be the case that a senior executive did not have the information that a problem was developing but cannot entirely escape responsibility for ensuring an appropriate organisation structure and information system are in place. In practice, this may be a very tough view of what a senior manager can achieve but it is surely reasonable and well within commonly accepted notions of what being a top manager entails.

Bishop attempts to argue that an executive who did not have the information that a disaster might occur is not morally responsible at the time but is professionally responsible. Larmer deconstructs the idea of 'professional responsibility' as a device intended to handle cases where the senior manager really was shocked that a disaster occurred but where some doubt exists as to whether he really had taken all sensible steps to guard against its occurrence. Surely the easiest way to handle such cases is to say that the executive is not morally responsible for the disaster but is morally responsible for his less than effective management over a period of time. He may also be unlucky to have his incompetence found out in such a way, particularly in view of the presumably large number of managers who keep theirs hidden!

We have arrived at a point similar to Larmer's and differing from Bishop mainly in the use of words, but have taken the opportunity to emphasise the dimensions of time, risk and information. This is part of our general theme that these are important in modern day business ethics. There are a few final points we make, however, on the subject of the moral responsibility of senior management, reflecting some comments made in passing by the above writers.

The first is that if we are to be so cautious and forgiving in attaching blame to senior managers, perhaps we should be similarly careful in linking the success of their organisations to their actions. Surely one of the reasons for the general public's distrust of the bosses who resist blame for disasters is the sight of their contrasting willingness to accept large salaries and honours for 'their' success. The practice of senior managers accepting large payoffs as severance packages when they have been unsuccessful is therefore even more distasteful.

A second point to note is that we have not even attempted to discuss or resolve issues of joint blame, even though the nature of corporate life is such that responsibility for effective risk management and information flows is hardly likely to rest with one individual. It may be convenient to identify one top person as a scapegoat but this does not reflect real personal moral responsibility. Some attempts have been made to consider the organisation itself as a 'moral person', similar to the way a company is a legal entity. Though this possibility has generated a complex technical literature (see Frederick 1999) it is simpler in an introductory text to see it as a metaphor with 'moral responsibility' being an essentially human attribute.

Finally Larmer points to the moral responsibility of executives to know their own capabilities and limitations. Is it morally responsible to take risks and engage in large and complex ventures which stretch your managerial abilities far beyond their proven boundaries? The resulting disasters may have wide ranging costs which make their heroic origins seem trivial and reckless.

Summary

By dealing with risk management in the context of operations and environmental management (see also Chapters 20 and 21), we have moved attention away from the management of financial risk to a sphere where it is of particular value and where ethical problems are evident. It should, however, be remembered that financial risk management is important in Corporate Governance (see Chapter 22) and it is this part of risk management which is most readily identified by many senior managers as a corporate strategic issue, except perhaps as far as it relates to Health and Safety. We would argue that all risk management is a corporate issue and is of ethical concern.

The final part of this chapter considered hierarchical responsibility, or 'where exactly does the buck stop?' This fascinating and important topic shows once again the importance of a consideration of information flows when carrying out ethical analysis and prescribing good practice.

Questions for discussion – Part III

The 4 discussion questions given below relate mainly to material covered in this part but may draw on earlier material and introduce new ideas and perspectives. These questions are intended to supplement the case-based exercises found in this part in providing an impetus for critical questioning.

Question 1

It can be argued that there are two types of potential ignorance in the context of bullying:

▶ the concept of what behaviour is to be classified as 'bullying';
▶ the fact of whether or not a specific person is being bullied.

The main thing we know about bullying (whether mental, physical, overt, covert, etc.) is that it is a bad thing, that is the term is invariably used as condemnation. The same behaviour would attract a different word if it was not to be condemned. We might also ask if a specific instance of bullying can have good consequences? Perhaps, for example, it leads to a fundamental change of behaviour, though we note that this will involve other causal factors. However, the original intention to bully is still not seen as good and 'bullying' in general can hardly be seen as leading to good consequences.

In the light of these notes, what is bullying and why is it wrong?

Question 2

When the Brooklyn Bridge was being constructed in New York in the 19th century, compressed air was used in the caissons where workers dug out the foundations for the bridge piers. This innovative working practice unfortunately resulted in severe illness and fatalities in the work force. There was no shortage of workers willing to participate as the pay was good. No other way of building the piers was seen as practical at that time and the extent of the health problems resulting from this working practice had not been foreseen. How would you assess the moral responsibility of the managers of this project?

The chief engineer was willing to undergo the same working conditions as his men and continued his work when seriously ill. Would this affect your view of moral responsibility in this case?

Question 3

One complication for workers making claims for compensation due to illness caused by asbestos is that if an individual worked for more than one company where they may have been exposed to asbestos, then they can not claim damages from any of them. Is it moral for institutions to actively pursue this point to the detriment of individual claimants? (i.e. to use the law to block what is otherwise a reasonable claim reflecting real harm done).

Question 4

Comment on the ethics of David Brent's management style. (*Note*: If you have never seen the television programme *The Office*, ignore this question.)

Part IV Functional perspectives and cases

Introduction

This final part continues the basic theme of Part III by introducing further topics and cases, though now within functional headings. This allows a consideration of ethics specifically related to areas of work, management and stakeholder concerns.

Chapter contents

Chapter 17 introduces a major change in direction from the generally applicable topics in Part III towards a consideration of topics related to general and personnel management. Here we meet performance management, training, discrimination, bullying, surveillance and a number of other everyday issues in organisational life.

In Chapters 18 and 19 we move our attention to marketing. These chapters include some important theoretical sections and we should note that 'marketing ethics' is in itself a substantial subject with its own specialist texts and theories focussing on ethics in a competitive market context. Of particular interest here is the concept of 'moral distance' which has a wider application, particularly in descriptive ethics. We then move to considering some instances of unethical behaviour based on recent events, in particular in the selling of financial products. If you find these examples interesting, you will have no difficulty following them up and finding new examples in the financial press.

Chapter 20 is based around some issues in Operations Management and the management of change. It also links with the ideas on quality in Chapter 14 as well as the theoretical work relating to 'moral muteness'. When considering marketing in Chapters 18 and 19 we restricted ourselves to 'business to consumer' contexts. In this chapter we broaden this to 'business to business' contexts and to the ethics of outsourcing overseas. In many ways Chapter 21 also relates to operational concerns, though now with a focus on the 'green' environment.

Chapter 22 begins with a discussion of the work of accountants in organisations and the ethical issues posed by these key roles. This is followed by some brief notes on Corporate Governance. We end by a discussion on whether morality may be confused with long-term expediency and a case study relating to a situation where strategic information from a source which the firm might not wish to disclose. This chapter also includes some discussion questions relating to Part IV as a whole.

Case studies in Part IV

The chapters in this part of the book explore ethics from a more functional or job-related perspective. There are a large number of textbooks devoted to each of these functional areas, some of which pay explicit attention to ethical concerns. Many of the cases found in such texts may be used as the basis of ethical analysis. This is also true of texts which focus on (Corporate) Strategy.

Chapter 17

Outward bound training – a case example

This case is placed before the section to which it refers as the intention is to motivate a discussion of some ethical issues in HRD before the reader is presented with a more formal set of ideas and issues. The underlying theme in the case is the extent to which an organisation may insist on the participation of its employees in 'training activities' which might seem peripheral to the tasks they normally undertake at work. It also explores issues of negligence and physical harm and thus relates to an employer's duty of care.

Bullying – a case study

There are few more emotive issues in HRM than bullying at work. We explore some of the ethical concerns through a short case. The tasks set emphasise the importance, once again, of language, description and reporting bias in a context where words may well be used in different ways within different working cultures. It may well lead to lively group discussion!

Controlling Internet usage – an exercise

A problem which frequently arises within organisations is when employees use 'company resources' for their own personal benefit. At one extreme this may involve actual theft while some will argue that any unsanctioned use of 'company time' is effectively theft. Access to the Internet has given many organisations a major problem of effective management and equity.

This case sets up a basic situation and asks you, as manager, what action you would take. Your choices are set in the context of a discussion of the issues which are likely to arise. This case should be of particular value to students with management responsibilities and might be explored through group discussion or role play.

Surveillance – some illustrative examples

This section includes eight illustrative situations where ethical issues arise in common work situations. Like the previous cases it explores issues of management control and well as bullying. Students might be encouraged to contribute their own similar examples.

Expenses claims – a case

This chapter ends with a more outrageous narrative which includes a wide range of examples of dubious expenses claims all within one example of escalating wrongdoing. This intention is to provide some light relief at the end of an exhausting set of moral problems, though the issue being explored is serious and potentially very damaging to an organisation. Students will no doubt contribute yet further examples of organisational misbehaviour!

Chapter 18

Chapters 18 and 19 both deal with aspects of marketing ethics. The 'theory' sections contain a number of anecdotes which may be used in a similar way to the cases listed below.

Selling disease – a modern fable

While referred to as a 'fantasy', this short case sets up an imaginary situation which is closer to reality than one might wish. It refers to instances when the need for a product appears to be artificially generated, which may be innocuous in many contexts but worrying when health products are involved. It might be used to generate class discussion and to collect similar, though real, examples.

The salesman and his contacts – an exercise

This case places you in the role of a Sales Director faced with a series of option for managing a difficult problem where dubious ethical action may be leading to short-term profitability. It asks what you would do and how you might avoid such a problem in the future. Students with less experience of managing a sales force may wish to focus on why 'John's' actions are wrong. Students with greater management experience might wish to explore perceived and real tensions between ethical and practical management.

Ethics and marketing strategy – an exercise

Using a context of the aggressive promotion of products aimed at children prior to Christmas, this short case focusses more on the ethics of market strategy than people management. It might be followed up with a selection of the many cases available in specialist marketing (strategy) textbooks. Even when such cases have not been written with ethical analysis and debate as the main intention, they almost invariably can be approached in this way.

Chapter 19

The text in this chapter contains much anecdotal material which may be used in a similar way to the more formally structured cases found elsewhere. The two 'cases' detailed below are unusual in structure and might best be used as starting points for wide ranging discussions or further empirical investigation.

The car payment plan – a personal narrative

The story which forms the basis of this case relates to an incident with which students may be able to identify and which raises a number of ethical and practical questions. However, the questions contained in the case are rhetorical in that one may simply never know the answers as they relate mainly to the knowledge, attitudes and motivation of the salesman. This narrative may simply be read as text, noting the points made, or discussed mainly in terms of generalising these points to other situations.

Precipice bonds – a discussion with case examples

The issue at the centre of this section is highly topical and therefore the material presented here might best be seen as an introduction to further research. The ethical points raised are important for a wide range of stakeholders.

Chapter 20

Is health and safety always a good thing? – a case exercise

This short case introduces the idea that debate about 'Health and Safety' may not always be as straightforward as it seems.

Chapter 21

Bhopal

There are a large number of texts and cases dealing with this tragedy, including the issues of long-term health damage and compensation which are a current concern. In this chapter we focus mainly on the operational causes of the incident. Students may wish to discuss this in isolation, to carry out research into the more general background of the case or to compare this with other industrial incidents which led to major loss of life and environmental damage.

Chapter 22

Information from a secret source – a case

This final case relates to a context of corporate industrial espionage. It raises a number of major issues, including balancing obligations to various stakeholders, and might therefore be seen in the context of the ideas introduced in Chapters 3 and 22.

17　The management of people

Purpose and learning outcomes

The purpose of this chapter is to apply theories of applied ethics to some areas of the management of people, with a continuing development of case analysis as a tool for the exploration of dilemmas.

You will be able to

▶ understand the importance of the concepts of business ethics in the context of some problems of the practical management of people;

▶ apply a structured approach to case study analysis.

Introduction

This chapter is the first of a series which focusses on different functional areas of management. It does not include new material on basic ethical theory, though it does include two sections relating business ethics to key areas of organisational life. It contains five case studies and exercises which introduce a number of key points and should therefore be seen as an essential part of the text rather than a set of additional activities. The cases vary considerably in their approach, presentation and intention, but it would be useful for you to look back to Chapter 11 and the advice given there on case study analysis before or during working with the case material in this chapter. You may also wish to refer to the list of ethical principles in Chapter 11 to ensure that relevant issues are being considered.

The first section of text is on Performance Management. In this chapter the topics chosen for discussion centre around the management of people, or 'human resources' to use the term favoured by the professions in this area. You might wish to consider whether the use of this term, and its associated management practices, is consistent with a Kantian view of respect for human dignity. Performance management can mean different things depending on the approach taken, but here is seen in the context of the routines of modern personnel management, that is selection, appraisal, performance review, resource planning and suchlike. There are a large number of texts on HRM and several which deal explicitly with the ethics of HRM. This chapter gives some flavour of the resulting debates.

We then include a case which challenges the ethical nature of a common form of management training. This case leads into a discussion of HRD in an organisational context, a key part of HRM strategies. We end the chapter with a further four cases illustrating common problems and concerns in any organisation. The reader is invited to apply ethical principles and theories to each case and also to consider how they would manage similar situations in practice.

The cases in this chapter are not based on direct reporting of identifiable events but they are based on experience and observation of practical management. Unless specific references are given, they are presented as imaginary situations, thus allowing for a clear statement of problems, something which may not be present in the muddle and complexity of a real business context.

It should be noted that the summary at the end of this chapter contains a number of reflections on topics which are not otherwise dealt with in this book and therefore might be considered as a separate section of this chapter. It is important to remember the breadth of material and range of management situations which might reasonably be included under the heading of organisational ethics but cannot be included here due to reasons of space.

Performance management

If you work in any modern organisation, in particular one with, or aspiring to, Investors in People certification, you will be familiar with appraisal interviews, which may in turn be linked with all manner of performance measurements and the development of action plans. This is all part of a web of policies and processes including performance management, HRD, rules for disciplinary processes and the development of performance improvement plans. It may also be linked to pay and promotion. From a HRM point of view the intention is partly to ensure fairness, that is a level playing field in relationships between managers and subordinates, but also to introduce formal processes of human resource planning which can be synchronised to business planning systems including financial and product output forecasts.

It is quite easy to view this whole set of actions in a mechanistic way, that is one forecasts future levels of business activity and then plans to have a suitably sized and capable workforce in place. As forecasts are inherently provisional, it can be useful to encourage flexibility and multi-skilling in your workforce in order to allow for most possible futures. Of course, if things do not work out so well, then there are severance packages available along with retraining and placement schemes. Now it can be argued that the existence of such plans are to employees benefit, in contrast to friendly if chaotic systems which are less effective in preserving the business and leave workers abandoned if the business fails. However, they are costly in terms of staff time and other resources and have an underlying consequentialist ethic which appears to give primacy to organisational goals and performance measures.

Alternatively we can view business planning systems as obviously necessary and seek to address legitimate personal goals and interests, for example the need for flexible working, personal development or career ambitions, within this context. If individual and corporate needs can be simultaneously satisfied, and this is often the case, then we have no problem. If this is not the case then we have the potential for a damaging ethical dilemma and a range of practical issues.

Though we have characterised this approach as consequentialist, we must assume that the legally defined employment and human rights of employees are properly addressed. However, if we take a more strictly Kantian view, it does appear that individuals are being viewed as a means to an end rather than full attention being given to their own ends. It is by no means clear how this can be fully resolved. If an employee's 'ends' can be fully summarised in their pay packet, then this can be addressed in a variety of ways, though even if we do consider the problem to be 'one dimensional' the solution may involve difficult negotiation at an individual or group (e.g. Union) level. Even a quick glance at the reporting of industrial action in the press will show that 'pay disputes' often have other dimensions such as working practices, flexibility, hours worked and plans for downsizing of the workforce.

A further issue arises with, typically, professional and managerial staff who see their own 'ends' to also include extensive personal development, career enhancement, new and challenging opportunities and other appropriate benefits (e.g. cars, status-related benefits, etc.) as well as pay. The negotiations surrounding such things, at appointment or appraisal, may be conducted in a ruthless fashion on both sides or may use a language of self-actualisation but will still have to take into account business and personal realities, including the relative power and negotiating position of the participants.

Many modern management techniques and the language for discussing such issues are designed to at least give the appearance that the needs of individuals and the organisation are being taken into account in an ethical fashion. An example is the presentation of multi-skilling to an individual worker as a positive personal development even though it has been introduced with workforce flexibility in mind. A comment I have noted on a number of occasions from shop-floor workers is the complaint that they have been taught some new skills but have not then been given the opportunity to practise them. One can see the employer as preparing a contingency human resource plan which involved such training but not carrying it through to the practice of these skills, which would have made the whole exercise of some benefit to the workers, for example in terms of future employment, bonuses or simply the motivational value of more varied work. Another similar example is the rhetoric surrounding flexible working.

More radical critiques of management practice seize upon such devices as examples of managerial hypocrisy, or the impossibility of 'the system' (e.g. a competitive, market context) ever being reconciled with a genuine workers' perspective. Thus the above issues in performance management and similar approaches to human resource planning are to be seen as symptomatic of an inevitable paradox in the employment relationship. This is in line with the radical critiques of management which characterise business ethics as irrelevant to a debate which is really about power and politics. You may wish to pursue this in Winstanley and Woodall (2000), in particular their Chapter 11.

Outward bound training – a case example

The task

The description of a situation given below is intended as an introduction to some basic issues in HRD and also to illustrate a dilemma relating to the moral right of employees not to be involved in activities which they may argue are peripheral to their work. It should be read carefully, noting the role of the narrator and considering any information bias the report may contain. The case ends with some points for consideration and leads directly into the following text on HRD.

Context and incident report

As the newly appointed training manager in a medium-sized company, you have noted a complete lack of any imaginative forms of staff training or development. Employees are a mixture of functional specialists (including a substantial proportion of IT staff with mainly technical skills) and administrative support. Though staff are generally regarded as professionally competent (and the company is profitable in a highly competitive software development market), they habitually tend to work as individuals rather than as a team despite frequently being encouraged otherwise. Some improvements in interpersonal and communication skills might also be welcomed as direct contact with clients is becoming more frequent.

It has been decided (in consultation with team leaders and senior management) that some short, residential courses focussing on skills development would be of benefit. The chosen external training provider is a local organisation which strongly recommends that some 'outward bound' style physical activities (including hill climbing and team-based initiative tests) should be included. This is agreed as being 'just the right sort of thing for our staff' by the Chief Executive, an ex-rugby player!

It quickly becomes apparent that few will volunteer for these courses and great ingenuity is shown by staff in avoiding particular events, citing appointments with key clients during the week and family commitments at the weekend. This is seen as typically evasive behaviour by the organisers and eventually groups of staff are brought together and the courses run. The events are moderately successful, except for a number of serious problems relating to the physical activities. The employees involved have a wide age distribution and show considerable variation in physical fitness and aptitude. In some cases, as intended by the organisers, this leads to mutual help and encouragement. Unfortunately, and despite some initial cursory health checks, several minor injuries to staff occur, followed by a serious heart condition becoming obvious in one participant and requiring emergency medical attention and an extended period of absence from work.

On the evening after this unfortunate occurrence, a furious row develops between a senior and highly respected team leader and the

Chief Executive, the former arguing that these events are not just a waste of time and money but also a serious infringement of the rights of individual staff. 'We're employed to design systems, not to be treated like schoolkids and subjected to trite and demeaning rituals in the vague hope we might learn something about how to work with people. I've spent the last 20 years learning how to work effectively in this industry and a lifetime interacting with people in all sorts of situations. Your bullying insistence we all conform to your idea of socialising has led to real hurt and injury.'

Discussion and points for consideration

Quite apart from any issues of negligence relating to the above, to what extent can a company expect, or demand, employees to participate in activities to which they openly object? How far should a company go in encouraging participation when there is an obvious unwillingness to take part? Note that both ethical and practical considerations may be relevant here and these may complement each other or may be in opposition. As training manager, what lessons might you learn from this situation.

Human resource development

A very basic classification contrasts training with education and with development. Training is seen as the mechanistic acquisition of skills, as typified by shop-floor manufacturing skills, basic administrative routines and the abilities to use computer systems effectively. The contexts in which skills are taught and learnt are reasonably well understood, though the acquisition of very complex skills such as language learning are the subject of much psychological investigation. Education is usually characterised through the improvement of analytical and critical faculties as well as the achievement of knowledge and understanding in a substantial subject area.

The use of the word 'development' in a business context is more contentious. We naturally feel personal ownership for our individual development, including our moral development, as we take this to include our feelings and judgements. It would seem pretentious to say we are involved in developing another person in this sense of the word, though we all do in practice have an effect on the development of others. The word 'development' may also be used in the sense of Organisational Development (OD), a professional activity concerned with bringing about changes in an organisation.

Now, if we reflect on the above, we can see that training, education and development are not watertight compartments even though their central thrust may vary. It may be nonsense to divorce skill development from knowledge acquisition and we might also note that the practice of very high levels of skill (e.g. in an art and crafts context) is demanding on the knowledge, feelings and judgement of the individual. Unless we unhelpfully define 'skills' as simple, mechanistic routines we cannot separate them from other forms of learning about the world and intervening in the world. We also should not split the exercising of a skill from the moral evaluation of the consequences of its use.

To separate education from personal development would also show an odd way of looking at the world. We should, of course, recognise the need to maintain objectivity when exercising the skills of analysis and discussion in an educational context, particularly in management and social areas of knowledge, but to be unaware of the influence of our subjective biases and the effects of our personal history and moral outlook on this activity is dangerous and perhaps intellectually dishonest. You will note the ways in which skills, education and personal outlook were mixed together in the previous sentence!

Now this is familiar territory for child development experts, psychologists and other education specialists. Our purpose in introducing it here is to consider its repercussions in the context of HRD. A great deal of the above type of activity takes place at work, or is sponsored by organisations, often specifically to meet organisational objectives. Indeed some techniques and approaches have been developed specifically in a work context. Examples are the notion of the reflective manager and approaches to learning which centre on action and evaluation of results.

An example of the use of a management development approach which is very popular in the context of teambuilding and leadership training, as well as selection and appraisal of new staff, is the residential outdoor activity programme, of which outward bound is typical. Participants may be subjected to physically rigorous training regimes, including activities which increase stress in order to encourage group support. There are some basic issues of safety and psychological well-being in this context but in addition it is not clear what right an organisation has to insist on such activities for employees or how fair would be to include them as appointment selection activities. Assuming that the core business of the organisation does not require actual competence in such real activities (i.e. we are not talking about the Armed Forces where such competencies are core) then the training activities used are devices to encourage 'character building', reflection on group working and problem solving. Even the more professionally run programmes must be considered ethically dubious unless genuinely based on volunteer participants.

A side issue is the extent to which, say, office workers should be physically fit. In the context of considerable publicity about excess weight and general physical unfitness in children and adults, an organisation may argue that it has the right to expect reasonable standards of fitness in its employees, even when such fitness is not directly linked to characteristics of their jobs. However, there is a difference between providing membership of a local health club or organising sporting events for employees to be enjoyed on a voluntary basis, and insisting on such activity. Though there is a grey area where to not volunteer and join in may marginalise an employee in their work teams, a policy should exist which protects the general rights of employees. At a practical level, attempts to coerce participation are likely to lead to ingenious and widespread subversion and political counter-manoeuvres, a traditional way in which an ethical balance is restored in the workplace!

An interesting contrast is the use of psychological techniques to improve work performance. An obvious starting point, well known to anyone who has taken a management course, is motivational theory. There are several basic models (borrowed from psychology and substantially critiqued in research-based literature) such as Maslow's hierarchy of needs and Hertzberg's hygiene factors idea which promise the manager some leverage in getting their staff to actually do what managers have decided is required. This is particularly evident in the literature on job design which, as well as including physical and ergonomic factors, addresses issues of motivation. If a job is designed as a coherent whole and allows some levels of worker autonomy this appears to be motivationally positive as well as ethically reasonable. Indeed if this design is carried out in consultation with all those involved we may have a situation which is seen as ethically positive, though critics of standard management approaches will still view it as manipulative.

More controversial are techniques such as NLP which involve a far more thorough approach to the study of human behaviour and attempts to modify it. The study of body language and of communication facilitating techniques in this methodology make it useful in contexts of sales training. This does leave it open to charges of being manipulative of customers (in the context of sales negotiation) and of an organisation's management ethically subverting their own staff by insisting on its use. NLP's use, along with the issues introduced above, is more fully addressed in Winstanley and Woodall (2000, Chapter 7).

Bullying – a case study

The task

It is suggested that you read the following short case and then carefully work through it in order to answer the following questions:

1. What items of information do you note in the case as being particularly significant, do you suspect any sources of reporting bias and what further information would you need to assess whether disciplinary action against the team leader was appropriate?
2. Comment on apparent differences in 'working culture' in this instance.
3. Assuming that the events detailed in the final paragraph could have been predicted, should this have affected the inquiry in any way?
4. What ethical principles can you bring to bear on this situation?

Case report

A well-respected and highly valued sales team leader in one division of your organisation has been accused of shouting at a female member of administrative support staff and making comments of a derogatory nature. The team leader is male, in his mid-fifties and usually regarded as being very friendly, if a 'bit of a character'. The female employee has been with this organisation for a number of years, though has only worked in this particular office for six months.

An inquiry takes place and this establishes that the actual words used by the team leader were actually somewhat guarded (e.g. 'you could have been more effective'; 'if you had been available'). The team leader insists that there was ample justification for such remarks and they were delivered in a way which was quite normal and accepted in that particular office, where both parties worked at that time. The female employee equally insists that the words were delivered in a sarcastic manner leaving no doubt that they were intended as a serious (though unjustified) rebuke. No previous warnings about her performance or behaviour had been recorded, though in point of fact this team leader had never resorted to the formal disciplinary processes on any other occasion, even when performance issues relating to other staff members were obvious. The female employee also commented that she had never been given a comprehensive job description, that training was minimal and that she had been given no clear work instructions or task for that week.

The inquiry supported the female employee in deciding that the actions taken by the team leader were inappropriate. Before any disciplinary action is taken, the team leader accepts an early retirement package and leaves the organisation. Following this several other team members leave and set up a small company doing similar work (though not in direct competition with your organisation) and with the team leader acting as a consultant. The division closes down.

Controlling Internet usage – an exercise

You are the manager of a purchase and supply office in a medium-sized engineering company. This office has always been highly regarded in the company as being helpful and productive, due in part to the good team spirit in a stable group of purchasing professionals and administrative support. Most individuals in the office are willing to put in extra time and effort in an emergency or when a major project is being undertaken.

One of the major changes to have taken place in recent years is the introduction of Internet access for all staff. This has led to major increases in productivity and the imaginative search for new sources of supply. Allied to this is the use of email, both within the office and business-to-business, and electronic data exchange with major suppliers, resulting in the office now operating with minimum paperwork.

However, it is gradually becoming evident that much time is being spent by some staff using the Internet for personal reasons, such as buying holidays and visiting sites of interest. This was initially viewed by management as a minor irritant; in fact, almost all staff used the Internet to some extent in ways which could be challenged of little immediate value to the company, such as checking on the news, weather forecasts and such like. Some staff have now become sufficiently annoyed by the perceived excessive and inappropriate use of this facility by others that they have made it an issue in staff meetings and informally mentioned it to senior management. Any specific individuals who have been accused deny that their usage is excessive or any different from other staff members. In the past, a similar difficulty arose with the unauthorised use of the telephone which resulted in an elaborate system of call-barring and permission being necessary for certain staff to make calls overseas. One advantage of the recent use of email and the Internet is that it has allowed a more flexible use of communications systems.

As office manager you have taken advice from senior management and benchmarked your practices with some similar offices, noting as always some unique features in your situation. The options appear to be as follows:

► An informal approach, appealing to team spirit and the need to maintain the profitability of the firm. Unfortunately the staff who are now complaining are likely to see this as a weak response favouring the culprits.
► A total ban on the personal use of email and the Internet and a determined use of existing disciplinary procedures.
► The allowed use of technology for personal matters at selected times or at specified workstations.
► Charging staff for the personal use of technology.

Initial discussions to sound out the response show two major problems with the above namely:

1. the need to define exactly what is permissible and what counts as personal use;
2. the need for systems which routinely monitor the usage of technology in order to enforce the agreed policy.

It appears that some definition of what is permissible could be achieved. Systems are in fact already available to monitor the use of technology but there is a suspicion that such surveillance is managerially heavy-handed and could equally be used to monitor other aspects of work performance.

The task

Having examined the issues and options, you seem to be no further forwards. It would be technically feasible to implement almost any of the above but this has now become a sensitive issue. What would you do, and can you produce an 'ethical rationale' for the choice you make?

Would your situation be easier if any one of the following occurred and a total ban on personal use was then enforced:

▶ Your company was taken over by a larger organisation which insisted on such a ban to ensure uniformity with its other operations.
▶ A major case of fraud was discovered to have been perpetrated by one of your buyers and rigorous security measures now had to be imposed to recover confidence.
▶ It was discovered that one of your employees had been accessing pornographic web sites and using the email system in a way which led to their dismissal.

We might reflect on the way in which such undesirable or even criminal events might lead to positive benefits. What does this tell us about ethical management?

Surveillance – some illustrative examples

The task

If your company has reason to believe employees are acting illegally, to what extent is it morally justified in undertaking covert surveillance of activities? Consider the following possible situations and assess how you would proceed, noting the need to balance ethical and practical considerations. You should also consider the more strategic issues raised, in particular how such situations may be avoided. Note that in many cases it would be advisable to seek up-to-date legal advice.

Illustrative situations and points for discussion

Case 1. An employee is suspected of accessing pornographic web sites from his workstation in the office. Should the company check the already existing records of his past activities? Should he be told this is happening? What further action should be taken?

Case 2. Employees are suspected of stealing goods when working on the delivery bay of a warehouse in a way which cannot be detected by existing CCTV cameras. Is the company justified in using anonymous security staff in the bay to attempt to uncover the extent of the theft?

Case 3. An employee is absent from work due to a debilitating industrial injury. It is suspected that the extent of the injury has been exaggerated. An inquiry agent poses as a market researcher to gain access to the employee's house and secretly videos the employee to see if any sign of this injury. Can this sort of action be justified in any situation, noting that a similar case has been criticised by the courts as an improper invasion of privacy?

Case 4. An employee is absent from work due to depression, allegedly caused by stress at work. An inquiry agent observes the employee doing the shopping, taking their children to school, attending a number of social gatherings and helping in a charity shop. Should the company proceed towards dismissal using this evidence as grounds?

Case 5. You are absent from work due to sickness. Looking out of the window during the day, you recognise an employee of your company who is delivering a television to one of your neighbours. The delivery is from a retailer's van and the deliverer is carrying official paperwork; that is, he appears to be working for this retailer. What factors might have an effect on any action you might now take? In particular, is this any of your business?

Case 6. Following allegations of drug use on company premises, hidden CCTV equipment is used in washrooms and recreational areas to monitor employee activity. This uncovered no evidence of drug use but did provide evidence of improper behaviour which is against company rules but not illegal. Should the company act on this information?

Case 7. The above surveillance also provided evidence of behaviour that contravenes the company's code of practice on behaviour at work in that some employees appeared to be engaged in the verbal bullying of another employee, who has not complained or brought this to the attention of management. How would you handle this situation?

Case 8. Would your approach (see Case 7) be different if the bullying was by the victim's line manager? What if the victim was female, with a male line manager? What if the victim was a member of a minority group?

Expenses claims – a case

The task

Though the imagined case below contains a large and rather extreme collection of examples of dubious 'expense claims' and perks for one rather ordinary employee, it might be seen in the context of the reported behaviour of some senior company executives with lifestyles that appear to feed on their organisation's revenues in far more extravagant ways.

No specific form of analysis of this case is suggested, though you might like to consider the extent of similar behaviour in organisations you are familiar with. The obvious question we might ask is exactly what expense claims are morally justified, remembering the economists' dictum 'there's no such thing as a free lunch'.

The case

For several years, Harold had followed the tradition set by colleagues in the past of adding 10 per cent to all mileage claims, using a map of the area which had been accidentally slightly expanded on the photocopier as evidential back-up if the need should ever arise. There was never seen to be any need to mention that his wife sometimes accompanied him on the longer trips, though this could easily be justified as essential to maintain his morale. He occasionally dined with colleagues from other companies, each submitting a full claim for the meal. The restaurant he usually used was most helpful in producing bills which showed only the total amount (including appropriately generous gratuities) and not revealing the alcohol expenditure officially frowned on by the company.

The purchase of several items for his office which were subsequently found at his home was explained by the occasions when he had to work from home, for example, due to a snowstorm; 'do you really expect me to carry a stapler around in my bag all the time?' In fact, this was a poor example for him to quote as a stapler would have been easier to carry than the company's computer, printer, leather executive computer chair and workstation also found at his home.

The Wedgwood crockery was even harder to comprehend, though at least it was found in his office. His explanation relating to the need to impress visiting clients might have passed muster for a couple of cups and saucers but he had no facilities at the office to cook a full meal for six. Of course it was accepted that his office computer could play films, but some of the DVDs found there had tenuous links to his work, though he could hardly have kept them at home either. His recent overtime claims, as well as those of his close colleagues, might now need to be re-evaluated.

In the light of the above, it just seemed so petty to alter a '1' to a '7' on a till receipt; £60 is poor recompense for a short stay in one of Her Majesty's 'hotels'. Harold was unable to substantiate his claim in court that 'everyone does it'.

Summary

As we move into this final section of this book, Part IV, it is useful to review once again the objective and style of presentation we are adopting. You will have noticed that the first ten chapters of this book were concerned mainly with the language, frameworks and theories of business and organisational ethics. The remaining chapters are different in the following ways:

▶ They deal exclusively with business and organisational ethics and situations rather than relating such work in more general theories of ethics or the social sciences.
▶ Each refers to either a professional perspective (HRM in the case of this chapter), an area of management application (e.g. international management in the case of Chapter 15) or a selection of topics of broad interest.
▶ These chapters contain material on specific topics in ethical management (e.g. performance management, bullying and HRD in this chapter).
▶ They contain substantial quantities of case exercise material which should be used in order to gain expertise and confidence in ethical evaluation.
▶ They invite the readers to reflect on their own employment situation and the ethical evaluation of work contexts as well as suggest answers to the inevitable question 'what would I have done in that situation?'

If your own learning style is to obtain a good understanding of theory before considering its application then you will probably have considered the material up to this point in the order it has been presented. If you prefer first of all to work with issues and dilemmas seen in practice before moving on to a consideration of theory then you will have found little baffling technical terminology in this chapter as a barrier to your appreciation of its contents. It is, however, important that you begin to relate this material to the preceding theories otherwise there is a danger you will miss the value of studying this subject in a structured way.

The work in this chapter can be related to any of the earlier materials but perhaps the most important links are the following:

► the advice on working with case studies to be found in Chapter 11;
► much of Chapter 2, though particularly the section on ethics and the law;
► employees are stakeholders and hence much of Chapter 3 applies;
► the theories of moral development in Chapter 4;
► the discussion of Kantian ethics and the discussion of fairness in Chapters 7 and 8;
► most of the material in Chapter 9;
► the material in Chapter 10 relating to power and politics, in particular the discussion of warrants and reputations;
► chapter 13 on diversity and unfair discrimination is highly applicable to HRM practice;
► a proactive approach to whistleblowing (see Chapter 14) is a good example of positive personnel management;
► the 'other cultures' perspective (Chapter 15) is obviously people related.

This list could have been longer and the ensuing chapters give rise to similar lists, which you may wish to construct for yourselves. The point being made is that there is a high degree of inter-connectedness of ethical management and theory.

This chapter has been largely concerned with organisational ethics, that is the focus has mainly been on internal issues of staff management which are common to both private and public management sectors. We can go further and say that the context is mainly related to management ethics through a consideration of the problems of managing staff and the dilemmas facing managers. There are a large number of other topics which could have been considered as part of this internal focus. Reference should be made to the specialist texts on ethics in HRM and to the publications and Codes of Practice of relevant professional bodies.

A major area which has not been considered here, nor elsewhere in this book, is the set of ethical issues surrounding the representation of employees by such bodies as Trades Unions. One reason for this omission has simply been that we have not had the opportunity in our theoretical chapters to set up an adequate foundation for such consideration in terms of an historical and social science framework. It would not be appropriate to consider the ethics of negotiating practices relating to pay and conditions without such a foundation. This is a major and highly challenging area of ethical concern, made more difficult by the perception by some that business ethics accepts an economic status quo that Unions should be challenging.

We could make some similar comments about the many topics within employment law which are not considered here. Once again their adequate treatment requires the appropriate foundations and considerable space which are given to them in other texts.

A number of the topics in this chapter are subject to current uncertainty due to changes in the law and in social attitudes. A similar point applies to Chapter 13 where we considered the area of unfair discrimination and diversity. Other topics, such as bullying, are becoming areas of considerable academic and applied research, though hardly new aspects of the experience of working in organisations. In other cases developments in technology are providing challenges, a typical instance being the opportunities and problems revealed by new advances in communications systems and in the working practices increasingly centred on terminals, email and the Internet.

Each of the above provides new challenges to the discipline of organisational ethics, perhaps even at fundamental philosophical levels in the same way that advances in bio-technology continue to lead to a necessary rethinking of the rights of humans and animals. In the context of rapid change one should not underestimate the resilience and conservative nature of many organisational working cultures.

There are a large number of texts dealing with organisational behaviour and with HRM and personnel management as areas of professional expertise. Some of these are explicit on their handling of ethical issues, though usually lack a comprehensive consideration of potential ethical theories. It is useful to consider such texts, as well as journal articles, in the light of ideas developed in this book. As in other chapters, the Annotated bibliography at the end of the book includes all the references, though the following might be singled out as particularly appropriate as a next step in following up the material in this chapter.

Ackroyd, S. and Thompson, P. (1999), *Organisational Misbehaviour*, Sage, London.

Buchanan, D. and Badham, R. (1999), *Power, Politics and Organisational Change: Winning the Turf Game*, Sage, London.

Larmer, R.A. (ed.) (1996), *Ethics in the Workplace: Selected Readings in Business Ethics*, West, Minneapolis.

Maclagan, P. (1998), *Management and Morality*, Sage, London.

Parker, M. (ed.) (1998), *Ethics and Organisations*, Sage, London.

Winstanley, D. and Woodall, J. (eds) (2000), *Ethical Issues in Contemporary Human Resource Management*, Palgrave Macmillan, Basingstoke.

An introduction to marketing ethics

Purpose and learning objectives

The purpose of this chapter is to introduce some of the concepts and issues in marketing ethics, illustrated by a range of case studies.
  You will be able to

► show an appreciation of the ethical issues raised in marketing and selling;
► understand some concepts of marketing ethics.

Introduction

We begin this chapter with a section on the theory of marketing ethics, presenting a model which places ethical issues in a competitive marketing context. This model is important in that it looks outwards from the business into a society which is organised on market economy principles. It therefore deals specifically with business ethics in the 'external' sense.

We then use discussions of two specific contexts in order to explore some issues of markets and management. The first area concerns some of the ethical problems which exist in advertising and product promotion, and is therefore concerned with management practice and the consumer as stakeholder. The second area is termed 'transplant tourism' and introduces a context where there is some doubt whether the mechanism of a market provides appropriate ethical protection for all concerned. It should be noted that a number of specialist texts exist which explore these, and other, areas of marketing ethics in far more detail, often with a particular emphasis on the defence of marketing practice. Our aim here has been to raise issues and draw attention to unethical practices as examples of the applicability of the methods of analysis particular to business ethics.

We follow these illustrative discussions with three case studies introducing new areas of problem and debate. The summary at the end of this chapter contains some new material and the next chapter introduces a further range of cases and issues in marketing.

Fundamentals of marketing ethics

Normative marketing ethics are prescriptions of the values, principles and ideals which marketing professionals should hold. It is interesting to ask if these are context dependent and whether they refer to individual marketing decision makers or to organisations. In particular, one interesting question which occurs in the literature on marketing ethics is the following: is there one overarching and universal set of principles from which the others can be derived (i.e. the 'Grand Narratives' of the Western philosophical tradition, see below) or should we proceed by 'case law' in deriving principles and practices which seem to embody common sense and decency?

Brenkert (1999), in the context of a brief survey of approaches to marketing ethics, tellingly comments:

> there is little agreement among marketers on what kinds of justification can be offered for normative moral judgments made regarding marketing. There is also considerable disagreement on whether marketing ethics is (or should be) separate from the rest of business ethics – or, indeed, from the ethics of (non-business) society.

As marketing is a central function within business as well as the source of many management and business strategy concepts, this semi-detachment of marketing ethics is alarming. What grounds can there be for such separation? It should be noted that there is an important strand of thinking which is highly critical of much management theorising, including business ethics. This is often referred to as a 'post-modern' approach which is at least partly based on a highly critical philosophical debate on the role and authority of ethical theory in general and the 'grand narratives' in particular (see Parker [1998, 2002] for a comparatively positive introduction to this material). One response to this might be to ignore ethical theory entirely and trust to common sense, judgement and decency. Much elementary ethical writing shows the dangers of such an approach. A more constructive way forwards is given in a paper by Robin and Reidenbach (1993) and summarised below.

By returning to meta-ethics we can probe more deeply into the nature of 'ethical marketing concepts' and how these might be justified. The paper by Robin and Reidenbach (1993) includes a classification of moral philosophies based on the scope of their application:

1. Individualised Ethical Principles (e.g. the Postmodernist approaches which completely reject attempts to find common ethical ground – the ultimate in moral relativism)
2. Bounded, Constrained or Directed Ethical Principles (e.g. approaches which recognise different understandings of justice but allow for networks of ethical agreement, e.g. within a professional sub-context such as marketing)
3. Universal Ethical Principles (e.g. the 'Grand Narratives' of Kant, etc.).

The first of the alternatives above is likely to be rejected in a systematic prescriptive account of an operationalisable theory of marketing ethics, that is if a theory is intended to guide action and not merely state that no guide for action exists. The central place given to individual freedom in the prescription given below should, however, be noted.

Following the work of such philosophers as MacIntyre (see Chapter 9 and the Annotated bibliography), the 'Grand Narratives' are seen as referring to different historical situations, that is as not being quite as 'universal' as intended! History, time and context are seen as essential factors in arriving at a working ethic. The standard approaches were developed using specific languages in particular contexts. Thus to take the usual example, the society and trading conditions of ancient Greece were so different from our own that basic words used by Aristotle (e.g. 'arete', etc.) are not easily matched to current ones (e.g. 'virtue', etc.).

The second alternative in the list above is therefore seen as the most appropriate and the following are proposed as constraints or boundary conditions:

▶ *Constraints from society*: including the norms of a democratic society (e.g. individual freedoms) and the legal environment.
▶ *Constraints from market capitalism*: the particular view of distributive justice inherent in a market economy, the encouragement of risk taking, hard work and creativity, and the implications of these in terms of unequal distribution of goods and the harm which the operations of markets may cause to individuals and sub-populations arc taken as a given part of the environment within which the profession of marketing operates.

▶ *Constraints from human capacities and limitations*: psychological egoism is taken seriously as a description of how people actually act. Therefore it is assumed that marketers have 'limited but positive sympathies towards others'.

Following on from this, the bounded ethical principles specifically for marketing are suggested to be:

▶ the improvement of human life (morality seen as a defence for the weak, etc.);
▶ recognition of Society's constraints (the law; consumer needs);
▶ working within a market economy, with its emphasis on the reward of risk taking, hard work and creativity (issues of distributive justice);
▶ recognising the constraints of human capabilities and limitations (e.g. the link between psychological egoism and theories of motivation).

It is argued that such an approach provides a practical basis for marketing ethics which connects fully with the real world in which marketing operates as a discipline. This does indeed seem to be the case as risk taking and human motivation figure strongly in this framework.

A counter-argument might be that this type of approach is too accepting of the status quo. It provides little critical edge for resolving the dilemmas inherent in a market economy (e.g. inequalities in rewards; effects on the environment) and no real critique of a market economy as such. Perhaps this work might best be viewed as a clear statement of an ethical position which might then be contrasted with more radical views. The gulf between the two can be readily seen.

This shows quite clearly a fundamental difference in perceptions of the purpose of marketing and business ethics. On the one hand emphasis may be given to decision-making support and the resolution of the routine moral ambiguities of business and organisational life. On the other hand business ethics might be seen as the source of a fundamental challenge to immoral business practice. The first takes the 'business world' as a given and tries to find tools and heuristics to help the individual manager act in a moral way. The second sees the role of ethics as providing a challenge to a given set of assumptions. It is difficult to see how these views can be resolved; perhaps we should accept they are two quite distinct disciplines, or at least the application of a common language and set of concepts to two different problems.

You will find it useful to reflect on the market-oriented ethical framework given above in all the remaining chapters of this book, noting that the two marketing chapters (18 and 19) explore mainly consumer issues while Chapter 20 includes some material on business-to-business market relationships.

Advertising junk food

The ethics of advertising and promotion are a considerable subject in themselves. In this section we will introduce some of the concerns usually expressed through a brief analysis related to some current examples. You may wish to consider further examples from the adverts you see every day; there is no shortage to the consumer of readily available advertising material to be ethically analysed!

One of the first tasks given to the new UK television regulator, Ofcom, was to draw up a tough code of practice on advertisements for junk food and drinks aimed at children. This is in response to a perceived crisis in child obesity in the UK. A ban on the advertising of unhealthy food products aimed at children is not out of the question. Is this simply a rational response by a government faced with the prospect of an increasingly unhealthy population, a trend related to poorer income groups, or a further example of the 'nanny state'?

At one extreme there are some items, such as drugs, which cannot be legally sold directly to consumers and therefore where issues of public advertising and promotion do not arise. However, there are also products which are for sale, with some age restrictions, where there exists considerable scientific evidence that they are harmful and addictive. The most obvious example is cigarettes. A few years ago, cigarettes were freely advertised in the UK. As evidence was gathered of their potential to harm both users and others in the vicinity of their use, a series of restrictions on their promotion were put in place, including the sponsorship of sporting events by cigarette manufacturers. It is argued that smoking in any quantity is harmful and that the long-term economic effects on the Health Service are considerable, that is the use of this product imposes a cost on society. We note also that cigarettes are taxed to a considerable extent, which produces a revenue stream to the government, and that the manufacture and sale of cigarettes is a source of employment. Currently the situation is being reversed by highly graphic government advertising showing the harmful effects of cigarette smoking replacing the previous cigarette promotions. One should be clear on the ethical justification of this unusual form of 'advertising'.

The sale and promotion of alcoholic drinks raises some similar issues, though alcohol is not considered a danger to health if consumed in small quantities. There is an issue of alcohol being illegally available to under 16-years-old individuals. There is an additional issue that even moderate levels of alcohol reduce our ability to effectively carry out some tasks, such as drive a vehicle, leading to prohibitions on alcohol consumption in some circumstances. Though subject to high rates of taxation, alcoholic drinks are freely promoted through advertisement and at the point of sale and are widely available. There is evidence of the considerable social and health problems and costs associated with high levels of alcohol intake. Can we be clear why alcohol is treated in a very different way to cigarette advertising?

Cigarette smoking is increasingly being banned from places of work and public areas. Most places of work will not allow the consumption of alcohol and many will not allow alcoholic drinks as part of expense claims. The similarities and differences between these two product areas show many of the problems facing business ethics. Though both are now considered to be harmful in a variety of ways, they were both at one time seen as socially acceptable. This perception has to some extent been changed for smoking but not for heavy drinking. A comparison could also be made with gambling which in its different forms (e.g. National Lottery, horse racing, casino gaming, etc.) are either promoted or restricted by the law! The debate could be, and often is, widened to prostitution, pornography of various types and to the use of some forms of recreational and medicinal drug.

These are examples of products and services for which there is a demand but which are the subject of various degrees of legal restriction. In general, the ethical debate on their sale and promotion relates to a balance between the rights of the seller and the consumer to freely engage in trade as opposed to the views of society that such trade should be restricted or banned. The latter may be based on general social and moral concerns in a given society and on scientific evidence relating to the consequences of such trade, either for the individuals involved or for society at large. Such consequences are often long term, for example, relating to the health of the individual consumer or the costs to society. For a given product or service, views may well change over time leading to apparent inconsistencies over time and between products and the social context in which they are to be used.

One of the strongest lines of argument in favour of allowing such products to be sold is the idea of freedom of choice. Assuming some restrictions are in place, usually relating to age and the assumption that the individual has the knowledge and ability to make a rational choice, it is argued that the freedom of choice of the individual is paramount. This will also apply to the long-term effects of using this product, though this may place a considerable burden on the ability of the individual to evaluate the long-term costs and benefits as well as on their will power! It could also be argued that such an individual would have to accept restrictions on the use of the product in order to protect other individuals as well as considerable taxation on the use of the product to compensate society for the long-term costs of its use in society. This is, roughly speaking, the situation with smoking if one accepts the need to guard against the effects of passive smoking and assumes the tax on cigarettes is sufficient to offset long-term economic costs. This line of argument might suggest a relaxation of legislation on prostitution and casino gaming and a tightening of restrictions on alcohol! This is where the social acceptability of various activities comes into play as well as views on the risks to individuals and society.

This 'consumers' rational choice' argument leads to an interesting problem where advertising is concerned. There is a decision to be made whether or not to engage in an activity as well as a choice between rival products. If we accept that rational choice can only be made if ample information is available, we appear to be led towards the view that such products should be widely advertised, provided that checks are available on the truth content of the adverts and that health warnings and so forth are also prominent. Advertisers will always claim that their activities are intended to inform as well as persuade, and the latter is perfectly acceptable in the context of competition and free consumer choice. It is not clear how logos of sponsors at sporting events carry information about product characteristics, except to suggest that such products are associated with desirable activities and feelings. It is difficult to see how many drinks adverts tell you much about the flavour or effect of the product! The reality is that much advertising of such entertainment products is concerned with repeatedly drawing your attention to a product, often in socially desirable contexts. Whether this promotes rational choice between products can be endlessly debated. What is certainly the danger is that drinks adverts, for example, not only contribute to choices between drinks but also encourage drinking to a greater extent and for a wider population. It is difficult to separate freedom to compete against rival brands from freedom to increase the size of the total market.

Let us now return to the original focus of this section, the advertisement of 'junk food' to children. If we try to isolate the key factors in this situation we might focus on the following:

▶ Can we define exactly which foods and drinks are to be included in the derogatory category of 'junk food'?
▶ Do we have good scientific evidence that consumption of such foods presents a danger?
▶ To what extent is any danger related to the amount consumed (i.e. most foods give some ill effects if consumed to excess)?
▶ Is the danger due to a particular product or cumulative over a number of products (e.g. salt)?
▶ Are the dangers widely known and well understood?
▶ Are there economically available alternatives, particularly for poorer consumers?

Increasingly the argument is that such foods can be defined and they do present a long-term danger to health if enough similar products are consumed over a period of time. It could also be argued that low levels of consumption are not harmful and public awareness of the need for health eating is such that rational choice can be exercised.

However, some further problems should now be considered which differ from the issues relating to smoking and alcohol. The first is that levels of awareness of food characteristics vary considerably over the population and there are a number of characteristics which are important, as any guide to dieting will show! The situation is considerably more complex than considering varieties, not brands, of alcohol, say. It is further complicated by personal taste (literally!) and the fact that decisions relate not only to the consumer but to families, including vulnerable groups such as children, the elderly and those with specific diet-influencing problems such as diabetes. The rational choice of what a family eats is very important and complex. Furthermore it is strongly affected by budget constraints and the pressures of children in particular to respond to advertising and peer pressure in what they want to eat and what they may consume without parental guidance.

Thus complexity, money and children figure prominently in the equation. It should also be remembered that the large amounts of money spent on food make large advertising and promotion budgets viable, particularly through TV advertising reinforced at point of sale and in packaging. Specific links to children's entertainment (e.g. plastic toys in breakfast cereals) reinforce the focus of promotional effort on the younger influencers of family decisions. Perhaps as important as any other factor is the cheapness of many 'junk food' products relative to alternatives, particularly if costs of meal preparation are also taken into account. Cheap, easy to prepare food which will be readily accepted by children is a very tempting option if the disadvantages appear minimal in the short term.

There is a further problem with obtaining scientific evidence, as the early opponents of smoking found out. Linking a particular form of consumption with a disease is not easy. We may find from general surveys that a particular sub-population is more prone to a specific problem but finding an actual causal link may be problematic. The fact that habitual smokers have a tendency to contract lung disease or suffer from heart problems when older will always meet with the examples of non-smokers who died from such causes and smokers who lived to a ripe old age. Nonetheless, if such causal mechanisms can be identified then acting on this information is a matter of public necessity.

The effects of diet on health have received considerable scientific scrutiny and we can be satisfied that the concerns relating to the excessive consumption of some chemicals and ingredients are well founded. The problem is often with the exact meaning of 'excessive' and the fact that a variety of very different products may have a cumulative effect.

The extent to which informed consumer choice is an issue may be gauged by the recent cases where typically a consumer attempts to prosecute a chain of fast food restaurants for allegedly causing long-term health problems. Whatever the legal niceties of such a claim, we might look at it using the ethical tools at our disposal. From a consequentialist point of view for the consumer in isolation we would have to be clear that the disutility of the long-term health problem outweighed the pleasure of eating in such outlets for a period of time. It is not easy to see how one might come to any conclusion on this unless the consumer was aware of the damage being caused, in which case we might infer that the operation of a personal cost–benefit calculus by the consumer took any responsibility away from the food outlet. If a broader utilitarian calculation is undertaken, the profit and employment benefits of the restaurant chain will also work in its favour.

If either was aware that there was some risk involved then this would also be part of the calculation, though the quantification of such risk at various points of time would not be easy. In this case we might move to a deontological framework. There is a difference between where the health problem results from harmful ingredients in the food offered by the restaurant and the situation where the consumer habitually over-eats. In the former case, if the restaurant knew of the potential harm then it was obviously in the wrong, though an 'everyone else does it' defence might be tried. If the restaurant did not know but had taken every precaution to operate at the highest standards then it would seem harsh to attach blame. On the face of it, the 'over-eating' scenario seems to place the fault firmly with the consumer, though would this be changed if the restaurant had aggressively promoted its products and always served large, cheap portions?

This whole situation seems to carry with it an assumption that the consumer has the right to freedom of choice, except when something goes wrong; then it's somebody else's fault! However, this does not take into account the information asymmetry of the situation. Surely we can reasonably assume that the restaurant chain knows far more about its products and how to motivate their consumption than most consumers. Using this knowledge to attract customers and encourage them to buy as much as possible may be regarded as normal business or an abuse of position, depending on one's perspective.

To take a different situation, how ethical is it to encourage people to buy high-performance cars? Having spent a considerable time discussing food, drink and smoking we will leave the ethical consideration of car promotion to the reader!

Transplant tourism

The trade in human organs, in particular from live donors, presents an interesting set of ethical problems where bioethics meets business ethics. There is little doubt that the shady world of illegal organ donation, usually kidneys, from poor third-world donors to rich customers in the West is undesirable and exploitative. The donors are likely to be paid a tiny fraction of the price such an organ can attract, and they receive little advice and care. The extreme case is the suspicion that children are abducted and killed to provide organs. The recipient, who will have to travel abroad for the transplant, may receive inadequate post-operative care, the Health Service of their country of origin of necessity providing an emergency response if things go wrong. It is not always clear whether the donated organ has been properly checked for match with the recipient or is clear of disease.

The above unregulated situation is obviously ethically undesirable even from the most 'profit-oriented' perspective of business practice. However, an interesting argument can be made that this could be replaced with a carefully regulated market which would care for all concerned. In the context of a considerable demand for organs for transplant, long patient waiting lists (with many dying before suitable organs become available), evidence that individuals are willing to sell organs for an appropriate price and on the assumption (consistent with current knowledge) that such donation carries little extra long-term risk then the conditions for a market appear to be in place.

It is possible to object to live donor situations on the grounds that your organs are not an asset to be traded but part of your being. The counter-argument would point to instances where organs are freely donated by, say, close relatives. This tends to suggest that one point at issue is the payment received for the donated organ, that is if the donation is altruistic then it is ethically correct but not if the motivation is financial. This is a point on which we will all have a personal position to defend, but it is important we ensure our beliefs are consistent. There are many activities involving caring for others, religious work and charities where many would like to feel that money does not change hands but this is hardly feasible. The caring professions are forms of paid employment. Of course, links between the standards of care and the ability of the wealthy to pay a high price may seem unpalatable to many but this does not usually lead to a ban on such activities.

The risk context is an important point to take into account. Presumably the risks to the recipient in receiving an organ are less than the risks of not receiving one; this is, after all, the whole point of the procedure. The extra risk therefore falls initially on the donor. At the very least we must be sure that the donor is fully informed and capable of freely giving consent. If the donation is forced to take place due to financial problems or social pressures then there is an obvious ethical problem. We should also be clear that extra risk does not fall on others, such as the family of the donor or the state who will provide care if things go wrong. It appears on current evidence that this is not the case.

There is also an additional benefit in a regulated market of removing the need for the criminal and exploitative actions accompanying illegal organ donation. This argument is similar to an argument for lifting the prohibition on the sale of alcohol in the USA in the early part of last century. It can also be used as an argument for the legalisation of recreational drugs, or in a milder case for the legalisation of some drugs with potential medicinal use. You might like to consider if these situations are indeed equivalent to live organ donation.

Selling disease – a modern fable

The following fantasy was inspired by reports of an increasing suspicion in some quarters that the idea of imaginatively generating a new market for an existing product might be morally unacceptable when applied to the pharmaceutical industry.

An imaginary situation

As a by-product from a major research programme, the pharmaceutical manufacturer (PM) discovered a new product which appeared to be effective in combating the Anxiety Effects of Social Interaction (which we will call AESI, thus imitating the practice of referring to common problems by impressive acronyms). Now it might be thought that an existing product, alcohol, adequately meets this need but some would argue that an alternative with different side effects might find a niche in the market.

Extensive research was commissioned by PM into the extent of AESI and the effectiveness of the new product in alleviating its symptoms. The product trials were a roaring success due to the discovery of some new side effects which we need not go into at this time. Past sufferers formed mutual support groups under the aegis of a charitable foundation set up by a subsidiary of PM, medical practitioners were encouraged to provide structured programmes of treatment (in return for supplies of the product to enable long-term research) and other commercial outlets were found to meet the needs of the obviously large target market for such a product.

When launched, the product was an immediate success...until the supplier of a threatened alternative came up with the slogan 'why bother – just have a beer'. Remaining stocks of the product were of great value to the ex-employees of PM in coming to terms with their more economically reduced life styles.

The task

Is it ethical to use all the paraphernalia of medical science and the health care professions in order to publicise a dubious 'social disease' in order to promote a product?

The salesman and his contacts – a case study

The case report

John Smith was recruited by a company as regional sales manager for the Northwest of England and quickly developed a good reputation for meeting his targets, mainly by using his extensive contacts from his two previous jobs in selling bulk cleaning materials to large- and medium-sized companies in the region. Though friendly, hard working and highly competent, management noted a ruthlessness in pursuing work which gave him the best sales performance figures (and hence bonus) along with a tendency to endlessly argue the case for expense claims. However, his single-handed positive impact on the company's performance could not be ignored.

This positive performance appeared to be immune to a slight economic downturn which affected market demand as a whole. John continued to find and keep clients to an extent which gave him considerable prestige in the company. Though he passed this off as the results of hard work, the Sales Director began to note a number of small concerns which suggested that John had some exceptionally useful, if possibly unethical, information sources. In addition, when some particularly large, and rather dubious, expenses claims were challenged by accounts, John simply threatened to resign if he had any more 'hassle' – 'if you want the business, this is what it costs!' The impact on profit was such that senior management allowed this situation to continue. The Sales Director was asked to 'have a word with him and sort it out', which he never quite found the opportunity to do.

As trading conditions worsened, John's performance began to decline dramatically, which John strongly argued was due to 'lack of support' by senior management. After a few more months, sales forecasts were dire with major financial losses predicted. Though the market was static, the company's market share nationally was declining. The Sales Director had a quiet chat with John, who was reputed to be looking for a job elsewhere, and asked him what more drastic steps could be taken to reverse the decline. John suggested some minor product changes and the need to expand their range of company contacts in a more targeted and effective way. 'That's obvious' responded the Sales Director, 'doing isn't quite so straightforward'. John then suggested how some useful information could be obtained, though there were 'financial implications'.

Though John was never explicit on his sources, it appeared that he could still obtain access to current customer data and market research from his previous employers.

The task

Should the Sales Director

▶ sack John for misconduct (though does he have any actual proof and how would an employment tribunal react to his weak management of John in the past?);

▶ negotiate an immediate termination with John (which would be expensive and would leave John free to work in opposition);

▶ actively pursue John's ideas, short of doing anything illegal, in order to preserve profits and jobs in his own company;

▶ do nothing.

Can you think of alternative action plans? In hindsight, what would you have done differently in the past?

Ethics and marketing strategy – an exercise

The situation

Your company manufactures a range of toys aimed at 3 to 7 year olds. Though a large and well-established company, recent sales have shown little growth while profits, though adequate, are declining.

You are considering the promotion of a major product which is to be launched for the next Christmas period. Two radically differing advertising strategies have been suggested:

▶ An aggressive sales campaign built around TV advertising aimed directly at children and promoting the product as this year's fashion. This campaign, along with point-of-sale promotion, will be very costly but should make a big impact and has considerable growth and profit potential.

▶ A more low-key campaign based on the safety and educational value of the product. This is similar to the approach used in previous years.

The task

What are the factors and issues to be considered in making a choice between these two approaches? In what ways might ethical concerns impact on this decision?

Summary

You may feel that the theoretical- and case-based material presented in this chapter and the next is somewhat negative in its portrayal of marketing as a professional activity. To state the obvious, marketing takes place in the arena of competitive markets! Many will interpret this context as necessitating aggressive and ruthless action; it is no accident that metaphors of war and competitive sport are often to be found in the practitioner literature. The pressures bearing down on marketing staff must therefore be recognised, which is why some writers will displace their criticisms away from such individuals and onto the market system in its totality.

However, this does seem a rather convenient argument for the unscrupulous: 'if the system cannot be changed, then anything goes and none of it's our fault!'. This is totally unfair to the many marketing professionals who sincerely wish to combine organisational success with treating clients fairly. The latter will emphasise the positive benefits of reputation and integrity; of building strong brand and corporate images and providing reliable value for money.

The section on ethical theory provided early in this chapter, the Robin and Reidenbach model, is supportive of the sincere marketer. It attempts to chart a path between a post-modern dismissiveness of any possibility of systematic ethical analysis within a market context and the strictures of the Grand Narratives, which are seen as giving an unreachable standard. The latter point is perhaps not true in that market theory can be allied with a sophisticated utilitarian analysis through the discipline of economics. This, however, can sometimes point to the failures of the market system rather than support it. It should also be noted that more modern theories of business ethics are more subtle than the Grand Narratives in the possibilities they uncover.

To develop this point further, one possible way of viewing markets and marketing is as a communication system with such activities as Market Research, advertising and the act of making a purchase been seen as a 'conversation' within a community of discourse. The result of such a model must be to focus attention on the flow of information and its reliability. If we add in to this mixture such notions as risk and complexity then we have some possibility of applying ethical concepts in a structured fashion.

Marketing ethics is a large subject in its own right. It may be argued that the moral evaluation of marketing action is best carried out within a detailed consideration of marketing theories, policies and practices. With this in mind, I would encourage marketing professionals to do exactly that. However, I would argue that challenging and critical inputs from outside the area of marketing are of value as an antidote to complacent and stereotyped thinking.

19 Moral distance – the selling of financial products

Purpose and learning objectives

The purpose of this chapter is to introduce some further concepts and issues in marketing ethics, with case studies mainly on the selling of financial products.

You will be able to

▶ show an appreciation of the ethical issues raised in marketing and selling;
▶ understand the concept of moral distance.

Introduction

This chapter continues the discussion of the previous one through the introduction of some further concepts and a range of new case contexts. The idea of moral distance has been mentioned or inferred a number of times earlier in the book. Here we give a fuller treatment using the context of marketing as a useful way of bringing the ideas to life.

In the remaining sections we use a mixture of discussion and case reports in order to explore specific topics. We begin with a discussion of privacy, introduced by some comments about telephone selling. The remaining examples explore the selling of financial products, beginning with a personal narrative which allows some details to be explored. We continue with some comments on credit card selling and end with an extended discussion of a financial product usually referred to as precipice bonds. Some unfortunate consumers have lost a considerable amount of their savings on such products, which have been sold by reputable, high-street institutions. This situation has been repeated over the years with such things as endowment mortgages and pension schemes. The issue we are exploring here is partly to do with reputation but also reflects the situation of consumers faced with complex products where some reliance on the advice they receive may be inevitable. This links with the personal narrative mentioned above and the idea of moral distance to produce a serious dilemma in a market context and a challenge for an industry to self-regulate in order to protect one group of stakeholders.

Marketing and moral distance

Though universalism is a key idea in most classical accounts of ethics, the idea that some individuals are more 'distant' than others, even to the extent that they need not be considered as 'moral persons' in ethical decision-making, can be seen as an underlying theme in many accounts of practical business.

The idea of moral distance is not new and can be seen as implicit in the consequentialist accounts of ethics which fall short of a full-blooded utilitarianism. To many people it would appear that their duties to family and close friends are more pressing than any consideration of unknown others. In a society (such as in East Asia) which places great emphasis on obligations to individuals within a social group, those outside the group may simply not count in any moral calculation (see Chapter 15).

One theme in applied ethics, which occurs in many accounts of unethical behaviour, is what view a perpetrator takes of the individual or 'victim' against whom some evil or injustice is to be committed. An extreme though often quoted example relates to the activities of the Nazis in Germany and occupied countries during the Second World War. On the one hand the holocaust is seen as a particular evil of the 20th century (though see Glover [1999] for some other horrific contenders). On the other hand the German people have a fine reputation for culture, efficiency and civilised behaviour. The two do not seem compatible, even allowing for the political aberration of the Third Reich. It is argued that the murder of large numbers of people could only be carried out in a bureaucratic organisational context (remembering the sheer scale of the holocaust and the 'operational efficiency' of its implementation) if the victims were thought of as morally 'non-people'.

The theorising which has resulted at least partly from a consideration of this dilemma has also been reflected in the previously mentioned radical views of business ethics, as seen from the quotation from the introduction to Parker (1998) given below:

the term 'adiaphorization' refers to the process of making something value-neutral. It can be argued that marketing is a dominant technology in contemporary society and organisation, and one that has often justified itself on the basis of a story of liberating consumers from constraints, yet it achieves its effects through distancing, objectification, effacement, disassembly and so on.

Customers are out there ready to be exploited as 'punters', or whatever term is being used to emphasise that they are different from the sales staff. Similar language is used for the labour markets of developing countries. Indeed the phrase 'to exploit a market' can be taken as indicative of the underlying attitudes as the 'exploiters'.

Effacement is literally 'removing the face'; the consumer is seen as an object to be manipulated through advertising, hard selling and other forms of persuasion. To push this view further we can argue that needs and preferences are created rather than discovered. The consumer is objectified to the extent that their view of the world is seen as malleable and capable of alteration along lines more suitable to the retail organisation's offerings.

Inside the organisation are 'the team', waiting to be motivated and carry out the selling, with success being measured in terms of daily 'hits' and commission earned rather than the much vaunted 'creation of satisfied customers'! The irony is that sales staff may be 'objectified' by senior management in much the same way as customers; seen as the cannon fodder of the organisation, receiving occasional big rewards and a medal as 'sales person of the month'. This may well be a radical view of the objective of internal marketing but it cannot be denied that 'selling' the product to the sales force is often a necessary prerequisite to selling it to the consumer.

A key term in modern marketing practice is 'relational marketing', where an organisation apparently seeks to build a lasting relationship with a client, a practice which might seem contrary to any talk of 'distancing'. However, an interesting question is whether relational marketing does in fact close the distance between buyer and seller. Many customer encounters are scripted and planned in detail and the supporting systems carefully programmed. Databases of customer preferences and previous purchases over a period of time can have considerable value in targeting customers with the most appropriate product or service from the range the company have on offer. This is 'getting closer to the customer' in a somewhat instrumental sense but is also an example of 'adiaphorization', with its sinister implications of exploitation. Proponents of relational marketing could argue that their approach is merely effective business practice, and is accepted as such by all parties concerned.

A related concept is the distance between an action and its consequences. A prime example is the selling of long-term financial products, as we have noted several times in this book. Consequences for the buyers of dubious financial products are only fully visible in the long term, while organisational profits and sales commissions are earned in the short term.

Organisational rules and procedures have a similar distancing effect where the means are separated from the ends. Unpleasant local effects can be justified as the means to achieving corporate objectives. The above, and similar concepts relating to other business functions, are part of a radical critique of conventional business and organisational practice. It is useful to ask what is the alternative if the benefits of a market economy are to be realised?

Silent phone calls and telephone sales – marketing and privacy

Imagine for one moment that you are an elderly person, living alone, and your phone rings. You pick up the receiver and all you hear is silence. You nervously ask 'hello, who's there?' but get nothing other than a continuing silence until the dialling tone comes back, or you put the receiver down. Who was at the other end of the line? A would-be burglar, checking if you are in the house?

The worry that one's house is being checked out prior to an attempted burglary has meant that some people have simply not gone out after receiving such a call, according to recent newspaper and other media reports. These calls are often repeated at frequent intervals throughout the day apparently confirming the above fears. In other cases an individual has become concerned that their partner has been receiving calls they wish to keep secret, for reasons easily imagined. A more extreme response might be to assume that someone you have had an argument with (e.g. a neighbour) is being an intentional nuisance, an assumption which might lead to undeserved retribution! Attempts to trace the number of the caller (e.g. by using the '1471' service in the UK) usually receive the 'caller withheld their number' response.

It appears that on a large number of occasions the caller is an organisation engaged in direct marketing, or to be more specific the call is being made by a computer 'power dialling' a number of phones from an electronic database. If you answer and an 'agent' (i.e. a human salesperson) is available at that instant then the agent will take over the call and it will appear to the receiver that the agent has just dialled their number. However, as it seems to be more efficient to make sure that agents have a ready stream of available clients than spend time waiting for dialling and answering to take place, the computer dials more numbers than agents are available. Any excess client availability is simply ignored: you answer the phone, no agent is available and hence silence! One can only assume this is more effective from the company's point of view than a recorded message apologising for the call. Occasionally a company will try to hold the call by using a recorded message of the 'I have a call for you from...' variety but this may cause even more confusion and annoyance.

The low costs of calls available to direct marketing organisations make this whole strategy quite efficient, particularly in the cost-effective use of the agents' time. This does, of course, ignore the costs to the recipients of the calls. Even assuming one is aware that there may be nothing ominous about silent calls, time is spent in answering the phone and one's attention to other matters is disrupted even if the call is silent. Of course, this may even be preferable to time spent listening to the laborious scripts used by telephone salespersons, though there is some amusement to be gained in noting the latest attempt to stop you putting the phone down as soon as the nature of the call is evident.

Few calls begin with 'I want to sell you a new kitchen'! A frequent opening gambit is 'We're doing a survey on...' or 'We're in your area demonstrating...' or maybe 'You've won a holiday to...'. Is this, perhaps, an area where inconveniencing and misleading the intended client is the norm? This would be strongly rejected by professional marketing specialists who condemn the 'silent call' approach. Others might note that an organisation has to sell to survive and meet the needs of its stakeholders. It has to find some way of reaching clients in a crowded marketplace and many people simply accept this type of call as part of life.

Another response is to note the existence of the telephone preference service, whereby a householder can make it known that they do not want to receive direct marketing calls. Reputable companies may well abide by this but the problem is the organisation which sees the cost advantages of 'power dialling' and can hide behind the fact that the recipient of a silent call cannot trace them. A response to this would be to make it mandatory for calls which are not connected to a human agent to alternatively give out a recorded message of who the call was from and a number to call back, however unlikely it is that the latter will be used. Even more radical would be an 'opt in' service where consumers register their willingness to receive calls from direct marketing firms. I leave it to your imagination to guess what proportion of the population would bother to 'opt in' and what effect this would have on the revenue generated by direct marketing.

The case for continuing with 'business as usual', seen from an industry standpoint, seems to be as follows:

▶ Very large revenues are generated by direct marketing, of which telephone sales are a substantial part. This revenue is essential for the survival of many organisations and of benefit to all of us, either as shareholders or as part of an economically successful society.

▶ In practice, many of the future customers who provide this revenue are initially ignorant of what is on offer, are resistant to sales activity and need to be persuaded and motivated to buy. Telephone selling is valuable in making first contacts as well as closing sales of many products and services.

▶ In direct selling (whether by phone, in the street or by home visits) it is the norm that many approaches have to be made in order to generate an economical number of sales. Therefore any form of technology which can effectively automate this laborious process of making the first contact is welcomed. Telephone selling based on large existing databases and using computerised dialling allied to call centres based in low-wage countries provide a cost-effective marketing tool.

▶ The use of 'opt-in' databases and the giving out of company details instead of 'silence' will increase costs and lower revenues. Such practices, including not withholding numbers, will simply not be observed by the less respectable companies thus giving them an unfair advantage.

▶ As people become more accustomed to this form of selling they will simply ignore silent calls as a fact of life. If this whole business is causing particular distress to a minority, this can be relieved by a combination of using an answer-phone to filter out unwanted calls, changing your number, going ex-directory and not giving out your telephone number to commercial organisations unless really necessary.

This discussion has taken us a long way from the elderly or nervous person fearing the attentions of a burglar. Such distress may be seen as a by-product of a successful commercial environment. Too much money is riding on the use of this technology to make its abandonment a realistic proposition according to the cost–benefit calculus of a commercial concern. This might change if the general annoyance with intrusive telephone selling became so great that it became less effective in generating sales.

There is an interesting comparison with door-step selling which is comparatively more expensive. It also opens the salesperson to face-to-face abuse from irate householders whose daily lives have been disrupted. Telephone selling not only uses technology to gain a cost advantage, can be cost-effectively used at times (such as evenings and weekends) when customers are traditionally more likely to be at home but also isolates the salesperson (or 'agent') from an abusive customer. This can be an advantage in cold calling, though could make the actual closing of a sale more difficult.

So far in discussing this situation, which relates to the specific problem of 'silent calls' as well as some issues in direct selling by phone, we have taken a 'practical' approach reflecting the reasons why this phenomenon exists. You might now like to try to relate these problems to the ethical ideas and models presented earlier. The paragraphs above reflect a broadly utilitarian perspective if the argument that telephone selling benefits society as a whole is seen as convincing. You might like to consider, for example, whether the rights of individuals are being respected and what this all means for the moral development of all involved.

The car payment plan – a personal narrative

In order to make some specific points about communication, I am including here an incident which happened to me a few years ago. I have used it on a number of teaching occasions to show the complexities of calculating Annual Percentage Rates (APR) and, as a side issue, to illustrate how this might be used to confuse purchasers of loans and payment plans. Let us now turn this around and focus on the role of the salesperson in attempting to sell a distinctly odd financial product.

I had just bought a car from a main dealership, and it is important to note here that the purchase decision had already been made and the deal closed. I had indicated that I would pay by cash but the salesman suggested I might consider a payment plan which he argued would have economic advantages. He then went through a long and highly structured spiel (the market trader terminology is very appropriate here to convey the impression I gained of a script delivered with fluency and enthusiasm!) which apparently showed that a series of payments made over a period of time would be of advantage to me by allowing the money I had intended to part with in payment, to continue to gain interest in the bank. Of course, this would have been a great idea if the payment plan had involved no interest payments (i.e. a zero APR, as is sometimes offered as a perfectly reasonable inducement to buy a product) but in this instance some interest was being charged. Nonetheless the salesman argued that the rate was very attractive compared with current rates which could be earned on a savings account (around 10% per annum at that time).

The delivery of this sales script was very persuading but as we moved towards the 'close' and my signature, a couple of things worried me. The first was that the interest rates quoted on the proposed plan were flat rates rather than compound (as would be reflected by a correctly calculated APR) and even my limited financial training was quite sufficient to ring some alarm bells, particularly when the salesman was unable to quote the APR and even suggested that such a figure was unintelligible and misleading! The second concern was, quite simply, why was I being offered this when I had already bought the car? The response was all about creating happy customers and doing me a favour. As this response was as unconvincing as the missing APR, I decided to give this 'wonderful opportunity' a miss, but I remained fascinated about how the very convincing data calculations had been done so misleadingly, much in the way we admire a conjurer making a large object vanish. Therefore I told him I needed to think about it and asked him if I could have a note of the calculations. He agreed to me making some brief notes and coming back to him with a decision on the payment plan in a couple of days' time, when I picked up the car.

I went away with enough data to reconstruct the plan, sought out a colleague (who is a chartered accountant) and repeated the sales pitch only to get the reply 'it's obviously a con but I can't see exactly how it's done!' The truth was revealed with the use of (recently invented) spreadsheets and the reconstruction of the full payment schedule for the plan compared with the immediate cash payment of the full amount. This showed an APR of around 19 per cent (which was quite an attractive borrowing rate at the time, but not in this specific context) and a loss to myself of around £400 (in net present value terms) compared to a phantom gain of around £500 if the sales pitch had been taken at face value.

When collecting the new car, I talked to the salesman (briefly, of course, as he had other customers to attend to) declining the offer, to which he responded with the best display of incredulity I have ever witnessed, leaving me with the interesting possibility that he really did believe the script himself! Of course I could have argued, complained and generally kicked up a fuss, though I have no doubt (remembering this is some time ago) that I would have run up against a denial that anything misleading had actually been said, reinforced by 'buyer beware'. So I chose the academics' option of influencing and educating through using this example to motivate people to pay attention to APR calculations. Since that time, anyone who teaches personal finance will have noted many further examples of the ability of the designers of financial products to confuse even quite knowledgeable consumers.

Points to note:

▶ Obviously it is important for a buyer to use common sense when faced with any sales proposition, but how far can this be relied on by the vendor of a complex product as a defence against misleading selling? In business-to-business transactions one might, perhaps unwisely, assume a high level of financial sophistication but how far can a consumer be expected to engage with such financial complexity. The clear statement of APRs would help in the simple case shown above, but investment decisions typically involve considerations of risk over long-time periods in the context of complex rules governing administrative and commission payments.
▶ Did the salesman in this case actually know what he was selling? Did he simply follow a script which he believed was above board, though he must surely have wondered where his commission would have come from, or did he intentionally bend a perfectly reasonable package, in effect offering a personal loan, by hiding the true interest rate situation?

▶ The financial package, its presentation, including what I have called the script or spiel, and documentation had been professionally designed. How far was it the intention to confuse the consumer or even the direct seller?

Advertising credit cards – does honesty pay?

In mid-October 2003, newspapers reported that the Chief Executive of a major high street bank, appearing before a Commons Treasury Select Committee, admitted that he did not use a credit card to borrow money and had advised his children likewise. The bank's Chief Executive may well have scored top marks for candidness but the reaction of the estimated nine million people who carry this bank's credit card may not be so favourable.

The topic being investigated by the Parliamentary Select Committee was the interest rates typically charged on outstanding credit card balances; around 18 per cent compared with the 3.5 per cent base rate. There was also criticism of this particular credit card promotion which carried the slogan '0% forever'. This in fact referred to a rate charged on balance transfers which could only be earned in the context of the cardholder paying the full rate on new borrowings. Whether this was clear to those attracted by the slogan was debated by the Committee. Such offers are not unknown from other credit card companies.

The Chief Executive is making a good point about the use of credit cards which would be echoed by any impartial advisor on personal finance. A credit card can be used without incurring any interest charges by paying off the balance every month and personal loans can be obtained at far better rates. Many consumers find it convenient and easy to use the credit card as the source of an occasional 'loan', the high interest rate being the cost of that convenience. The attitude of mind this banker is advising against is the habitual use of an expensive source of long-term finance.

The '0% forever' slogan presents a different issue. One side of the argument is that this slogan is misleading as it reflects only part of a complex package. The other side is that slogans do exactly that, and we all know it! A genuine '0%' deal with no strings attached is impossible to imagine – somebody must pay the cost. All the credit card deals which offer similar incentives (and there are many on the market) do so within some inventive context. In fact, many consumers play the game of moving their negative cash balances around between cards in order to take advantage of the best current deals.

Therefore the financial meritocracy of bankers and wily consumers are playing a game they both understand. The potential losers in all this are the less financially aware, the less self-disciplined and the poor or desperate individuals or families which grasp at any deal which seems to offer hope, even though it will, in fact, push them further along a spiral of financial decline.

The unfortunate banker mentioned at the start of this section joins a colourful list of business executives and entrepreneurs who have made comments about their customers or products they might have subsequently regretted. The most famous and oft quoted is a retailer's comment that the jewellery sold in his chain of high street stores was 'total crap'. While the banker was under pressure to explain his company's policies to an acutely demanding audience, other comments may have been made in situations where the speaker naively thought they would not be reported.

It is doubtful if such comments are often made openly and clearly to stakeholders as part of a policy of ethical management, as it might be seen as ethically dubious to say things which disadvantaged other groups of stakeholders, such as providers of capital.

So the question which must occur to customers of many companies, whether banks or retailers, is 'do the bosses of these companies have similar opinions which they have been careful not to share with us!' We might welcome such honesty as a breath of fresh air, but is it practical and ethical?

Precipice bonds – a discussion with case examples

When most of us place our savings in a bank or building society account we expect to be paid interest, though not at a high rate at this moment in time (mid-2004), with the amount invested remaining intact. There might be some restriction on the withdrawal of this capital but this will usually only be a loss of interest. If we invest in the stock market we really have little excuse not to be aware that we may lose some or all of the capital. We accept the gamble in return for a hoped for higher reward. Recent problems with endowments may have shaken the faith of many who used them as part of a mortgage payment plan but even then their long-term nature means that a reasonable amount of money is still available on maturity, if less than expected or needed. We would hardly expect to go into our high street bank, be advised to buy a savings bond with a good rate of interest and then discover that in three years we had lost most of the capital!

In 2001, Anne received a mailshot from a reputable firm of Independent Financial Advisers (IFAs) offering a savings plan which promised an annual rate of interest of over 10 per cent. At this time, interest rates in normal high street risk-free deposit accounts were around 4 per cent. The wording of the mailshot was very positive so Anne decided to invest £10,000 in the three-year plan. By mid-2003 the capital invested was worth around £300, though this might recover a little by the time the plan matures.

The plan involved a bond which was linked to a stock market index. The capital was safe if this index fell up to 20 per cent in value but any further fall would have a dramatic effect on the capital invested. A fall of 50 per cent would have wiped out all the capital, hence the term 'precipice bond'. The actual fall in mid-2003 was over 40 per cent. Anne had, in effect, gambled against a fall in the index of this magnitude.

Because she had replied to a mailshot and not requested advice from the IFA who sent this advertising material she is classed as an 'execution only' client and has therefore apparently given up the right to formally complain. We also note that such a complaint against advice given by an IFA can only be made when a bond matures. She is, however, in the process of setting up a protest group. It is possible that a case could be made that the advertising was misleading.

Betty is a pensioner who invested £15,000 expecting around 9 per cent income for three years with the capital remaining intact. In fact, over half of the capital was lost when the bond matured recently. The bond was bought through an IFA who has now ceased trading, their assets but not their liabilities having been taken over by a new owner. There are estimated to be around 30,000 similar clients of this IFA with around £300m invested.

A number of highly reputable organisations are involved in the business of selling products such as the ones now referred to as precipice bonds. The basis of these financial products is a stock market index, such as the FTSE 100, or Eurostoxx50, though more idiocyncratic portfolios are evident in some cases. A bank or building society then designs a 'product' (typically a three-year bond) based on financial derivatives such as options and swaps. The bank then sells these either directly to customers or through IFAs, who earn commission on the sale.

The customer, often a retired person with little experience of equity-related products, will be attracted by the high interest rate and not understand the risks involved in terms of the loss of capital. It appears that these were not always fully explained to them by IFAs and bank employees. After designing the product, the bank would also create advertising and other promotional material outlining the merits and risks of the products. It appears the former descriptions were more prominent and, in practice, some IFAs appear to have used such copy as a template when creating their own promotional material, such as mailshots.

A high street bank at the centre of this affair (not the same one as in the section above) sold much of its bonds (the first issue of which brought in £120m) through its branch network. Branch staff would be aware of customers who had cash in deposit accounts with the bank and who could therefore be targeted as potential buyers of a product offering a far higher rate of interest. Customers have typically lost around half of their capital. The bank has been fined £1.9m and made to pay £98m in compensation by the Financial Services Authority. It is estimated that around 22,500 customers could be compensated, though 28,500 will not be. This is because the compensation rules relate to the advice and not the product as such. Compensation is automatic only if certain conditions relating to the customer's lack of experience in equity investment, amount invested as a proportion of capital or age are met. Other customers might complain to the Financial Ombudsman Service if they can argue they were wrongly advised in their particular case.

The bank was particularly criticised for its lack of staff training and lack of control of its sales staff. The underlying portfolios for the bank's products seem inappropriate when viewed retrospectively.

There is, of course, another way of looking at this and similar situations. Whatever the advertising, the customer was being offered an interest rate of at least double that available in ordinary, risk-free savings accounts. How can this be the case? If these bonds are such a good deal, why have they not been bought up already by the financial sophisticates? One answer may be the time conditions; your money is tied up for three years, say, with its resulting implications for liquidity. Otherwise the only possible answer relates to the increased risk accompanying the purchase of this product. The customer must have known there was a catch somewhere! However, it is not as if an interest rate of, say, 50 per cent was being offered, when we can all guess that a scam or a gamble is involved. Though the extra rate is financially very significant it does not look totally outrageous if presented to you by the friendly bank or building society adviser or the very skilled and persuasive IFA who, after a long discussion of your needs and lifestyle, tells you this is an important source of income in your portfolio and worthy of investing 30 per cent of your savings while some of the rest can be in long-term growth investments which are risky in the short term! It is an indication of the power of mailshot advertising that many individuals were persuaded to invest substantial amounts of their lifetime savings in such products without even seeing the need to obtain independent advice.

Finally, let us remember the instances where banks and IFAs have avoided penalty. Having gained the profit margin on sales turnover and the commission paid on individual sales (a couple of per cent of sales totalling billions of pounds), many people who have invented, designed and sold these products have had the benefit of the revenue that such activity brings. Perhaps they will now be looking out for the next opportunity.

Notes

1. Particular financial institutions have not been identified in the details above as their specific identity is irrelevant to the argument presented. It would also seem unfair to name some but not others equally involved. The individual case histories are fictional but consistent with actual cases.

2. This extended argument against some providers of financial products and services illustrates why many consumers are becoming more than a little disillusioned with the activities of some parts of the financial services sector. It shows how ethical issues may exist within mainstream economic activity and why balancing duties towards stakeholders may not be simple. Other than the 'personal narrative' it does not reflect the author's direct experience but like so many issues in marketing ethics could easily affect anyone.

3. You may wish to consult the original sources of the facts underlying the above argument. Considerable attention was given to this issue in the serious press in September 2003 with continued updating to the time of writing. You may usefully consult the archives of *the Guardian*, *Financial Times* and *Sunday Telegraph* and use appropriate web searches.

4. It would be wise to view the above as only an introduction to this troubling situation, whose ramifications will no doubt unfold in the

future, along with a range of other stories affecting this industry. The nature of many of the financial products on offer is such that some problems associated with them will only become evident to the consumer in the long term. Company profits, however, will have been earned in the short term.

Financial product design and sales – analysis

An understandable company response to the above might be to argue that this is how business is conducted in this industry. Therefore, in order to explore the ethical implications of the precipice bond selling case, let us try to develop an 'ideal situation' from an ethical perspective in order to try to see the ways in which real practice might be improved. There is, of course, an assumption here that an ideal moral situation is possible to find.

This characterisation of an 'ideal situation' could no doubt be improved by further lists of obligations on each of the actors involved, and even by extension of the list of actors; at the very least, a number of financial institutions and sources of advice could have been included. The details below are enough to show how far adrift the key players in the precipice bond situation actually are from such an ideal.

The actors and the events from the point of view of each actor are listed below:

▶ *C is a financial institution which designs financial products for sale to consumers and also creates the necessary promotional material.* Based on comprehensive market information and knowledge of the financial environment, C designs a product for a given purpose (defined in terms of such features as interest rates, risks, life, etc.). C does not design products which are unlikely to be of benefit to customers, or if a product is designed for a particular narrow market niche (e.g. high growth and high risk) C notes this feature as a prominent warning on all promotional material. C creates appropriate descriptions of the product for the customer and for the seller and also develops suitable training materials and programmes for the seller. After launching the product, C checks whether or not it is being sold in line with its intended purpose and if the supporting information is being correctly used. C determines the rates of commission to be appropriate.

▶ *F is an organisation which sells financial products designed by others or by itself to consumers.* F ensures that its sales staff and advisers are fully trained and competent and conducts audits of their performance. F ensures that sales targets and commission do not encourage inappropriate selling on the part of its staff. F reviews the suitability of the product for its client base and creates its own promotional materials as appropriate. F trains its staff in the sale of this product in the context of the full range of products on offer from a variety of financial institutions. When advising clients F fully explores relevant aspects of the customer's position (in particular their grasp of risk and time factors), explains the features of this and other products as relevant to this situation and gives advice only based on the appropriateness of the products in question. When advertising products where advice may not be taken by the customer, F is explicit in terms of risk factors in terms which are intelligible to the customer. F audits the take-up of products (including customer feedback) in order to be sure the product is finding its target customers.

▶ *S is an individual salesperson, probably employed by F though might be self-employed.* S has been thoroughly trained to sell this product, though his or her background knowledge in finance need not be extensive. He or she is well aware that the product is suitable only for customers with specific attitudes to personal risk and then only as part of a balanced portfolio. He or she is supported by promotional materials and 'scripts' and though part of his or her remuneration will be through commission he or she will not make sales on the basis of maximising commission. He or she will not close a sale if the customer is unclear on the implications of buying this product or is reluctant. Having sold the product he or she will normally have little further contact with the customer but will be available if necessary.

▶ *Z is a customer.* Z recognises his or her responsibility to be informed to a reasonable extent on his or her own needs and how these might in theory be met by various types of financial product. Z actively enters into a dialogue with S (and with other information sources as appropriate) in order to fully understand the implications of the specific products on offer.

It is interesting to note the extent to which all the actors in the various cases mentioned earlier failed to meet at least some of the above-mentioned conditions. The conditions are not based on abstruse philosophical analysis but on simple notions of fairness, openness and responsibility to clients and other actors.

However, the earlier theoretical section, dealing with the distancing of human subjects, may either be seen as strongly critical of current marketing practice or as pointing to the need for marketers to carefully review their own moral development in the context of how they view and characterise other people. This is particularly true when the consumers are disadvantaged and vulnerable in some way. It is sometimes said that the key point of ethics is how we view the less privileged in society and what we do about it. To view those with less knowledge of the dangers of the products and services we are selling as a potential revenue stream, and no more, hardly signifies moral maturity at a corporate or individual level.

One might note at this point the effects of a morally neutralising use of language. 'Safeguarding a revenue stream' sounds so much better than 'ripping off the punters'! You may be the judge of the underlying intention behind that well-known phrase 'exploiting the market'.

Summary

The early discussion centring on moral distance used marketing contexts as examples, though similar arguments could be made relating to the 'distance' between managers and employees, large manufacturers and small suppliers and other business contexts. Much of philosophical ethics is based on the idea of the universal application of moral principles. If one feels this is idealistic and that some notion of 'insiders and outsiders' is necessary (at least in descriptive ethics) then we may be led towards some very muddy, and ethically treacherous, waters.

The rest of this chapter was devoted to the presentation and analysis of a variety of specific contexts. Privacy was explored through telephone selling, where the low costs of this form of communication are increasing its use. An alternative discussion could have centred on the use of 'spam' and a whole range of other issues associated with selling on the Internet.

Most attention is given here to financial products, chosen due to the increasing disquiet which is currently being expressed by consumers and the press relating to what was once a fairly sedate sector of the economy. Pension funds, endowments, credit cards and the like have become major concerns. We have chosen here to explore the world of precipice bonds; financial products sold by major players in the market which have led to crippling losses for many vulnerable people. Perhaps the most disturbing aspect of this situation is that the companies which have sold these products have previously enjoyed a reputation for being solid and safe. While most people will realise that direct investment in the stock market carries considerable risk, it will have come as a shock to many that dealing with major high street institutions may also have unforeseen financial dangers.

20 Ethics and Operations Management

Purpose and learning outcomes

The purpose of this chapter is to consider the ethics of Operations Management, including project and change management.
   You will be able to

▶ show an understanding of the ethical issues raised by Operations Management;

▶ appreciate some of the particular problems of public sector management;

▶ show an understanding of ethical issues in partnership and overseas sourcing decisions.

Introduction

This chapter introduces a range of issues in the practical management of operations along with some case studies. We begin with an outline of ethical issues in the various branches of Operations Management, followed by a comparison between the philosophy of continuous improvement (often referred to as kaizen, reflecting Japanese influences) and more radical ideas of process re-engineering. This is followed by a short discussion of ethics in project management, with a particular emphasis on public sector procurement projects.

We then move the discussion into the supply chain, an emphasis on Business-to-Business (B2B) relationships rather than Business-to-Consumer (B2C). We first consider some ethical and power issues in the context of partnership sourcing, an area generally considered of positive value to industry due to attempts to reach 'win–win' relationships. Is this reality or the rhetoric used by large companies? Finally we consider some difficult ethical issues evident when manufacturing, previously in a company's home country, is relocated to another part of the world.

It should be noted that Chapter 14 introduced quality management in a discussion on moral muteness. Quality management is often seen as a branch of Operations Management and therefore the first part of Chapter 14 might be read in conjunction with this chapter. In contrast, discussions of organisational change are often seen as part of 'people management' while we have focussed on kaizen, Business Process Re-engineering (BPR) and project management. This once again shows the pervasive nature of management, organisational and ethical concepts and issues.

Ethics and Operations Management

In any organisation much effort is spent on the actual design and delivery of products and services for the customer. While this is most obviously the case for a manufacturing concern, where the basic concepts and models of Operations Management were developed, it is also true of any public service or private sector organisation. Hospitals, schools and social services departments have customers with a legitimate right to expect high-quality service and must organise themselves appropriately to deliver such service.

Therefore Operations Management is a very practical discipline concerned with:

► the design of products and services;
► the design of the work processes necessary to manufacture and deliver goods and services;
► the design of planning and control processes to ensure appropriate delivery, quality and cost control;
► the implementation of operational plans including the management of risk and the emergency action needed if things go wrong.

It can easily be seen that Operations affects large numbers of employees, has responsibility for the effective use of capital tied up in facilities, incurs costs and generates revenue on a large scale. It is at the 'sharp end' of many of the ethical concerns mentioned in this book, even when we have previously associated such concerns with, say, Personnel or Marketing.

Few texts on Operations Management deal with ethical concerns explicitly and at length. Indeed many appear to be somewhat technical and quantitative in approach with an apparent emphasis on performance, efficiency and cost reduction. However, this can be misleading. Many of the original thinkers in this area have had a strong intuitive grasp of the need to provide good working conditions, give a fair deal to customers and make efficient use of resources. This reflects the engineering training of many of the original practitioners and the obvious need of practitioners to be close to the point where actual work is being carried out and fully aware of the problems it entails. Being 'close to the workers', like being 'close to the customers' (advice frequently dispensed by popular writers), should give one a powerful incentive to understand the issues involved from a wide range of perspectives.

Though usually seen as simple common sense, there is an important ethical issue here. In Chapter 19 we were concerned about moral distance and the objectification of the consumer. Here we can see the dangers of viewing a 'workforce' in a similar way, particularly if a state of conflict over pay and conditions has continued for some time. There is an opposite danger, however, of management being close to working processes with the sole objective of control. An example in this context might be workers in a call centre where electronic surveillance of their work, in terms of productivity, quality, mistakes made and other parameters management finds interesting, is coupled with a distancing from the workers in a moral sense. The fact that a great deal of data passes between workers and management does not mean that any real moral dialogue is taking place.

Whilst the originators of the techniques of work study may appear to have instituted a soulless system for exploiting labour they can also be seen in a very different light, that is as engineers who carefully studied the nature of work and designed ways of carrying out tasks which were safe, efficient in the use of the workers' energy and provided a fair rate of pay linked to the time and effort required to do the work. The fact that this also increased management's visibility of the tasks being performed and therefore the control of the work may be seen as an advantage or a disadvantage depending on one's point of view! For many years this has been one of the most fiercely debated areas of organisational theory.

Similarly if one looks more recently at the development of ideas such as TQM one can see tensions between a paternalistic and management-oriented view typical of the 'quality campaigns' and the emphasis placed on the dignity and knowledge of all employees by such writers as Deming.

It is not our intention here to fully explore all the potential ethical problems of Operations Management but to list some of those which are typically mentioned in texts and to relate these to our ethical models and language. Based on a structuring of Operations Management in one popular text (Slack *et al.* 2001) we note the following as areas of potential ethical concern:

Product and service design
Many of the decisions made at this stage have tremendous implications for environmental concerns (such as the use of appropriate materials and energy) as well as the potential effectiveness of the product or service to meet customer needs and to be safe. The key issues of cost and quality must be addressed, particularly as this relates to the effective life of the product and its maintenance costs.

Location and layout of facilities
There are a number of employment and environmental issues in the location of factories, warehouses and retail outlets. Facilities management is a growing area of concern with particular current attention placed on disabled customer and staff access.

Process technology and job design
In parallel with issues of product design are the equivalent, and often similar, issues in process design, including the plant and equipment needed as well as the design of work tasks. Issues of safety, pollution, stress, unpleasant and unsocial work are obviously important. Similarly in operational contexts where the customer is present (from hospitals to supermarkets) there are issues of the management of the customer experience, including safety.

Planning and control
Though the usually computer-based systems which plan and monitor work in real time will seem a somewhat esoteric subject for most people, they have a considerable effect of the experience of workers (in terms of work intensity and hours), of customers (in terms of delivery performance and prioritisation) and on cost (through warehouse capacity, inventory levels and suchlike). It is often possible to reduce costs and manage demand fluctuations at the expense of security of employment and unsocial working hours. Public sector disputes, such as those recently

affecting the Fire and Rescue Service and the Royal Mail, may centre on pay but have a background of 'increasing productivity' which may well involve changes to working practices and shift patterns as well as the total number employed.

Supply Chain Management

An important development in Operational thinking in recent years has been to move the focus of analysis from the organisation (or a particular factory, say) to a supply chain. For instance we might consider the flow of materials from the suppliers to a main manufacturing concern right through to the end-user. This often involves a range of organisations involved in making things, transporting them and selling them in high street locations. By co-ordinating all these activities along the supply chain (through negotiated contracts, effective liaison and the use of information and communication systems) the aim is to reduce wastage and delivery times to the benefit of all concerned, similar to the 'Just-in-Time' concept which originated in Japan in the 1960s. Whether the comparative power relationships between all participants in a supply chain do in fact ensure that all partners benefit equally is a source of much academic debate.

Risk management

As we show in Chapter 16, risk management is a key issue of ethical concern in operations as well as in financial management and business strategy.

Implicit within the literature in Operations Management is an attention to ethics as briefly shown in the following models and approaches:

► Utilitarian frameworks – through the use of cost–benefit analysis and the attempts to operationalise the concept of quality, particularly as this relates to 'quality of life' in a health care context. Environmental management attempt to do this through environmental audit and analysis (see Chapter 21).
► Deontological frameworks – through the law relating to employee rights, health and safety, discrimination and so forth. The development of such things as customer charters and codes of practice are attempts to make explicit the rights and duties of all parties involved. If these are developed through a process of consultation, this may be seen as contractarian.

▶ Virtue ethics – through the emphasis on staff development and knowledge management, though whether this relates to moral development or is merely instrumental to the processes and required behaviours determined by the organisation depends on context.

Is health and safety always a good thing? – a case exercise

The task

Carefully read the case, in particular noting any potential bias in the use of language. How would you manage this situation as operations director? If you could start again from the beginning, how would you now approach this obviously difficult change in operating systems?

The case

Your company is in the process of re-equipping a major manufacturing site. Your Health and Safety committee (including employee representatives), backed up by a consultant's report, have insisted on the implementation of rigid guidelines on the use of certain essential new machines and the development of a dedicated training programme for all operatives and direct managers. This will also involve higher than planned manning levels when the machines are put into operation.

The equipment maker insists these are quite unnecessary, in particular as this machinery is intended to be safer than that previously used. Indeed it is unlikely your company would have bought such machinery if it was known to require such attention. Other factories use similar machinery in line with the maker's recommendations, though the consultant's report reflects allegations that safety is being compromised in these situations.

As operations director, your instinct has always been to ensure a high level of safety, but in this case it is obvious that the use of this machinery in the way suggested by Health and Safety is unprofitable. Negotiations are underway suggesting a compromise can be reached which is just about profitable, would benefit employees financially but which appears to conveniently ignore some of the safety problems raised. You are suspicious that Health and Safety issues are being used as a lever in what is actually a bargaining process relating to pay and conditions of work.

Discussion

This case illustrates the way in which what at first appears to be a tightly defined, technical problem, the safe operation of a new machine, is in reality a major change in a 'human activity system' with wide-ranging implications. The management of change is one of the most demanding challenges for all employees, both at a strategic and an operational level.

The management of operational change – Kaizen or BPR?

Two performance improvement techniques which have generated a considerable amount of interest in recent years are Kaizen and Business Process Re-engineering (BPR). The term 'Kaizen' originates from Japan and formalises the notion of continuous improvement in business activities and in life in general. It recommends a long-term, never-ending search for improvement, the antithesis of the 'if it's not broken, don't mend it' approach. In a work context it is usually based on team effort, working to find a series of small, incremental changes which, if successful, are then embedded in normal working practice. The emphasis is on the improvement of human processes through the involvement of the people who normally do the work, rather than 'experts' coming in from the outside.

Kaizen and other techniques such as 'Just-in-Time' can be seen as arising from the historical situation of Japan after the Second World War, when the country was short of capital and had an industrial infrastructure damaged by the war. Japan did, however, have a well-educated and resourceful population and the use of this resource was the foundation for its industrial success in the second half of the 20th century. While much of the Japanese approach to management has been adapted for the West it has also been the subject of considerable debate and criticism. Techniques of team working and quality management can also be seen as the adoption of particular forms of social control in the workplace. Even within Japan in the 1960s there was criticism of the ferocious drive towards productivity and the toll this was taking on workers and managers (see Chapter 15).

In contrast, BPR is a more recent concept which originated in the USA, particularly in the context of innovation in the use of Information Technology. BPR rejects the use of incremental change in favour of top-management-led radical change in the search for productivity breakthroughs to be implemented within a short time-frame. Such change is seen as affecting a business as a whole and involves the use of a structured approach to process analysis and the implementation of change. In practice, this often involves the introduction of new computer-based systems and the 'downsizing' (or 'rightsizing' if a gentler term is thought necessary) of the human operational resource.

The originators of BPR claim a number of successes, though its opponents point to expensive failures. It is often difficult to arrive at a view of its overall value in terms of implementations, as a great deal of money and consultancy activity rides on the perceived value of such techniques. It is perhaps easier to comment on its stated benefits and note the reported risks. Potential benefits are said to include:

- ▶ aligning core operational processes with business strategy, in particular as groups of customers are targeted and processes or products designed to meet their needs in total;
- ▶ asking naïve and challenging questions about the 'way we have always done things' in order to promote change through staff involvement;
- ▶ increasing staff flexibility, as multi-skilled staff are often desirable within new IT-based processes;
- ▶ eliminating non-value-adding activities;
- ▶ encouraging networking and information sharing by staff;
- ▶ emphasising benchmarking, that is internal and external performance and process comparisons in order to improve the system (though it should be said that this is also part of other approaches to quality management);
- ▶ managing successful change improves organisational confidence and capability.

This is all very well if the change is successful at both an operational and a financial level. Some writers have pointed to risks, as seen in some less successful attempted implementations:

- ▶ For a variety of reasons a BPR project may fail, which can be very expensive, lose key staff and lose customers due to the disruption of the attempted improvement.
- ▶ Even a project which succeeds in terms of short-term operational and financial performance may sow the seeds of failure due to the downsizing and loss of skills and knowledge that occurs.

▶ Many projects have in practice had a very strong technical flavour with little attention being paid to organisational culture. Indeed projects may simply result in the creation of a new operational system, for example, with the location of call centres in other countries and hence with new working cultures and norms of behaviour.

▶ As the environment continually changes (e.g. in terms of market need and available technology), then BPR projects must be carried out repeatedly. This may lead to an increased capability for radical change ('continuous revolution' rather than 'continuous improvement'?) or to excessive cost and organisational confusion.

A series of papers exploring BPR are given in Burke and Peppard (1995). As you may well imagine, most organisations will attempt to adapt any use of Kaizen and BPR in order to gain the advantages they promise while avoiding the problems detailed above for each technique. This is far from easy to achieve in practice. If you consider these techniques with a sensitivity to the implications of the language they employ as well as the potential for ethical dilemmas then moral issues are not hard to find.

Managers will, however, quite reasonably argue that the competitive environment, and the need to deliver effective public services, faces them with a series of challenges in maintaining and improving operational systems. These challenges will not go away while we debate their ethical implications. Another set of techniques associated with operational change management goes under the heading of Project Management, though the literature in this area shows some further ethical problems as we explore below.

Project management ethics

A retired senior executive of a large engineering company was speaking recently on his attitude to gaining government contracts for weapons systems. This was following the news that four key weapons procurement programmes were both late and massively over-budgeted cost. The executive blithely commented that it was the norm for this to happen as contractors tendering for such contracts played a game whereby they deliberately offered a low price secure in the knowledge that changes during the life of the design and manufacturing project would inevitably give them the opportunity to recover revenue and make a profit.

To some extent this game suited the end-user of the designed system, as they may not have been able to gain approval to go ahead if the true final cost had been known at the outset. The users may not, however, be quite so happy about the delays which seem typical of such situations. The final cost, of course, is borne by the taxpayer, either in the form of tax or the lack of other public services which might have been obtained with this money. We have been assured that new controls are in place to prevent this happening again!

For many years this scenario has been typical of the public procurement of major systems and large buildings around the world. Such developments involve considerable risk, particularly when highly innovative design is involved. Recently this is often associated with computer-based information system design, such as air traffic control or nationally based systems for tax and benefit administration. In all fairness to the designers, such systems may require tremendous ingenuity, original thinking and sheer hard work to make them operational at all. However, between the worthy designers and the needy customers there appears to be ample opportunity for profit for other individuals feeding off the mistakes, uncertainties and general confusion inevitable when really advanced and difficult tasks are attempted. Much of this extra cost (or revenue, depending which side of the fence you are on) accrues to managers, lawyers and other agencies on the fringe of the technical work.

We may therefore first of all ask whether such chaos is inevitable. The best answer would seem to be that large complex projects are almost always susceptible to problems both in the original definition of what needs to be done and during their execution. The purpose of project management, as a practical discipline, is to protect the stakeholders in such situations by managing the three basic parameters of any project: the quality of the output, its cost and the timescale of delivery. Though this may well mean some cost and time overruns, and perhaps some compromises for some stakeholders, these will arise from the agreed risks which have been taken rather than profiteering by some of the parties involved. This is why project management is widely regarded as a highly challenging role, requiring not only technical expertise but political judgement in managing both external stakeholders and the design and production team.

There is also a considerable moral dimension to the role of the project manager. We have already pointed to the need for an even-handed balancing of stakeholder perspectives, requiring political sensitivity.

Some project managers might be tempted to take a differing view, for example, as employees of one of the agencies involved to aggressively pursue the objectives of that agency. If management inadequacies exist in the other agencies (e.g. a funding public sector authority) then the project manager may well be able to use the up-to-date information at their disposal to favour their employer. Though the final result of such actions may be arrived at only following post-project legal proceedings or negotiated compromises there is a fair chance that short-term advantage will have been gained.

There are a variety of professional bodies which aim to prescribe standards of education and behaviour for project managers. Such bodies typically produce codes of ethical behaviour for their members, though whether they are in effect able to monitor and enforce compliance with such codes (in the manner of medical and legal professional bodies, for example) is doubtful. However, even if such codes are only built into educational programmes in the form of guidance for professional practice, then they will have an obvious value. Not surprisingly, much of the influence on professional practice is through standard forms of contract. This does, however, suggest that the law is being used to set the rules of an adversarial game which is then played with gusto by the professionals involved – a view of practical morality in business seen as inevitable by some writers on business ethics! The danger is that the weaker or less organised stakeholders, the consumer and the general public, will inevitably lose out in the short term, gaining some limited satisfaction only when reports of wrongdoing are produced by central agencies or the press long after the event.

In a private sector context, the ultimate control on this and other undesirable, if legal, activities will be customer choice in the market. Companies are well aware of the effects of damage to brands and to a company's reputation when customers finally see they are getting a poor deal. Provided competition is maintained and there is a good flow of impartial information to consumers (e.g. from independent product surveys) in order to counter advertising, then companies will see that some sanctions do exist if they mismanage their operations. The difficulty in project management contexts is that the timescales for the exercise of market choice may be highly protracted. To say that all will be sorted out in the long term may be of little value to the losers in such situations.

In the public sector, changes in consumer choice may not be an appropriate control, though attempts to make this work are at the centre of much policy-making by political parties. The alternative is effective audit by central and local public bodies. The danger, as always, is the timescale of action.

In these contexts we can clearly see how time, risk and information set a demanding context for ethical decision-making. Where an individual or company can get away with egoistic and biased actions for a long period of time, there is a premium placed on reputation and justified trust as the safeguards of decision makers acting fairly. The practical alternative is active investigation and disclosure of dubious practice. It would seem sad if our only guarantee of basic ethical standards in business and public sector management is the actions of audit bodies and the press. You may have an opinion on whether this is in fact the case, and whether or not it is inevitable. Timely investigation and open access to information may be the only remedy in a society where high standards of ethical behaviour in business and public life are not seen as widespread.

You might wish to use reports published in the press or other media to explore issues in the effectiveness of project management. The public sector inevitably uses project management extensively to manage change and published reports often make very interesting reading. The anecdotes and points made above are all based on published reports of public sector projects.

Partnership sourcing – 'win–win' or domination by the large firm

In much of our discussion in this book there has been a tacit assumption that we have been referring to the management of an organisation. Of course we realise that much management activity relates to the environment of the manager's employer but the assumption has been that managerial decision-making and control refer to the organisation in question. In recent years, much attention has been given to the notion of Supply Chain Management (SCM). A supply chain is usually defined in material terms as beginning with basic raw materials and extending through a range of operational processes, such as manufacture, storage, transportation and so forth, until a product is in the hands of a customer.

While a particular manager will still be employed by one or another firm within a supply chain, there is an assumption that they will pay considerable attention to the operation of the supply chain as a whole. This is not to detract from their major responsibilities to their employer but is based on the assumption that an effective supply chain will be to the benefit of all the firms involved in its various stages.

Now supply chains have existed as long as manufacturing industry. One key to SCM is to consider the relationship between neighbouring firms in the chain. This may be on the basis of participation in an open market, that is each purchasing transaction is separate. The buyer acts in much the same way as a customer in a normal consumer market. In practice, however, in B2B (as opposed to B2C) contexts there may be much to be gained from more stable relationships. This might take the form of supply contracts and a variety of similar, close relationships. A key phrase now used is the notion of partnership sourcing.

One aspect of Japanese operations which was noted in the 1980s by Western organisations was the way in which car manufacturers in particular formed stable and dominating relationships with their suppliers. Much has been written, for example, about Toyota's relationship with their supply base. It was seen that the purchasing staff in such companies did not simply buy goods when needed but used long-term stable partnerships with suppliers as a key part of their 'Just-in-Time' manufacturing philosophy. This was seen in contrast to the adversarial relationships which appeared to be the norm in B2B material procurement in the West.

This is one context in which the notion of 'win–win' relationships were trumpeted as a positive way forwards for industry; profitable for all concerned with the partnership and based on an ethics of trust and integrity. Of course it can be argued that partnerships also exclude and interfere with the operation of a market but this can be countered by noting that in practice the partners will always be looking for alternative sources and customers. However, the fact that a partnership exists does provide a measure of medium-term stability.

If working well, such a partnership will involve a degree of openness and communication not seen in a more adversarial and nakedly competitive context. The purchasing organisation will typically give their suppliers a lot of information on their future requirements and plans. This should make production planning by the suppliers far more cost-effective and successful in terms of delivering goods on time. Part of the deal, however, is that suppliers will be more open with their cost data and the expectation will be that a 'learning curve' effect takes place whereby costs in the supplier are lowered over time and this benefit is transmitted to the buyer in terms of lower cost of goods bought. Western firms who agreed to innovative supply contracts with Japanese companies in the early days of this approach were often shocked by the extent to which the Japanese buyers really did expect high quality, precisely timed delivery and dramatic cost reductions over time. If the supplier found this hard to achieve, the Japanese would help with strict advice on the operation of quality systems and other operational processes as part of the partnership approach. A further benefit was the sharing of information on future products and a sharing of design expertise over a period of time.

The above, lengthy description has been included in order to fully convey not only some flavour of the way in which B2B relationships are different from B2C but also to show how competition can be made to work in a practical context of inter-firm dealing. It should not, however, be thought that such a context is inherently more ethical because a partnership is involved!

The first point to note is that a number of business researchers and writers have noted that the West may have misunderstood the true basis of Japanese manufacturing strategy. The industrial structure in Japan is based on a small number of extremely large conglomerate organisations which may well, in effect, own most of the supply chain in question. It is usual for one firm in such a chain to be highly dominant and, in practice, manage the chain in an authoritarian fashion. The suppliers are simply not going to act independently! Studies of factories operating the Just-in-Time approach have also raised issues of the extent to which a benign and participatory ethics is in fact in operation. There is a big question mark over the transferability of such a system in its entirety to the West.

Furthermore, researchers have increasingly begun to understand the strategic dynamics of supply chains. A key concept here is that of value added at each stage of the chain. Concepts of power, dominance and value appropriation have been used to provide economic models and prescriptions of how to maximise profitability when operating in a supply chain context. What is revealed, not surprisingly, is a highly sophisticated game which is as strategically cut-throat as any other market. The power, reputation and integrity concepts we introduced in Chapter 10 form a natural part of the language which seems to be used to describe such a context rather than the more traditional models of business ethics.

As Cox [1999] comments in a useful summary article on the strategic issues in SCM:

Essentially business is about appropriating value for oneself...the theoretical ideal in business (from an entrepreneurial perspective) is to be able to put oneself in a position where neither customers, employees, competitors or suppliers can leverage value from you, while putting yourself in a position to leverage all of them.

While admitting this is a rarely achieved '...idyllic business situation...' (Cox 1999, p. 171), such power is seen as desirable and at the root of strategic SCM rather than the softer notions of trust and openness. This style of exposition is typical of the hard-headed strategic and economic approach where the analysis of power relations is seen as providing the key explanatory variables and practical prescriptions. It says little about the ethics of actually managing in such a context and may even feel that there is little to be said.

Overseas sourcing

In the UK, as well as in other Western economies, there has been a considerable trend towards overseas sourcing of components and finished goods as substitutes for products previously manufactured here. Where there has been a direct replacement of manufacturing capacity, for example when a factory has shut in the UK and identical goods then made overseas, this has often led to considerable protest. Less emotive, though just as real, have been increases in the general level of import of manufactured goods at the same time as a decline in UK production. The reasons given for such changes usually revolve around the major parameters of manufacturing performance; reduced cost, improved quality and more reliable delivery.

A more recent trend has been the substitution of jobs in the service sector, for example the location of call centres overseas. This type of change has been facilitated by improvements in the cost-effective use of communication and information technology. This change might also be seen in the context of the recruitment of overseas labour in many parts of the service sector. The political responses to such changes are highly visible in the media and a cause of concern in many communities.

This is, therefore, a highly emotive and politically charged area of concern. In the past it might have been argued that the quality of the overseas produced goods was lower than those produced in the UK. This is no longer a persuasive argument. The basic ethical argument is

323

therefore quite straightforward, though a separate argument about the exploitation of the workforce in other countries will be considered later.

From a utilitarian perspective, assuming the decision to source goods overseas was economically and operationally sound (i.e. there are real cost, quality and other benefits), then several categories of stakeholder will benefit. Providers of capital will see an improved return on their investment and customers will get a better deal in terms of price or quality. Within the heading of 'customer' we may include the retail outlets which will benefit from lower costs and buoyant demand. Furthermore the remaining employees of the firm will benefit from improved profitability and security of employment. The potential losers will be employees who have lost their jobs, including future employees who will not benefit from continuing employment vacancies. An important part of utilitarianism is protection of the losers in any economic calculation from extreme disutility. In such a case in the UK there are considerable redundancy benefits, redeployment possibilities and the advantages of a generally buoyant economy. The argument given in this paragraph is essentially that employed by any firm in such a situation. It might even be sharpened if the alternative to overseas sourcing was the closure of the firm. The above argument is also the general one employed to justify a free market which will inevitably involve winners and losers.

A deontological approach would naturally be concerned with the rights of existing workers and the fairness with which redundancies are managed. There is considerable legislation available to ensure that appropriate consideration is given. Employee representation through Trade Unions is likely to figure strongly in such a process of change. This type of situation does, however, provide something of a challenge to a contractarian style of dialogue with a workforce. The boundaries of a community of discourse will be altered by a substitution of a workforce and any implicit 'social contract' will no longer apply. Dramatic organisational change may well involve redrawing the boundaries of an organisational community's membership. Who should do this and who agrees to a plan of change?

The answer, of course, is that the owners and managers of an organisation have the responsibility for making such a change happen. The fact that organisational membership is potentially uncertain and changing poses considerable problems for the effective dialogue that discourse ethics assumes must take place. This is not to say that dialogue should not take place; indeed it should surely increase as a matter of good management practice. The issue is who is involved in such a dialogue during the different phases of the proposed change? At what point are the new suppliers and workforce entitled to consider themselves part of the conversation?

The obvious answer to the above questions would be that the part of the management of the firm that is unchanging, often senior management and a project team commissioned to manage the planning and implementation of change, form the group engaged in real dialogue. Fact finding and briefing of other employees and stakeholders will take place, and openness combined with honesty would be desirable features of such processes. However, the decision-making community has in effect shrunk down to a stable core. A theme we explore earlier in the chapter was the difficulty of managing change. Overseas sourcing is yet another example of this and clearly shows the challenges facing ethical approaches based on dialogue within a community in a context of radical change.

It should be obvious from the above that change management provides a useful arena for moral development. It also provides a context where the ethical basis of actions should be challenged using the language and concepts of ethics, that is situations in which moral muteness is unhelpful.

Our discussion up to this point has focussed on the ethical concerns of the parent company. A very important alternative perspective is gained if we move our attention to the overseas supplier. We may be dealing with a wide variety of situations here, but it is interesting to consider the situation of sourcing from a less well-developed economy where lower wages provide at least part of the competitive advantage. Perhaps the most desirable context is where wages and working conditions (in particular safety) in the factories of the supplier are good when compared with others in that country, though obviously costs are lower than in the destination country. The workers in the supplier will then consider themselves to be getting a good deal. It is possibly the case, however, that such wages and conditions would seem exploitative in the West. Should we judge such a situation in terms of the ethical norms of the destination country or of the supplier's country? This issue can be further explored through the mechanism of integrative social contracts theory given in Chapter 8.

However, many commentators in the West have noted the poor working conditions and the exploitation of child labour in some countries which supply goods to the West. In particular this seems unjust when fashion items, sold at premium cost, depend for their manufacture on the skills and labour of young people who are paid a pittance even by the standards of their own country. The economic response might be that such manufacture still provides some work and wages which may be essential to avoid starvation. A further response is that the consumer is always free to protest through not buying the goods.

At the root of this difficult argument is the picture of global economic inequality which provides a setting for much misery as well as competitive opportunity. A firm in the West may simply argue that this is how the world is at the present time so exploiting economic possibilities is the name of the game. Those who are outraged at the results of such actions may then use the media to provide negative publicity for such firms, thus giving a disincentive to such exploitation. Thus a very public discourse takes place and it could be argued that this is the way in which ethical concerns are translated into action in some contexts.

As we have noted several times in this book, some radical opinion is sceptical of the ability of business ethics to address such problems. You might wish to consider if the tools of ethical analysis we have been using do in fact need to be supplemented by others in order to enable a debate regarding the global effects of market economies.

Summary

Unlike marketing, there is no widely recognised subject called operations ethics, though the ideas and models of marketing ethics will have an obvious relevance to operations carried out in a market environment. Operations shares with HRM a concern with organisational behaviour though naturally focusses attention on a narrower range of concerns and uses a number of techniques and concepts specific to this context. Because of its practical nature, there are a large range of case studies and articles available on problems and issues in Operations Management, and many of these have considerable ethical import.

To reflect this we have focussed first of all on the management of change and on Health and Safety as areas of work where some ethical analysis is useful for both private and public sector management. The concept of moral muteness, mentioned in Chapter 14 in the context of quality management, is of wide general value in ethical evaluation and could in fact have been introduced in several chapters in this book.

The final sections of this chapter relate mainly to the management of material supply. It is interesting to note that most traditional texts on management make the assumption that the 'unit of analysis' is a company and that a manager in such a company has both internally and externally oriented roles. A quite different and fruitful approach is to take a supply chain as the 'unit of analysis'. In some ways this is quite awkward as simple notions of ownership and control do not apply in quite such a clear way. These must be replaced by ideas of negotiation and comparative power in relationships between companies. A manager might now have roles within the company which employs them, roles defined in terms of the partnership relationship and further roles with other organisations, which may be prospective partners. However complex this may sound, it defines the working world of many company employees at this time and is likely to become more widespread in the future.

The final section relates to overseas sourcing, a highly emotive issue where the needs of various stakeholders, past and future, may place them in inevitable conflict situations. Thus in a UK context, the loss of manufacturing jobs has been taking place for some time, with the more recent publicity regarding the loss of service jobs (e.g. in call centres) showing considerable anxiety. However it could be argued not only that the need to protect shareholder interests over-rides those of local workers but that the increase in employment opportunities in other countries is a positive gain in utility which must be taken into the equation. This issue is often confused with another ethical concern, namely the economic exploitation of workers, in particular children, in other countries by large Western corporations.

It should be noted that the material in Chapter 15 on other cultural perspectives is also relevant to operations, partly due to the Japanese influence mentioned above and also to the increasing prevalence of global operations as companies seek to locate manufacturing, service and distribution facilities in low wage countries.

Environmental management and Intellectual Property Claims

Purpose and learning objectives

The purpose of this chapter is to apply ethical principles to environmental management, including some discussion of environmental and quality standards. As much environmental management is concerned with the effects of new technologies, we also include in this chapter an introduction to some ethical issues surrounding Intellectual Property Claims (IPC) and a case study involving the Bhopal disaster.

You will be able to

- ► understand the link between ethics and environmental management;
- ► appreciate some of the issues which arise in the area of environmental and quality standards;
- ► understand some of the principles underlying Intellectual Property Claims in an international context.

Introduction

The first topic in this chapter is the interface between the activities of organisations and environmental management. This is an area which has achieved a deserved prominence in recent years and has obvious ethical implications. We follow this by some notes on the use of inter-national standards (ISO) and competitions in the area of quality and environmental management (thus providing another link with the material in Chapters 14 and 20). After a discussion on Intellectual Property Claims we include a summary of the events at Bhopal, one of the most unfortunate disasters to occur to the human and natural environment in recent years.

At first sight this may seem a somewhat disparate set of topics but two underlying concerns, in a context of sustainability, are third-world economies and the management of new technologies. Not all environmental management is concerned with new technology, an example being the effects of tourism on natural landscapes and local economies. However, the spread of industrialisation round the globe, the use of non-renewable energy and material sources, the dumping of wastes and the operational challenges posed by the use of recyclable materials will often have a new technology dimension. In contrast to this, the restriction of the use of patented technologies can have a dramatic effect on the economies of developing countries.

Environmental management

Within the general area of CSR (see Chapter 3), a number of key concerns are identified as follows:

- ► Environmental sustainability
- ► Respect for basic human rights
- ► Treating employees fairly and equitably
- ► Operating ethically in the marketplace
- ► Ethical investment
- ► Business relationships in the community.

The first of these, environmental sustainability and associated management practices, is the focus of this section. It will be noted that the management practices mentioned also rate positively in terms of the other concerns above. A great deal has been written on this topic in recent years and the intention here is only to mention ideas and practices which relate to our general themes in business ethics.

As we saw in Chapter 3, the ideas of 'environmental sustainability' or 'sustainable development' are used in an attempt to characterise and sharpen up what is meant by a concern for the environment in an organisational context. Some 'green' approaches are strongly opposed to many aspects of business practice and are hard to reconcile with a market economy. The notion of sustainability signals a more constructive approach and is defined, roughly, as business activity which does not compromise the ability of people in the future to meet their own needs. Thus current activity which uses up natural resources and pollutes or irrevocably changes the environment is viewed negatively. Whether this is achievable through the operation of free market economies (with limited legislation) or requires dramatic intervention in world markets is a debate which is beyond the scope of this book. We might note that the 'green business' approach which believes sustainability can be achieved through free markets, technological progress and good environmental management has much in common with the 'ethical business is good business' view of the world.

However, at a macroeconomic level, environmental debate is entwined with issues of comparative living standards and economic success in countries round the world. Developing countries may see a route to economic success through manufacturing or tourism, which may in turn have considerable detrimental effects on the environment. Attempts by the wealthier countries to insist on the limitation of such activities for 'environmental' reasons may appear hypocritical, a situation further complicated by the activities of multinational corporations in exploiting countries with lower levels of environmental legislation.

Returning to a concern with the management of an individual organisation, the next point we should note is the extent to which an organisation's objectives are consistent with environmental concerns. The most basic position is a sole concern with share price and short-term profitability. In this case the most obvious driver of some limited environmental concern is the avoidance of legal action due to non-compliance with environmental legislation. In addition to this, many of the examples of good operational practice mentioned below are also cost efficient and the publicity value of being seen as a company with some concern for the environment may bring increased revenue.

It is a small step, particularly for the larger organisation, to see advantage in longer-term strategies of innovation in products, processes and services and the issue then arises of anticipating future environmental legislation. The implications of failing to develop essential technologies (e.g. in the use of alternative fuels and materials or in the reduction of pollutants) can be considerable and therefore the major manufacturers of such things as cars and domestic appliances will have to spend much time and money in this area.

Linked to this is the idea of the total cost of a product through its life in terms of its impact on the environment. A simple example (in concept though not in application) is a car. Consider the total cost impact on society of mining raw materials, production processes, obtaining and distributing fuel, the use of the car (in terms of road maintenance) and disposing of the finally discarded product. If we then envisage legislation which will put the onus on the manufacturer and user to bear that cost, to a greater extent than at present through direct costs and taxes, then we can see type of design challenge currently being addressed by Research and Development in the car industry.

Improvements in risk management and crisis handling will also come into the picture for the responsible organisation, as will the choice of suppliers with appropriate environmental management profiles. While still working within the 'green business is good business' framework, and assuming future legislation and public pressure for responsible environmental practice, we can see some prospect of sustainable development hand-in-hand with evolving good practice.

Many environmentalists would consider this a very limited objective. Furthermore it is very dependent on legislation, which can be blocked or delayed by political pressures from the business community as a whole, worldwide agreement on trade and on technology continuing to produce solutions to problems without causing increased problems itself (e.g. the positive advantages of nuclear energy balanced against the issues of nuclear waste disposal).

The ordinary business manager may well appreciate these issues but can only influence their own operations and future plans to any great extent. A strength of current ideas in environmental management at an operational level is that it places emphasis on simple and feasible improvements relating to material and energy supply, efficient processes, the disposal of waste and effective transportation (from a manufacturing perspective, with equivalent concerns in other sectors, e.g. tourism).

A useful technique in this context is 'Life Cycle Assessment' (or 'cradle to grave' impact analysis), which also provides us with a link to our earlier discussion on the problems of utilitarianism (see Chapter 6). Briefly, this consists in taking an existing or proposed product (or service, with appropriate adjustments) and carrying out the following explorations:

1. *Information gathering*: collect all the facts relating to the supply chain and manufacturing process, that is what materials and energy sources are used in manufacture, maintenance and disposal at the end of the product's life.
2. *Impact analysis*: establish the environmental impacts of all the items listed in Part 1. This can be very difficult as the chains of cause and effect and potentially open-ended.

3. *Impact assessment*: quantify the extent of the environmental impacts listed in Part 2. This can be even more difficult, involving complex scientific and economic analysis.
4. *Improvement analysis*: based on the results in Parts 2 and 3, the products and processes are now redesigned in order to improve the environmental impact profile.

Looking at this positively, such a radical review of an existing situation may be worthwhile if it encourages conceptual design breakthroughs or provides an economic cost justification of capital expenditure. Even at a basic level it may remind designers and managers of issues which should be receiving higher priority. If one is committed to implementing the idea of a 'learning organisation' this may be one of the practices which could bring this about. The major problem is the open-endedness of this type of activity and the considerable cost and time which can be involved.

At a more everyday level, much emphasis is now placed on perform-ance measurement, that is the regular gathering of data on how much things cost and how effectively existing systems are actually performing over time. Internal measures of material usage, waste rates, supplier performance and a wide range of other factors can be routinely collected along with external measures of stakeholder reaction, levels of complaint and so forth. Particularly useful here are measurements of risk factors, including such basic things as Health and Safety data. The regular reporting of such measures and linking them with performance manage-ment and improvement plans can be an indicator of real grass-roots concern for environmental management.

ISO standards in quality and environment

Both operations and environmental management are areas which have benefited from the development of formal systems of audit and assessment. These have their origins in the standards of product and material inspection which were developed for suppliers of military equipment and with the formal documented systems put in place by major manufacturers, such as Ford, in order to safeguard the standards of material supplies to their factories. Gradually it became known that a company which met such standards had the engineering expertise and organisational capability to maintain high-quality supply, and this became a good selling point when tendering for supply contracts to other organisations.

Originally these standards were mainly concerned with measurement of key quality characteristics and sampling schemes for process and product control. The aim was often to avoid duplicate inspection of a supplier's output by the supplier's quality inspectors followed by goods inwards inspection at the receiving factory. However, as the example of Japanese Total Quality became better known and as the philosophy of TQM became accepted, formal systems tended more and more to concentrate on product design and continuous improvement processes as the route to reliable quality.

The systems outlined below are covered in detail in many texts on Operations and Quality Management, a good introduction being Slack *et al.* (2001). The current accepted standard worldwide for quality systems is ISO 9000. For a company to register as ISO 9000 compliant will require third-party assessment of its policies, standards and procedures as well as recurring audits. Such an assessment will include a comprehensive view of formal systems (i.e. written and computer based) from top management policies to detailed operational methods. This is a massive undertaking when first attempted, but in practice almost all substantial manufacturing companies will find it necessary and valuable. As well as documenting good practice in maintaining quality, reducing customer complaints and holding down costs it acts as a signal to other organisations of effective management.

There are, however, some potential drawbacks in such a system. As registration involves third-party assessment, which will usually take place primarily during a specific visit by outside quality experts, there can be a tendency to pay lip-service to the agreed procedures. This can range from a blatant cheat whereby the systems on view are simply ignored in day-to-day practice (thus gaining the PR advantages of registration while avoiding the costs of real implementation), through a surface implementation which gradually decays back to inferior practice to a situation where the formal system was not thought through and is unworkable. This can leave workers and supervision in the awkward position of having to implement non-standard working methods in order to achieve any real output. Of course, any well designed system will encourage corrective action to take place in such a situation and also allow for conditions and working methods to change but the potential for shop-floor ethical dilemmas ('should I follow an inadequate set of rules or bend them to improve results?') remains.

To develop this theme a little further, it should be remembered that ISO registration is not only very expensive and time-consuming but is seen as the work of 'experts'. Indeed when such standards were first introduced some companies made the disastrous mistake of investing heavily in consultants and specialists for a short time while system design and third-party assessment were being carried out. This may have been a route to short-term success but could well leave workers and indigenous management feeling left-out and undervalued, particularly if they were the people who really knew how things could go wrong! In such a situation can one blame 'the troops' for subsequently just following the rules, as imported from outside, whether or not they were actually appropriate?

Such standards were originally used mainly within engineering manufacture but as time went by more organisations felt the need to achieve this type of recognition. This included service and public sector organisations, with this type of approach being applied to service encounters as well as administrative tasks. Fairly obviously such approaches can be matched with the structured design and change management procedures used by computer systems designers. It increasingly began to be seen that this activity had to be tailored to the organisation and strongly led from the top, itself something of a challenge to senior managers whose careers had avoided operations and engineering!

The ethical point to be made here relates to leadership, learning and involvement. It is all too easy to see ethics as constituted by bans on some activities and top-level decision-making. It can be unethical for management not to get involved in areas which they would like to avoid due to lack of practical experience, expertise or even a feeling that such details are beneath them. One misuse of delegation is to distance oneself from the tasks you do not like, using the excuse that one cannot be involved with everything. Of course, in some ways, this is true and the incompetent senior meddler is also unlikely to be effective. However, one of the difficult parts of senior management is to accept responsibility for a wide range of areas and to find effective ways of discharging that responsibility; a real ethical challenge!

In the light of this it is interesting to note the criticism of TQM in Slack *et al.* (2001) as going too far in developing a quality bureaucracy and pushing too much responsibility down to the shop floor. In practice this combination of rules, procedures and continuous improvement for everyone and everything can become a source of stress, particularly if seen as one of the more exploitative forms of 'knowledge management' where the ideas and skills of workers are taken over by the company and automated.

A curious aspect of all this activity has been the promotion of a variety of 'quality awards'. The Deming Prize is named after an influential if idiosyncratic American quality guru who made his name in Japan after the Second World War. Deming's writings have a strong flavour of ethical evangelism and should be consulted if researching the debate of ethics in quality management. The Deming Prize is highly prestigious and is competed for by Japanese and other companies. The American equivalent is the Malcolm Baldridge Award while in Europe the European Quality Award (EQA) is run by the European Foundation for Quality Management (EFQM).

It should be noted that the EFQM and EQA promote the benefits of self-assessment. While at first glance this may appear to remove one of the main advantages of quality assessment, that is external involvement, in practice such self-assessment follows a rigorous framework with a natural tendency to benchmarking and outside comparison and involvement.

It should come as no surprise after this exploration of formal quality systems to discover the existence of a standard for environmental management, ISO 14000. This has similar objectives to ISO 9000 in promoting good practice, including the setting of environmental objectives and encouraging the good practices. Slack *et al.* (2001) does, however, comment that this sort of activity can lead not only to similar problems as in quality management (e.g. over reliance on a burgeoning bureaucracy) but also to what they term a 'badge for the smug'! Environmental concerns are highly emotive and newsworthy so it can be very good public relations at both a local and national level to have a reputation as an environmentally friendly organisation. However, one of the main points to be noted about poor quality is that customers complain, kick up a fuss and even sue you, particularly if matters of health and safety are involved. The equivalent 'policing' in matters of environmental mismanagement is less obvious unless a disaster occurs or a particular pressure group becomes involved. It can be all too easy to roll ambitious environmental objectives over from year to year with little progress being made, though keeping a caring reputation. In the equivalent quality management context customers will leave and the competition should make your life difficult. This shows the value of tough legislation and committed, and persistent, environmental campaigners.

Intellectual Property Claims

One area of intense disagreement in the world of business and commerce is the extent to which being the inventor and developer of an initially unique product gives one the right to block its exploitation by other parties. The history of technology is full of arguments and lawsuits about patents. On the one hand we can see inventors such as James Watt preventing rivals for many years from manufacturing steam engines which incorporated some of his particular innovations. It could be argued that this inhibited the continuing development of some useful mechanisms and kept the price of his engines at a high level due to a reduction in competition. On the other hand we can also see the unfairness of inventors not gaining benefit from what might have been a life's work if some form of protection is not available. Indeed, why should individuals and companies invest in the production of new ideas and useful knowledge if it immediately becomes commonly available for anyone to exploit?

An area of particular concern is the development of pharmaceutical products, particularly where their distribution at an affordable price really is a matter of life and death. As products become available to treat such things as AIDS, their distribution on a worldwide scale becomes a major issue. This becomes even more of a problem if the prices of such products are high not due to manufacturing costs but because of the need to recoup investment costs. This may well mean that the manufacture of similar, far cheaper products is blocked by patents on the original product until those patents reach the end of their lives or cheaper alternatives can be developed outside the scope of the legal protection of the originals.

Of similar concern are the Intellectual Property Claims surrounding scientific knowledge in such areas as genetics, along with the possibility that particular organisations may 'capture' areas of massive human interest as well as profit. It is the very real 'life and death' issues which make this area so important a concern for applied ethics to the extent that bio-ethics has developed as a discipline which engages with these problems.

Of course, not all issues of 'intellectual property' are so obviously emotive. The distribution of pirate copies of films and music, for example using the Internet, is a major issue in the media industry. Here the rights of the artistic originators are threatened, in effect, by the technology which makes mass copying and distribution economically viable.

The issue here is more one of the straightforward theft and receiving of material which is readily available and not essential to life!

For many years, the manufacturers of household products have played a game whereby items made by rivals are bought, stripped down and minutely examined in order to facilitate the design of an alternative, similar though legal product. For the industrial engineer, imitation remains the sincerest form of flattery as well as often being cost-effective. The best protection for the original manufacturer may be the advantage of being first to market in terms of revenue and brand reputation. Unfortunately radically new products can have quality problems in the early stages of their product life cycle; the imitator may therefore also benefit by allowing others to solve such problems.

To return to our concern with business ethics, it is difficult to make a case that such imitation is unethical. Imitation and improvement is one of the ways in which individuals and companies learn and eventually create new knowledge and artefacts. Few companies make a point of doing everything 'from scratch', though some notable examples, such as Apple computers, develop a reputation and a market based on radical thinking and implementation.

Similarly the exploitation of copies of entertainment products, such as CDs, is either legal or not depending on the context and possible loopholes in the law. If illegal it is hard to see where there is an ethical dilemma unless one takes a radical view of freedom and the non-existence of property rights. As we are arguing here within the context of a market economy and the social institutions of the democratic world, the legal framework defines the 'rules of the game'. The main difficulty arises if an action is legal within some countries and illegal in others.

If for some reason activity such as producing unauthorised copies is on the right side of the law then we might argue as follows. The widespread, cheap distribution of such products creates 'happiness' for a large number of people which may well exceed the 'unhappiness' caused to those who lose out, particularly if the latter are artists (with an already flamboyant lifestyle) and large corporations. Therefore a utilitarian calculus might suggest that this is a good thing. The difficult part is gauging the long-term effects of such actions. If the result is that corporations then become unwilling to invest in these businesses we may end up with an industry in decline. This illustrates the perennial problem of using such a consequentialist framework; causes and effects are very hard to model and predict even if we feel we can quantify costs and benefits. Perhaps we should leave such concerns to the economists who traditionally take such an approach and attempt to unravel such knots.

Western notions of entrepreneurial freedom might suggest that such actions, if legal, are ethical and industrial economics can take care of itself. This rather ignores the real harm that can be done to original thinkers and innovators (both individual and corporate) and perhaps places the emphasis on legislators and trade negotiators to develop frameworks for international commerce which provide a reasonable balance.

Finally we may end our brief exploration of these issues by considering the real problems for developing countries in trying to promote their own industries in the face of existing products originating from the developed countries which are surrounded by patents and copyrights. Developed countries will no doubt argue that such protection is only reasonable as their industries put in the effort and investment needed in the first place, and will not continue to do so in the future unless the fruits of further investment are protected. What arguments can you produce to counter these assertions?

You may find this very difficult, particularly as it entails escaping the mindset of 'Western style' Intellectual Property Claims. Here are some lines of argument you might try to develop:

▶ We have a fundamental right to survive which is at a higher level than intellectual property rights relating to the means to survival, such as food and medicine. (*Note*: How does this relate to 'defence technology', i.e. the armaments a developing country might argue are essential to its security?)

▶ Many of the technologies which are critical to the needs of developing countries (e.g. relating to basic industries such as food production) are far less important in developed countries. Though a particular industry might be vociferous in protecting its patents and jobs, this may contribute very little in total to the economic well-being of the developed country. Thus there is a disproportionate effect between the great benefit a technology might have in a developing country and the small loss to the originating developed country.

▶ Knowledge in all forms (scientific, technological, etc.) cannot be 'owned'; it is the property of us all. It may be reasonable to protect a human artefact such as a picture, book or piece of music as these have been put together based on the subjective judgement of the author or composer. However, knowledge is 'objective' and is discovered rather than invented. Though an individual may deserve some reward for the effort of discovery, this reward is not ownership. (*Note*: Are you entirely convinced that all knowledge is 'objective' in the above sense of the word? If not you might be interested to explore the philosophy of science. This is part of the very tricky area of philosophy called 'epistemology' (or theory of knowledge). Even if knowledge is not objective, it is not clear how you can own it!)

▶ In some branches of science (e.g. mathematics, physics, etc.) knowledge is considered to be freely available in order to encourage the global community in these difficult disciplines to be open about discoveries, to share information and to be creative. The fear of being wrong is a quite sufficient incentive to behave professionally without, in addition, the fear of breaking the law!

▶ Historically the developed world has economically benefited through exploitation of the rest of the world. It is only fair that there is some form of payback!

Bhopal

The case

In the 1960s there was seen to be a need to improve India's agricultural productivity and the use of pesticides was promoted as a key component in a 'Green Revolution'. This led to the construction of an industrial facility at Bhopal in central India by the Union Carbide Corporation (UCC), a company with headquarters in Connecticut, USA.

This plant produced pesticides using the chemical methyl isocyanate (MIC). It is important in understanding this case to know that MIC has a boiling point of 39 °C, that is it exists as a gas at a possible ambient temperature for the city. As a gas it has a density twice that of air, and therefore will tend to keep close to the ground. It is highly toxic and reacts violently with other substances, including water, producing heat which in turn speeds up the reaction. Such properties make it of great value in industrial scale chemical reactions but also make it highly dangerous to living populations. For this reason it was stored at Bhopal in stainless steel, refrigerated tanks, partly below ground and covered by earth and concrete.

Bhopal is an industrial city and major rail junction with a population of around 800,000, some living in poorly constructed accommodation within 100 m of the chemical facility. The Indian Government saw the production of pesticides in India to be of value not only in terms of the product but also in the development of engineering expertise essential to the country's future. It has also been noted by some commentators that as the Bhopal facility included the storage of MIC in substantial quantities rather than its immediate use it is possible that other uses were intended, for example, by the military.

The plant was designed and funded by UCC and operated by Union Carbide India Ltd (UCIL), a subsidiary of UCC. Despite the incentives of operating in India (including lower labour costs and the operation of local safety protocols) the plant did not meet the financial expectations of UCC. The locally managed UCIL provided management training and ongoing operational management.

It would be obvious to any chemical engineer that stringent safety measures must be designed to be in place to prevent the escape of MIC. An analysis (see Fortune and Peters 1995) shows that ten such measures were designed:

1. Safety valves
2. 'Slip bind' metal sheet
3. Refrigeration unit (to keep MIC in its liquid form)
4. High-temperature warning alarm
5. Pressure gauge on the MIC tank
6. Pump to move MIC back to an earlier stage in production
7. Pump to move material to a reserve tank
8. Vent gas scrubber
9. Flare tower to burn off the gas
10. Gas alarm.

Late in the evening on 2 December 1984 water entered a tank containing MIC, probably due to an inexperienced technician flushing out a nearby pipe incorrectly. This produced a reaction in the tank, increasing heat and pressure and resulting in the escape of MIC gas for around an hour into the still air surrounding the facility. In the early hours of 3 December, an MIC gas cloud rolled slowly and quietly over the parts of Bhopal adjoining the plant.

As large numbers of people tried to obtain medical assistance for a variety of symptoms (including burning sensation in the eyes and choking), local doctors were unsure of the cause of the problem as there was no past history of treating the effects of MIC poisoning in the city and no standard procedures in place to identify and deal with this problem. By the time the cloud had dissipated, over 3000 people had died, though the eventual official death toll is 5325 with some estimates nearer 15000. It is estimated that at least 250,000 have suffered permanent disability with around 100,000 still seriously ill 10 years later. Typical long-term damage includes impairment to the respiratory system, miscarriages, children with birth defects, breathing problems and mental illness from the memory of the incident and its effects as well as the fear that other problems (cancers and genetic damage) will be revealed in the long term.

If we look back at the safety measures which should have been in place to stop such an event occurring, we note the following:

1. Safety valves (not used correctly or not working)
2. 'Slip bind' metal sheet (not used)
3. Refrigeration unit (to keep MIC in its liquid form) (not operational since June)
4. High-temperature warning alarm (incorrectly set)
5. Pressure gauge on the MIC tank (showed pressure but not how it was changing)
6. Pump to move MIC back to an earlier stage in production (process not running)
7. Pump to move material to a reserve tank (reserve tank full)
8. Vent gas scrubber (faulty meter)
9. Flare tower to burn off the gas (corroded pipe to tower; closed for repair)
10. Gas alarm (sounded at 01.00, long after the leak had started).

Recriminations and litigation over compensation and criminal negligence have continued for years since this tragic event with victim's families beginning to receive some compensation by 1992. Medical appeals continue in an attempt to provide relief for the victims. The plant no longer makes pesticides and UCC have had considerable financial difficulties. Guilt or sympathy felt by their executives appears to have been lost within that arena of combat called litigation and self-preservation.

Discussion

There is a very large literature on the Bhopal tragedy, reflecting both the technical approach to risk management and also the political concerns underlying UCC's involvement. You are invited to explore this in order to make a fuller moral evaluation of the actions (and inactions) of the many stakeholders. As in many major disasters, the ethical issues surrounding the ensuing compensation claims are a major case study in themselves.

Summary

In this chapter we continued an operations and risk theme, but in the context of environmental management, another area where disasters occur and therefore of public and ethical concern. Operations and environmental management share a tendency with engineering to spawn international standards, codes of practice and even competitive awards for the organisations which score highly in achieving best practice. We discussed these in the ensuing section.

The discussion on Intellectual Property Claims raises different issues but within a similarly international context where less-developed economies may appear to be at a disadvantage.

22 Ethics, accountancy and Corporate Governance

Purpose and learning objectives

The purpose of this chapter is to introduce some discussion relating to the roles played by accountants in an organisation. These range from information gathering and presentation within a company to the essential auditing role which aims to protect stakeholders from being misled by an organisation's annual performance information. This leads naturally into a consideration of Corporate Governance, a topic mainly concerned with the ethical functioning of the most senior levels of management in an organisation. The chapter also includes some observations, and a case study, on management expediency.

You will be able to

▶ understand the ethical importance of the various accounting roles in an organisation;
▶ appreciate the need for Corporate Governance and top-level accountability in an organisation.

Introduction

In this final chapter we briefly examine some further ethical issues facing the management of a company as a whole. We begin with an introduction to a very large and complex area of practical management; the role of accountancy, performance reporting and audit in an organisation. The term 'accountant' in fact covers a range of professional institutions who are chartered to qualify individuals who are suitable to carry out such roles and whose professional codes of practice are intended to show the standards of behaviour expected of such individuals. There is also a large amount of legislation relating to some of the work of accountants in organisations, that is accounting roles are some of the most regulated forms of management. We will not be focussing specifically on some other financial planning and management roles often carried out by qualified accountants.

In Chapter 3 we introduced some ideas of CSR and Corporate Governance. In recent years this has been extensively explored with a number of reports and codes of practice aimed at curbing instances of what are seen as grossly unethical ways of managing major organisations. Quite apart from the strictures of moral theory, there is considerable danger to the reputation of quoted companies if shareholders feel they cannot believe the information presented to them by company directors and senior executives. Any general lack of confidence in the financial probity of companies could be very damaging to the economic system as a whole. If entrepreneurs and senior managers are seen to be paying themselves unjustified large salaries while not paying attention to the wishes of shareholders then conflict, particularly with the more powerful groups of shareholders such as financial institutions, will be the result.

We follow this with another exploration of a theme which has recurred in this book: whether morality in a business context is in effect the same as long-term practicality, here termed 'expediency'. We then include a case study reporting an instance when strategic behaviour may well be expedient and profitable but it is hard to see how it can be described as ethical, particularly if the 'what would happen if everyone knew about this' maxim was applied. The chapter ends with a set of discussion questions for Part IV as a whole.

Accounting ethics

Accountancy is one of the most prominent professions in the organisational world, partly due to the economic nature of business activity (accountancy can be seen as the operationalisation of economics in the firm) and partly due to the need for organisations to produce reliable performance data to satisfy their owners (e.g. shareholders, the government, etc.) that their interests are being safeguarded. Investment is risky enough without exposure to corrupt management working in their own interests rather than those of the providers of capital. This latter point shows the importance of firms producing financial statements and of the audit process which checks and validates such information.

The term 'Chartered Accountant' refers to a qualified member of the Institute of Chartered Accountants in England and Wales (or similar bodies in Scotland, Ireland and other countries). Other professional accounting bodies now also have charters but the specific term 'chartered accountant' traditionally applies to a member of an accounting firm providing auditing, taxation and other related services. The other chartered accounting institutes tend to relate to specific areas of activity (e.g. management accounting) or sectors (such as public sector management). All the accounting bodies have detailed codes of professional ethics with legal sanctions in place to combat serious professional misconduct.

Management accountants are usually employees of an organisation or of a consultancy providing services to an organisation. They are key players in systems which support pricing decision-making, project management, budgeting and cost planning and control. Their work is often closely involved with computer-based management information systems. In specialist financial organisations their role becomes even more central and often involves focussing on such key aspects of financial management as currency or risk management.

Thus whatever their specific duties, accountants in general have responsibilities relating to recording financial data, its analysis, the communication of information and the support of the decision-making process. The recipient of such information may be an external stakeholder (e.g. shareholders, taxation authorities, business partners, general public, etc.) or the management of the organisation where the accountant works or who have retained an accounting firm to provide services. The intelligibility and trustworthiness of such information is critical to a range of key decisions, which in turn implies a need for clarity and honesty in terms of information preparation and presentation. It is also important to remember that an organisation routinely generates a vast amount of accounting data which must be summarised and simplified for reporting purposes. Leaving out key items of information may be as damaging to the interests of stakeholders as presenting false information or presenting information in ways which may be technically defensible but are likely to mislead, say, shareholders and other providers of finance, goods or services to an organisation.

One key to the process of providing reliable accounting information is the work of the Accounting Standards Board which sets accounting standards in the UK. Similar bodies exist in other countries and there are important issues of comparability between countries, noting that accounting standards relate to the legal infrastructure supporting business and public sector activity in a given country. In particular when preparing its annual financial statements, an organisation must be clear about the accounting policies it has adopted where legislation allows some leeway, for example, relating to goodwill, research and development and similar matters where firms in particular industries may argue that quite specific ways of reporting financial information are appropriate. For example, some firms will engage in very long-term investments or argue that much of their worth lies in some intangible factor such as brand image or reputation. Such factors may be crucial when valuing a firm during a take-over battle, for instance. It should not be thought that the choice of accounting policy is arbitrary and governed by only public relations concerns; taxation authorities necessarily have strong views on how profitability is established!

There is always the possibility of engaging in 'creative accounting', usually defined as potentially misleading, though not illegal, accounting practices which take advantage of grey areas in the law to present a firm's activities in a way which furthers management's current objectives. Though some have argued that if a specific example of creative accounting is legal then it is permissible (similar to the distinction between tax avoidance and evasion), such practice may diminish the reputation of managers and can hardly be ethical if a bias against some stakeholder interests is at work. The work of the Accounting Standards Board and the streetwise vigilance of investors is a valuable antidote to such manoeuvres, particularly large, financially based bodies such as banks and insurance companies, though some small investors have shown great determination in harrying organisations with dubious practices.

However, despite legislation, regulation and vigilance, accountants and managers working within (or too closely with) an organisation may be able to create some short-term advantage through financial reporting ranging from misleading to criminal. While in the long term such activities may be uncovered, vast sums of money may have been made or lost in the meantime. This situation of 'information asymmetry' shows clearly why the professional and ethical role of the accountant is critical.

We should, of course, remember that auditing services tend to be supplied by firms of accountants, which themselves need to make a profit, may be large in order to provide economies of scale and also may provide other services such as financial consultancy. This can lead to a dangerously close relationship with a client, to conflicts of interest and to a lack of control within the accounting firm. Unfortunately instances do exist where auditors give a company a clean bill of health only for it to quickly fail due to factors which should have been visible at the time of audit. Certainly some such cases may be defended as unfortunate judgement calls (accountancy is not a purely mechanical exercise) but unfortunate investors may not be so charitable and reputations may suffer. In the long term an atmosphere of deep distrust (beyond the traditional, healthy suspicion of investors) is to everyone's disadvantage; trust is essential to the workings of a market economy and the continuing provision of reliable information feeds trust. The reliability of the external auditing process as well as justifiable trust in the probity of internal management accountants as well as managers leads to a more effective market economy.

A more radical critique might argue that the above optimistic picture is misplaced. At a basic level there is an assumption on the part of many people that accountancy is a technical exercise; given basic financial transaction data and accounting principles, accountants (or computers) can find the 'right answer' relating to performance (e.g. profit) and the valuation of an enterprise. An alternative view is that financial reporting is always a social process with political and ethical dimensions, the latter referring to more than whether the reporting and auditing process were carried out in accordance with professional norms. This, in effect, says that there is always a large 'grey area' where management may package the results while keeping within the law (or avoiding any reasonable chance of getting caught!). This problem may even be more acute within areas of public service accounting where, for example, moving a health care organisation forwards based on financial numbers is a narrow conception of providing a public service. Even the 'balanced scorecard' idea, where financial information is balanced with other performance data, both with a forward as well as backward looking perspective, may be seen as only a partial alleviation of a heartless attitude.

We can also refer back to the adiaphorization discussion in Chapter 19 and ask whether this apparent mechanisation of performance measurement does not also demonstrate a distancing of the technocrat from the stakeholder. Certainly within a company, management may find reference to 'the numbers' a useful device to block one project or favour another in a way which can be presented as simple, objective and clean decision-making as opposed to the messy politics of debate and discussion. Few have the technical ability or determination to argue with 'the numbers' or to challenge their guardians, who may unfortunately enjoy the power and prestige of the senior accounting and financial management roles. Of course engineers and technocrats (e.g. the guardians of computer-based systems) may enjoy similar advantages but the prestige and centrality of financial information to the management of all manner of organisation puts the accountant and financial manager in a powerful position. Not surprisingly, some of the most rancorous debates one may witness are between engineers and accountants, though it is useful to remember that the most senior management body of any organisation will almost inevitably include a financial specialist who is certain to have a strong voice in key policy debates.

Accountants and financial specialists will always have considerable power and influence within organisations. Therefore such professionals provide a critical case relating to the need for ethical action within and between organisations. Though this is an area where substantial work has been carried out by professional bodies, the rewards for unethical behaviour, in accountants or those they advise, can be sufficiently great for some to risk legal sanctions and damage to reputation. The technical nature of accounting and of computer-based financial systems can also lead many to feel alienated and distanced from financial decision-making, a situation which can be exploited by financial managers in organisational power struggles. We may see this situation as potentially problematic for an organisation which tries to pursue a path of ethical debate and openness.

Corporate Governance

In 1992 the Cadbury Report set out guidance for Corporate Governance, addressing the issue of the accountability of the managers of companies to the shareholders. This code of practice, with which stock-exchange listed companies must comply, relates to information provided by the company in its Annual Report and includes guidelines on the separation of the roles of chairman and Chief Executive as well as the role of non-executive directors. This addresses the felt need that in some companies there had been an imbalance of power favouring current management to the detriment of shareholders.

A further issue addressed by Cadbury is the process for deciding on the remuneration of directors and senior managers (through remuneration committees made up of independent directors) and the disclosure of the full remuneration package of all the directors in Annual Reports. Whether these provisions will be sufficient to end the series of reports of excessive director payment, fraud, misappropriation of pension funds and similar dubious practices prior to Cadbury remains to be seen.

It has certainly provided ammunition for journalists intent on exposing what is seen as corporate greed.

An example is a report in the press (see *The Guardian*, 9 May 2003 for details) listing 30 cases of top managers receiving large remuneration packages, often including payoffs in the event of failure, while running companies which were performing badly. Such payments are unlikely to be seen as fair and reasonable by the shareholders of these companies or by employees newly made redundant.

This draws attention to some of the problems faced by Codes of Practice aimed at self-regulation. No doubt each of the above cases, and others similar, can be supported by detailed justifications drawing attention to the specific circumstances the companies find themselves in. The result may well be that independent directors will feel they have no choice but to agree the payments. Searches for more radical solutions may be beyond their scope, unless shareholder meetings vote against such packages and force a rethink or resignations. This is where the reporting aspects of Cadbury may be of value in giving large, institutional shareholders ammunition to stage a revolt.

The ethical principles at work here are openness and the promotion of information flow as well as addressing concentrations of power at boardroom level. There can be no hope that such Codes of Practice will finally solve problems; rather they attempt to make fairer the game being played. For further examples you might wish to search for references to the Higgs Report (January 2003) which relates to the role of non-executive directors of companies.

Morality or expediency

Some writers on business ethics have promoted the view that there is a convergence between acting morally and the long-term business objectives of the firm. In a competitive environment it is easy to find situations where the pursuit of short-term objectives may seem morally dubious, for example:

- Selling poor quality products
- Using creative accounting (i.e. adopting accounting practices which are legal but potentially misleading) to increase short-term profit figures
- Over-optimistic advertising prior to a product launch
- Reducing staff development budgets.

It can be argued that each of these is counter-productive in the long term. Thus we meet arguments such as the following:

▶ If a firm develops a reputation for moral integrity this will create loyalty in its stakeholders and lead to long-term success.
▶ The development of moral integrity in marketing is essential in the building of long-term customer relationships.
▶ Adopting a positive attitude and set of personnel practices for employees will increase their commitment to the mission of the organisation.

A similar argument is sometimes met in the 'green business' literature where the pursuit of positive environmental policies is argued as being in the long-term interests of a business. One interesting point we should note here is that legislation to promote good environmental practice may lag behind the initial promotion of such practice, for example it may be some time before new technologies in controlling harmful waste emission become required practice as part of the law. Some car makers are far ahead of others in terms of developing clean engines or in making cars with recyclable parts. When such good practice does become law then the 'early adopter' firms will be in a very strong situation in terms of market reputation, proven technology and working practices. Therefore the anticipation of future good practice leads to organisational learning which develops such good practice and this form of investment will usually be seen as a sign of a moral enterprise.

This argument can also apply in other areas of business ethics. An instance might be the provision of access to all facilities for employees with some form of disability, or similarly provide access for customers to all sales areas. This may be far easier to achieve when a building is being designed or radically remodelled rather than converting an old building. Hence the anticipation of legislation in this area is good business economics as well as demonstrating a positive attitude.

Therefore we have the idea that if we look to the long term, good business is inevitably based on sound moral principles. However, there are a number of practical problems with this line of argument:

▶ The long term is made up of a series of 'short terms', each of which have to be survived! If we invest too much in the long term our firm may become uneconomic and we may never get there. A counter-argument at the level of the industry may be that our investment in, say, research and development will not be wasted as the failing firm may be taken over and its technology exploited. However, at the organisational level this remains a problem, particularly for the smaller enterprise.

► Long-term planning is based on forecasts that include political, economic and technological dimensions in complex and large integrated systems. The resulting scenarios and quantitative forecasts may be dubious in the extreme.

► While there are examples of firms which paid considerable attention to employee welfare and customer support enjoying long-term success, there are also examples of organisations which have adopted far less enlightened attitudes in the past (e.g. the builders of railways; manufacturing in poor conditions; manufacture of dangerous products) and the present (e.g. use of very low cost labour and the exploitation of natural resources in other countries) and yet are large, profitable and appear little troubled by the moral indignation they arouse. There appears to be no strong empirical link between the adoption of moral policies and long-term success.

► It may be asserted that a link between moral integrity and organisational success will occur in an enlightened future, perhaps due to the increased availability of information on company practices and stronger lobbying by reformers. This remains to be seen, as companies may also develop more sophisticated tactics to resist such intrusions.

Finally, there is also an important philosophical point about moral motivation. Even if we were sure that good business performance was based on moral integrity, would acting in this way actually be 'moral', that is if our reason for acting in a moral fashion is expediency (obtaining a profitable outcome), are we actually behaving morally? A comparison might be made with publicly making a donation to a good cause. Many would argue that the moral reason for making such a donation is that it is our duty, not that we are seen to be generous by our peers nor that we get a nice, warm feeling from being a 'good person'! Similarly we could argue that the moral reason for obeying the law, instituting good working practices and giving customers a good deal is not the avoidance of sanctions or being promoted as a good manager but simply that we have a duty to do these things (see Chapter 7 on Kantian ethics).

Therefore if we argue that asserting there is some link between ethical business practices and long-term success will at least encourage businesses to be ethical, we could be on dubious ground. Immoral practices can lead to long-term success. Moral practices may not lead to success. If we can show clear ways in which particular ethical practices will be good for organisational performance then this is to our advantage but we must also be able to handle instances when ethical practice is expensive and time-consuming.

Ethical practice may turn out to be organisationally expedient but that is no reason for its adoption. In the final analysis the reason for acting in a moral way in business and organisational life does not rest on the practical achievement of business goals but on the reasons for moral action shown through ethical analysis.

Information from a secret source – a case

The task

Ethically evaluate the action taken by the company, the equipment manufacturer and their parent organisation in the case below. To what extent is it ethical for a company to provide and use such industrial intelligence?

In such a context it is possible that a company which avoids all such covertly gathered information will end up in financial difficulties, to the detriment of its stakeholders. Is it ethical to disadvantage yourself in this way?

The case

A company manufactures a commonly used household material and is part of a privately owned, and somewhat secretive, international organisation with headquarters overseas. Like its competitors, there is a considerable amount of technological innovation taking place at this time (the late 1980s) with computer-controlled machinery being introduced to improve both quality and productivity. However, the market is fiercely competitive and it is unlikely that all current rivals will survive.

The group which owns the company also owns the leading equipment manufacturer in this sector, a fact which is not widely known. This latter firm works with many of the company's rivals in the UK and overseas in developing new systems and maintaining them during use. All the competitors in effect gain from this arrangement as successful machinery is made more widely available. However, there is a suspicion that the equipment manufacturer passes on information to the company about its rivals' investment plans, manufacturing performance and financial health.

Company management argue that, whatever rules governments may wish to enforce to preserve fair competition, sensitive and valuable information will inevitably flow between organisations by all sorts of mechanisms. Following this line of thought, the best thing the company can do is to become good at playing this game, though without resorting to grosser forms of illegality such as theft and blackmail!

Summary

The areas of management covered in this chapter may seem remote from ordinary employees and members of the general public, except for the financial pages of newspapers and the not infrequent reports of dubious senior management activities. This impression is reinforced by the mathematical nature of accounting and the complexity of published company information. Yet we would all agree that it is of crucial importance to the individual employee, customer and investor as well as the economy that the activities of corporations are open to scrutiny so we can all have confidence that they really are performing as reported. Unfortunately there are many situations where senior management may see things differently; where they may even feel it expedient to do and say things they might not wish to be made public 'for the long-term good of the firm'. Perhaps it is not surprising that the wealth and careers of senior executives are sometimes seen to be entangled with such expediency.

Questions for discussion – Part IV

Note that the 9 discussion questions given below relate mainly to material covered in Chapters 17–22 but may draw on earlier material and introduce new ideas and perspectives. These questions are meant to challenge rather than review basic learning of the material in these chapters.

Question 1

Consider the following examination question, to be set some years in the future:

'Up to the 21st century there existed a peculiar form of work organisation called "employment", now seen as outmoded as slavery seemed then. Rather than working as free agents in the context of a negotiated agreement, as we do now, individuals were classed as "employees". In exchange for money, they submitted to a quasi-military regime whereby they were "told what to do" and disciplined if "non-conformance" occurred. What are the ethical implications of this practice?'

Discuss!

Question 2

Suppose an organisation has a problem with 'flame-mail' (abusive emails). It has implemented a set of rules to deal with this problem, but the abuse is perceived to be continuing within these rules by a more subtle use of threat and innuendo.

How can one evaluate the success of the existing rules? How can you set objectives for the design of new rules?

(Note that a key issue is exactly what defines wrongdoing in this type of situation.)

Question 3

Carl is the manager of a bar in a medium-sized town with many similar bars and a reputation for catering for a 'good night out'. He works around 90 hours a week and his performance is measured by the turnover of the bar. As the supply cost of alcohol reduces with volume sold, he must get as many customers as possible into the bar and encourage consumption. To do this, on some nights the bar offers £1 entry plus £1 per drink. Local residents are increasingly complaining about the rough and drunken culture which now seems to be the norm on most nights in the town.

Can this be justified on a utilitarian basis as the pursuit of pleasure? Is the bar an ethical business?

Question 4

The discipline of business ethics comes under attack from a number of directions. The business practitioner may view its analytical methods as time-consuming and its prescriptions as soft and impractical. In particular, the recommendation to engage in dialogue with stakeholders is seen as detracting from the right to manage.

Some academics and consultants often seem to prefer more 'objective' methods of analysis and modelling, for example, as seen in texts on Business Strategy. For instance, it is currently fashionable to use concepts of power, sustainable competitive advantage and value appropriation in modelling competitive action, all notions with little linkage to ethical theory. Often ethics only comes into the picture when discussing strategy implementation, when it appears little more than Public Relations!

Other radical critics of the business world view business ethics as tainted by its accommodation to a market philosophy and hence not capable of taking an independent and critical line.

What use is business ethics?

Question 5

According to a recent survey (*The Guardian*, 17 November 2003), the UK's leading quoted companies gave 0.8 per cent of pre-tax profits to charities, voluntary organisations and community projects. In what circumstances are such donations an ethical use of company resources?

Question 6

'Fair Trade' is the name given to the practice whereby small producers worldwide, operating to high environmental and social standards, can sell their goods at a higher price in the developed consumer markets with extra cash going back to the producer rather than being lost in the supply chain. Consumers appear willing to buy such products in order to support this way of doing business.

Does this point the way towards global business in the future or will it always be a minority enterprise of limited value to less developed economies but acting as a salve to consciences in the west?

Question 7

Investigate the ethics of fast food production. You may find Schlosser (2002) helpful in this enterprise.

Question 8

According to a recent report (*The Times Higher Education Supplement*, July 2002) a businessman who endowed a University chair in Corporate Governance has been charged in the USA with tax evasion and tampering with evidence.

Should the source of such an endowment affect whether or not it is accepted?

Question 9

Since buying the business nine months ago, Dan had run a small car repair garage with 15 employees. A couple of weeks ago he was given £1M by his father who had won the jackpot in the National Lottery. When his employees turned up for work on Monday morning they found the garage shut, despite customers waiting with their cars. Representatives of a firm of liquidators eventually arrived and told everyone that Dan was winding up the firm and they were now unemployed. Dan had not discussed his intentions with any of his employees and was not available for comment.

Assuming that Dan's actions are legal and the employment rights of his workforce will be respected (perhaps with a new owner being found for the business), is Dan's action ethical? What further information would help you with your evaluation?

Annotated bibliography

Below we include the full set of references for books and journal articles included in this book, along with some brief comments. You may also wish to make use of materials on the web. We have not included explicit web references as these have a tendency to change. However it is usually a straightforward matter to search the web for material related to business ethics provided a few appropriate keywords are known.

A useful start is to explore the 'Business for Social Responsibility' web site (search 'bsr' or use www.bsr.org). Another good search keyword is 'eiro'. You should avoid using keywords such as 'business ethics' or 'Kant' unless you are in, say, a publisher's site or some other specialist web location. Of course, if you are experienced in carrying out web searches you might start with a fairly general keyword and then experiment with narrowing the search.

University and library resources sites are likely to be of most use for academic references while professional bodies and trade associations will usually have something to say about codes of practice for the ethical conduct of their members. Newspaper and other media sites contain much incisive material on managerial conduct, which can be contrasted with organisations' own sites. Some useful references for philosophical ethics are given in Baggini and Fosl (2003).

Ackroyd, S. and Thompson, P. (1999), *Organisational Misbehaviour*, Sage, London. [A useful source of anecdote and organisational behaviour theory.]

Allinson, R.E. (1993), *Global Disasters: Inquiries into Management Ethics*, Prentice-Hall, New York. [An approach to business ethics based on a detailed analysis of disasters and influenced by Japanese management thinking.]

Aristotle, trans. Crisp, R. (2000), *Nicomachean Ethics*, CUP, Cambridge. [A Modern translation of a classic – surprisingly approachable.]

Axelrod, R. (1984), *The Evolution of Co-operation*, Basic Books, New York. [A ground breaking study on trust based on Game Theory.]

Baggini, J. and Fosl, P.S. (2003), *The Philosopher's Toolkit: A Compendium of Philosophical Concepts and Methods*, Blackwell, Oxford. [A resource for the philosophically minded with an emphasis on sound methods of analysis and argument. Also contains useful web-site references.]

Baldwin, T. (2001), *Contemporary Philosophy*, OUP, Oxford. [A general introduction to modern philosophy with a useful chapter on trends in ethical theory.]

Benn, P. (1998), *Ethics*, UCL Press, London. [A useful ethics text which complements the more basic introductions in this book.]

Bernstein, P. (1996), *Against the Gods: The Remarkable Story of Risk*, Wiley, London. [A witty and interesting general introduction to the history of probability theory and risk.]

Blackburn, S. (2001), *Being Good: A Short Introduction to Ethics*, OUP, Oxford. [A useful quick read to complement any text on ethics.]

Bowie, N.E. (1999), *Business Ethics: A Kantian Perspective*, Blackwell, London. [Though intentionally narrow in its use of theory, this very useful book addresses a wide range of contemporary issues in business ethics.]

Brenkert, G. (1999), 'Marketing Ethics', in Frederick (1999), Blackwell, London. [A useful article, referred to in Chapter 18 of this book.]

Broome, J. (1999), *Ethics out of Economics*, CUP, Cambridge. [A specialist text which shows how consequentialist theory can be used in business and related disciplines such as health care.]

Buchanan, D. and Badham, R. (1999), *Power, Politics and Organisational Change: Winning the Turf Game*, Sage, London. [An essential reference for Chapter 10 of this book.]

Burke, G. and Peppard, J. (eds) (1995), *Examining Business Process Re-engineering*, Cranfield Management Series, Kogan Page, London.

Cannon, T. (1994), *Corporate Responsibility*, Pitman, London. [A useful, if dated, introduction to Corporate Governance and social responsibility.]

Carroll, S.J. and Gannon, M.J. (1997), *Ethical Dimensions of International Management*, Sage, London. [An interesting complement to Chapter 15 of this book, with a number of cases.]

Cohen, B. (1997), *The Edge of Chaos: Financial Booms, Bubbles, Crashes and Chaos*, Wiley, Chichester. [A business oriented introduction to chaos theory.]

Cohen, M. (2003), *101 Ethical Dilemmas*, Routledge, London. [A student friendly ethics text with a few business dilemmas.]

Cottingham, J. (1998), *Philosophy and the Good Life*, CUP, Cambridge. [A more advanced ethics text which explores personal moral development.]

Cox, A. (1999), 'Power, Value and Supply Chain Management', *Supply Chain Management: An International Journal*, Vol. 4, No. 4, pp. 167–175. [Referred to in Chapter 20 for its use of ideas of power in a strategic competitive context.]

Cragg, W. (1997), 'Teaching Business Ethics: The Role of Ethics in Business and in Business Education', *Journal of Business Ethics*, Vol. 16, pp. 213–245. [Referred to in Chapter 2 for its discussion on the use of language.]

Crane, A. and Matten, D. (2004), *Business Ethics: A European Perspective*, OUP, Oxford. [Focuses on corporate citizenship, globalisation and sustainability with extensive text and cases relating to European issues.]

Davies, P.W.F. (ed.) (1997), *Current Issues in Business Ethics*, Routledge, London. [Contains some useful articles and a different perspective from this book.]

Easterby-Smith, M., Thorpe, R. and Lowe, A. (2002), *Management Research: An Introduction*, Sage, London. [A leading text on research methods with chapters on ethics and on power.]

Fortune, J. and Peters, G. (1995), *Learning from Failure: The Systems Approach*, Wiley, Chichester. [A comprehensive approach to risk and failure.]

Frederick, R.E. (ed.) (1999), *A Companion to Business Ethics*, Blackwell, Oxford. [A large collection of useful articles, a good complement to this book.]

Fritzsche, D.J. (1997), *Business Ethics: A Global and Managerial Perspective*, McGraw-Hill, New York. [Develops systematic models of international business behaviour.]

Gatley, S., Lessem, R. and Altman, Y. (1996), *Comparative Management: A Transcultural Odyssey*, McGraw-Hill, London. [A challenging book on cultural diversity in business and management.]

Gensler, H.J. (1998), *Ethics: A Contemporary Introduction*, Routledge, London. [An unusual introductory ethics text which makes a great effort to be student friendly.]

Gladwell, M. (2000), *The Tipping Point: How Little Things can Make a Big Difference*, Abacus, London. [Useful in the context of showing how cause and effect may have problematic links in a social context.]

Glover, J. (1977), *Causing Death and Saving Lives*, Penguin, Harmondsworth. [Contains some early discussions on the idea of moral distance.]

——. (1999), *Humanity: A Moral History of the Twentieth Century*, Jonathan Cape, London. [An alarming book, ideal for countering any complacency that the world is becoming a nicer place.]

Grisham, J. (1995), *The Rainmaker*, Random House, London. [A fictional account of practical professional ethics!]

Hampden-Turner, C. and Trompenaars, F. (1993), *The Seven Cultures of Capitalism*, Piatkus, London. [A useful early text on international cultural difference.]

Hargreaves Heap, S.P. and Varoufakis, Y. (1995), *Game Theory: A Critical Introduction*, Routledge, London. [A useful introduction to the principles of this difficult subject; little mathematics and some philosophy.]

Hidden, A. (1989), *Investigation into the Clapham Junction Railway Accident*, The Stationery Office Books, London. [A readable account of an accident which is concerned with senior management as well as operational responsibility.]

Hinde, R.A. (2002), *Why Good is Good: The Sources of Morality*, Routledge, London. [An account of the development of ethics based on social science theory and evolution rather than philosophical argument; interesting theory and anecdote.]

Hollis, M. (1994), *The Philosophy of the Social Sciences*, CUP, Cambridge. [Social science theory cannot be divorced from ethics; an interesting argument using game theory.]

——. (1998), *Trust within Reason*, CUP, Cambridge. [Trust is a key issue in business ethics.]

Hood, C. and Jones, D.K.C. (eds) (1996), *Accident and Design: Contemporary Debates on Risk Management*, Routledge, London. [Sophisticated theorising on risk and organisational management.]

Horton, J. and Mendus, S. (1994), *After MacIntyre: Critical Perspectives on the Work of Alasdair MacIntyre*, Polity Press, Cambridge. [A critique on the work of MacIntyre, useful if one wishes to pursue his approach to virtue ethics.]

Hume, D. (1998), *An Enquiry Concerning the Principles of Morals*, OUP, Oxford. [The original text with a useful, and necessary, introduction.]

Jaggar, A.M. (2000), 'Feminist Ethics', in LaFollette (ed.) (2000), Blackwell, Oxford. [A comprehensive guide to a varied subject.]

Jenkins, T. (ed.) (2002), *Ethical Tourism: Who Benefits?*, Hodder and Stoughton, Oxford. [A short set of introductory articles relating to an interesting topic in marketing ethics.]

Kant, I., trans. Gregor, M. (1998), *Groundwork of the Metaphysics of Morals*, CUP, Cambridge. [A translation with introduction; not for the faint hearted but useful for the serious student.]

Kaptein, M. and Wempe, J. (2002), *The Balanced Company: A Theory of Corporate Integrity*, OUP, Oxford. [A long and detailed account of integrity theory; very interesting.]

LaFollette, H. (ed.) (2000), *The Blackwell Guide to Ethical Theory*, Blackwell, Oxford. [A useful sourcebook containing many short articles.]

Larmer, R.A. (ed.) (1996), *Ethics in the Workplace: Selected Readings in Business Ethics*, West, Minneapolis. [Though oriented to USA practice and law, this text contains a number of well argued topics and interesting cases.]

Machiavelli, N., trans. Bull, G. (1961), *The Prince*, Penguin, Harmondsworth. [Already used by some as a primer on management, a logical if chilling view of the uses of power.]

MacIntyre, A. (1985), *After Virtue: A Study in Moral Theory* (2nd edn), Duckworth, London. [One of the original texts which provided a new impetus to the study of virtue ethics and its use in organisations, though the author is somewhat disparaging of management practice.]

——. (1998), *A Short History of Ethics: A History of Moral Philosophy from the Homeric Age to the Twentieth Century* (2nd edn), Routledge, London. [A challenging, though readable, introduction which argues that ethics depends on historical context.]

Maclagan, P. (1998), *Management and Morality*, Sage, London. [A useful and detailed text with a people management focus.]

Mill, J.S. (1972), *On Liberty*, J.M. Dent, London. [A highly influential 19th century view of utilitarian ethics.]

Norman, R. (1998), *The Moral Philosophers: An Introduction to Ethics* (2nd edn), OUP, Oxford. [A good, modern ethics text.]

Paine, L.S. (1994), 'Managing for Organisational Integrity', *Harvard Business Review*, March–April (1994). [An early and useful article on integrity.]

Parker, M. (ed.) (1998), *Ethics and Organisations*, Sage, London. [A selection of readings, very critical and challenging in their exploration of ethical theory and practice.]

Parker, M. (2002), *Against Management*, Polity Press, Cambridge. [A radical challenge to business and to business ethics theory.]

Pratley, P. (1995), *The Essence of Business Ethics*, Prentice-Hall, London. [Contains some useful cases and makes a number of trenchant points.]

Rawls, J. (1972), *A Theory of Justice*, OUP, Oxford. [The original and important text, though hard to read.]

Resnick, D.B. (1998), *The Ethics of Science: An Introduction*, Routledge, London. [The ethics of scientific practice and the interface between science and business are important topics.]

Riddall, J.G. (1999), *Jurisprudence* (2nd edn), Butterworths, London. [The philosophy of law provides a different view of the implementation of ethical concepts in practice; this student friendly text contains useful explanations of many ethical concepts.]

Ridley, M. (1996), *The Origins of Virtue*, Penguin, London. [A short introduction to evolution and ethics; very interesting with useful parallels in business.]

Robin, D.P. and Reidenbach, R.E. (1993), 'Searching for a Place to Stand: Towards a Workable Ethical Philosophy for Marketing', *Journal of Public Policy & Marketing*, Vol. 12, No. 1, pp. 97–105. [Referred to in Chapter 18 for its marketing ethics theory.]

Rowe, D. (1997), *The Real Meaning of Money*, HarperCollins, London. [A psychologist's view.]

Schlosser, E. (2002), *Fast Food Nation: What the All-American Meal is Doing to the World*, Penguin, London. [An antidote to complacency about the ethics of business practice.]

Shaw, W.H. (1999), *Contemporary Ethics (Taking Account of Utilitarianism)*, Blackwell, Oxford. [A systematic introduction to ethics which takes a more positive view of utilitarian theory.]

Singer, P. (ed.) (1993), *A Companion to Ethics*, Blackwell, Oxford. [A useful collection of readings.]

Singer, P. (1997), *How are We to Live: Ethics in an Age of Self-Interest*, OUP, Oxford. [A strongly argued view on ethics in modern society.]

Slack, N., Chambers, S. and Johnston R. (2001), *Operations Management* (3rd edn), Prentice-Hall, London. [A standard text on Operations Management as referred to in Chapter 20.]

Statman, D. (ed.) (1997), *Virtue Ethics*, Edinburgh University Press, Edinburgh. [Some useful further reading on virtue theory.]

Stroud, D.I. (1980), *Magna Carta*, Paul Cave Publications, Southampton. [A translation of the original, with notes.]

Thompson, M. (1999), *Ethical Theory*, Hodder and Stoughton, London. [A straightforward and clear introduction to ethical theory.]

Trompenaars, F. and Hampden-Turner, C. (1997), *Riding the Waves of Culture: Understanding Cultural Diversity in Business* (2nd edn), Nicholas Brealey Publishing, London. [An interesting text on international cultural diversity; does business ethics depend on the society you live in?]

Vardy, P. and Grosch, P. (1994), *The Puzzle of Ethics*, HarperCollins, London. [A good basic introduction to ideas in ethical theory.]

Verstraeten, J. (ed.) (2000), *Business Ethics: Broadening the Perspectives*, Peeters, Leuven, Belgium. [A useful reference to corporate ethics.]

Webley, S. (1997), 'The Business Organisation: A Locus for Meaning and Moral Guidance', in Davies (ed.) (1997), Routledge, London. [A short note with a useful model on the ethical development of the firm.]

Whitehill, A.M. (1992), *Japanese Management: Tradition and Transition*, Thompson Learning, London. [A good background to Japanese management, though should be complemented by reference to current articles showing changes in business practice.]

Winstanley, D. and Woodall, J. (eds) (2000), *Ethical Issues in Contemporary Human Resource Management*, Palgrave Macmillan, Basingstoke. [A very useful collection of articles on HRM and ethics.]

Index

LIBRARY, UNIVERSITY OF CHESTER